TELLING TALES

*The Fabulous Lives
of Anita Leslie*

This book is dedicated to Anita Leslie's children, Tarka King and Leonie Finn, and to her grandchildren, William and Olivia King and Jessica Ottaine, Heather Oriole and Cian Merlin Finn

TELLING TALES

*The Fabulous Lives
of Anita Leslie*

Penny Perrick

BLOOMSBURY CARAVEL
LONDON · OXFORD · NEW YORK · NEW DELHI · SYDNEY

BLOOMSBURY CARAVEL
Bloomsbury Publishing Plc
50 Bedford Square, London, WC1B 3DP, UK

BLOOMSBURY, BLOOMSBURY CARAVEL and the Diana logo are trademarks of
Bloomsbury Publishing Plc

First published in 2017 in Ireland as *Telling Tales* by The Lilliput Press
This edition published 2018

A catalogue record for this book is available from the British Library

Library of Congress Cataloguing-in-Publication data has been applied for

ISBN: PB: 978-1-4482-1721-2; eBook: 978-1-4482-1722-9

2 4 6 8 10 9 7 5 3 1

Typeset in Perpetua by Deanta Global Publishing Services, Chennai, India
Printed and bound by CPI Group (UK) Ltd, Croydon, CR0 4YY

To find out more about our authors and books visit www.bloomsbury.com
and sign up for our newsletters

Contents

'The lies we tell are part of the truth we live.'
Michael Holroyd, *Works on Paper* (1998)

'Do what you want to do and then pay the price.
That is the only bargain which fate understands.'
Frances, Countess Lloyd-George of Dwyfor, CBE

Introduction

Six months before she died, on 5 November 1985, Anita Leslie wrote to her daughter-in-law, Jane, asking for the loan of a khaki shirt. She wanted to pin on the sleeve the two decorations that she had won in the Second World War, the Desert Star and the Croix de Guerre, when the artist Theodore Ramos painted her portrait. 'I was the only woman in the world to get both,' Anita pointed out. On the battlefield with the French army as it slowly pushed the Germans back across the Rhine, she was probably the only woman, perhaps the only person, to keep her cousin Winston Churchill, the wartime prime minister, informed about what was happening on the ground: the behaviour of the retreating Germans, the thoughts of ordinary combatants. Her respectful but idiosyncratic letters obviously touched Winston's heart. After the war he kept in close touch with his young cousin and assisted her in writing a biography of his American grandfather, Leonard Jerome, having previously vetoed Anita's father, Shane Leslie, from writing the book.

The portrait was never commissioned in the end, although an earlier one by Ramos exists, showing Anita looking old, ill and wispy-haired. The decorations have been mislaid. Anita Leslie is remembered not for her wartime heroism but as the author of larky biographies, many of them of members of her family, including her great-aunt Jennie Churchill, mother of Winston, known as 'the Panther' because of her smouldering dark eyes and, possibly, her predatory ways.

Born in 1914, Anita led a haphazard life apart from her heroic war service. She may have suffered from akrasia, a mental condition that leads one to act against one's better judgement. Her bewildering behaviour, bewildering even to herself, suggests a chronic disposition for taking the wrong road. She knew this. 'Now I kick myself for having taken the wrong decision,' she wrote after one mishap. And, during a fraught period in the Desert War: 'I want to marry two men.' Her editor once commentated: 'Miss Leslie does get herself into the most fearful muddles.'

Perilous dithering ran in the family. An associate of her younger brother Desmond described him as having 'a foot in two clouds at once'. Anita was at her most akratic when she handed over to her brother Desmond Glaslough, the estate in County Monaghan that the Leslies had owned since 1665. She then spent years trying to get it back. The Leslies were Anglo-Irish, a tribe described by Declan Kiberd as 'a hyphenated people, forever English in Ireland, forever Irish in England'. A confusing condition to be in.

Anita was a hybrid of a hybrid class. Her father, Sir Shane Leslie, had, as a young man, renounced his inheritance to become both a Catholic and an Irish Nationalist in a betrayal of his family's Ulster Protestant values. This could have been seen as an embarrassment but, as Elizabeth Bowen, that superb chronicler of the Anglo-Irish, has pointed out, this class had a gift for 'not noticing', a stance both arrogant and brave. Among the things it determinedly didn't notice were those that R.F. Foster describes in a section called 'Lost in the Big House' in his book *In Words Alone*, as a combination of 'loneliness, uncertainty ... an implicitly threatening countryside, unknown natives, the threat of death'. Anita's cousin Winston, not being Anglo-Irish, noticed. During the 1921 treaty negotiations that followed the Irish War of Independence, Winston, as Colonial Secretary, supposedly asked the Irish delegate Michael Collins to ensure that Castle Leslie in Glaslough wasn't harmed, since it was the home of his favourite aunt, Leonie Leslie, Anita's grandmother. It was left intact. On the whole, the Anglo-Irish were not persecuted as a class, merely enduring what Kiberd calls the 'tragedy of irrelevance' and subject to increasing taxation and loss of land while, as John Banville described it, holding on to a 'languid but valiant mode of life at the Big House'.

They didn't quite know what to do with themselves. The essayist Hubert Butler wrote of the way that families like the Leslies floundered in the new Irish State: 'Sometimes they seemed not to live in Ireland at all but in a little cocoon of their own making.' 'We have no code,' Anita wrote in her diary, referring to the Leslies. She was visiting her mother's family, the Ides of St Johnsbury, Vermont. The Ides were diligent, hard-working, influential in public life and emotionally stable. In Vermont, Anita realized that her mother Marjorie came from a milieu that 'admired men for their individual achievement and where women were married for love and expected to be virtuous!!' How different from the society into which Marjorie had married, 'where inherited titles and wealth were adored, where poor men looked around for heiresses and it was "chic" to sleep with everyone on the right "snob" level.' The Ides' 'sincerity, trueness, lack of sophistication allied to love of culture and instinct for training of the intellect' made Anita feel ashamed of the pleasure-seeking Leslies who 'lived in such different airs and morals – in many subjects we would have been Chinese to each other.'

In 1937 when she was twenty-four, Anita made a catastrophic marriage, without deluding herself that it would bring her anything but misery. The exiled Colonel Paul Rodzianko was thirty years older than she was, dispossessed of his Ukrainian lands and considerable wealth by the Russian Revolution, whose leaders regarded aristocrats like Paul as 'former people'. He was a brilliant horseman but such a hellish husband that, thirty years after their divorce, Anita could hardly bear to mention him in her memoirs. From the start of their marriage Anita wanted to get away from it but she was such a useful wife that Paul wouldn't let her go. She ghosted his books – an autobiography and a manual on horsemanship, helped him train other people's horses and inexpertly kept house for him in a mean little flat in west London. She claimed not to be able to make a cup of tea and her culinary skills didn't improve. Decades later a luncheon guest at Castle Leslie was surprised when the meal cooked by Anita turned out to be only a half-cooked baked potato.

Paul infected Anita with his vicious anti-Semitism. He blamed the Jews for the loss of everything he had once had and saw the downfall and murder of the Tsar and his family, whom Paul had served and loved, as inspired by Jews. The word 'Jew' was synonymous with 'communist', equally loathsome to him. Anita, who sympathized with her dispossessed husband, even while wanting to leave him, was influenced by his attitude. Their shabby marriage was played out in the 1930s, W.H. Auden's 'low, dishonest decade', that inter-war interlude 'born of exhaustion' according to the historian Tony Judt: fertile ground for racial prejudice and class warfare.

It is hard to reconcile Anita's courage, generosity and intelligence with her hatred of Jews. The American writer Adam Gopnik faced a similar problem with regard to a particular heroine of his, the nineteenth-century feminist food critic and anti-Semite Elizabeth Pennell. Gopnik came to the uneasy conclusion that 'to demand that our ancestors be right about everything in advance is as mad as hoping that our descendants will think us right about everything in retrospect.' In his book *The Table Comes First* he addresses the shade of Pennell: 'Would you have seen a wiser way, with better company and a larger view?' Anita too might have seen a wiser way in those circumstances. As it was, throughout the late 1930s, her opinion of Hitler veered between admiration and amusement: 'We may go to Nuremberg as Hitler's guests,' she wrote to her friend Rose Burgh in 1938. 'Rather fun to meet all the Nazis!' And in April 1939: 'I thought Hitler's speech brilliant, sane and dignified, the best he has ever made.'

We all see the world in our own time. Felix Frankfurter, the Austrian-born Jewish lawyer whom President Franklin D. Roosevelt appointed to the Supreme Court the year before the war, said in 1945: 'If the judgement of the time must be corrected by that of posterity, it is no less true that the judgement of posterity must be corrected by that of the time.' Like many people, Anita hoped for peace at any price. Her uncle Norman Leslie had been killed in the Great War and her much-loved grandmother,

Leonie, had never recovered from the death of her favourite son, keeping his room at Castle Leslie exactly as he had left it.

After the war, Anita admitted to having been 'an idiotic debutante' but not to her earlier anti-Semitism. In a memoir, she described a highly improbable scene from the 1930s, in which Leonie 'shaking with emotion' holds a newspaper clipping that shows a man stripped to his underwear, to which a large yellow star was pinned. Anita's letters, always more truthful than her published work, tell a different story. She wrote of Leonie joking with a customs official about sending Jews who had recently escaped to Ireland back to Germany 'and let Hitler sort them out'. While Winston Churchill, Leonie's favourite nephew, warned about the coming horrors of Nazi Germany, few members of his family, including Anita, took much notice of him. The war changed her attitude: Winston became her hero and the recipient of lively and informative letters about life on the frontline as Anita, now an ambulance driver in the French army, drove through a ruined France towards the Rhine.

Not that Anita became particularly philo-Semitic. She regarded Jews, along with intellectuals and the professional classes, as 'clever' – not a compliment. Perhaps because of her scanty schooling, people who led swottish indoor lives and failed to be amusing rattled her. The writer Logan Pearsall Smith maintained that: 'Quality folk are seldom at their ease with intellectuals, among whom they make a great deal of mischief.' Anita didn't make mischief; she just chose to live among the descendants of those members of the aristocracy who were the subjects of her biographies, a choice that intellectuals such as the historian Hugh Trevor-Roper would have deplored. In his wartime journals, he wrote: 'When I … observe the lack of education and values amongst most of them [aristocrats], and their dreary pleasures, the sickening triviality of their lives, I despise them.' They may have been empty-headed but they were amusing, a word that Anita held dear, and shared her love of horses, hunting and the countryside, as, incidentally, did Trevor-Roper.

Writing was what the Leslies did. Dean Swift, a visitor at Castle Leslie, noted the Leslie-authored books on the shelves, 'all about themselves'. Diaries, memoirs, essays and, long after the dean's visit, Shane's novels and poetry, which were all rather self-centred, even when he was writing about other people. Anita, not a self-confident woman by any means, never doubted that she could write. Living briefly in Paris, after a predictably unsuccessful debutante Season, and getting to know some elderly sculptors who had worked with Rodin, she produced a biography of the artist which, with bad timing, was published just as war was declared. By then the success or otherwise of her first book didn't matter. The war was an opportunity to leave Paul. She joined the Mechanised Transport Corps (MTC), a snobbish but efficient service that attracted upper-class young women, whose beautifully tailored uniforms were designed by the couturier Hardy Amies. As she sailed from Glasgow to Cape Town on board the *Union Castle*, Anita wrote to Rose Burgh: 'Only I could invent this way of running away from a husband.'

The husband wasn't mentioned in her wartime memoirs. 'How lucky I was to be husbandless, childless, unloving, unloved,' she wrote untruthfully. The running away from Paul was a mixed success and he followed her to various postings: South Africa, the Middle East and Italy, to be finally shaken off when Anita joined the French army in 1944. It is in Anita's letters that we learn of Paul's pursuit, the lovers who relieved the boredom of hanging around waiting for the next battle to start by courting her while a suspicious and vengeful husband hovered nearby. It was like an ooh-la-la French farce with Russian overtones.

Anita's real war, the one that gave her the reputation of '*une anglaise formidable*', began when she landed with the French forces at Marseilles in August 1944. As a front-line ambulance driver in the 1st French Armoured Division, she played a vital part in the liberation of France. The French were unique in allowing female ambulance drivers on the front line. Had Anita stayed in the MTC, now incorporated into the ATS (Auxiliary Territorial Service), she would have been stuck in Alexandria. Anita wrote in *Train to Nowhere*: 'Whatever the achievements of the ATS, the tendency of male authorities was always to scoff, and keep first-rate women subordinate to second-rate men.' The second-rate men withdrew the iconic 'Blonde Bombshell' recruitment poster for the ATS, designed by Abram Games, as being too glamorous.

They did things differently in France. *Train to Nowhere* is dedicated to Jeanne de L'Espée, Anita's commanding officer. Jeanne's first command to Anita was: 'Whatever happens, remember to use lipstick because it cheers the wounded.' Amid the sound of shellfire and kitted out in American soldiers' outfits, including 'comic underwear', eating tinned beans off tin plates, the *ambulancières* listened to Jeanne, who had run the salon of the couturier Jean Patou before the war, lecture on the perfect wardrobe: '[A] well-cut black *tailleur* will get you from breakfast to midnight and the hat is of great importance.'

Anita gave Winston her opinion of the Germans: 'Pleasant kindly people, they are so tolerant they'll let children be tortured if someone in authority says so.' When the war was won at last, she lunched with Winston at Potsdam in July before rejoining her unit in Moselle where in 'ironed shirts, polished boots and our best white gloves' Anita and three other *ambulancières* were presented with the Croix de Guerre. In September, demobilized and trying to find unobtainable knitting wool for the baby a French officer's wife was expecting, she applied for 'the discarded fighting lines' from Winston's map room. It arrived in the form of 'pink wool of best Churchillian quality ... I reflected happily that little pink pants need never grow obsolete'. *Train to Nowhere* ends on this hopeful note.

A German wartime joke: 'Better enjoy the war – the peace will be terrible.' Anita certainly found it so. In 1948, a war heroine with a leftover life to kill, disconsolately trying to breed greyhounds at Castle Leslie, she wrote to Rose:

> It's the mental depression that gets me down now ... the utter futility and nerviness of everything ... I know that I long for the feeling of life and comradeship that I had during the war and have now lost ... that I am terribly tired and the last three years have been exhausting disillusion so that I don't even know what to grasp at any more ... And that I who used to have something to give others now have nothing.

The letter ends: 'I am so sorry to go on being in such a bad state like a lead weight to my friends ... I just got all broke up and am bad at mending.'

She had been betrayed by one wartime lover, which led to half-hearted suicide attempts, airily dismissed as 'the sulks', lived unhappily with a second, by whom she became pregnant and then, the fates finally smiling on her, married the ideal husband, Commander Bill King, another old admirer. An odd household was set up at Oranmore Castle on the west coast of Ireland, where Anita, Bill and Peter Wilson, the father of Anita's son Tarka, attempted to farm beside the wild Atlantic shore. When it became clear that Anita's brother Jack, who had spent most of the war in a German prison camp, was not able or willing to run Glaslough, the estate was offered to Anita and Bill. The reasons for them relinquishing the estate a few years later are confused and confusing. Having handed it over to Desmond, Anita spent years buying back the farmland, almost acre by acre, so that Tarka could inherit it. Most of the money she made from her books was spent on Glaslough's fields and meadows.

Anthony Powell in *At Lady Molly's* ascribed to the fictional Lady Warminster biographies that delighted readers because of 'their engaging impetuosity of style and complete lack of pretension to any serious scholarship'. He might have been describing Anita's biographies. So might Michael Holroyd when he described another biographer, Hesketh Pearson: 'He often wrote as if he had to catch the next post.' What makes Anita's rather breathless books so readable is her knack of putting her subjects, from the sexpot Jennie Churchill to the gruesome Marie Tussaud, convincingly in the world about them. Like Theodor Adorno, she recognized: 'Even the biographical individual is a social category.' Mme Tussaud's biography was commissioned by the Tussaud company and Anita wrote it only for the money. She thought Marie 'a dismal little bore obsessed with waxworks' and never again wrote about a person she disliked. Her books sold well and led to overseas book tours and appearances by their author, now described admiringly as 'a racy old girl', at literary lunches.

Bill had only a small naval pension and any money he made from farming was spent on buying and repairing the boats that he sailed single-handed around the world. After six perilous and exhausting years as a submarine commander he counteracted the stifling confines of submarines by sailing and skiing as often as he could. Anita would never admit that she was the one who kept the family afloat, in every sense of the word. Although she was the author of fourteen books, she presented herself as a lady dabbler, more involved with horses than literature and emulating the Edwardians, the subjects of many of her gauzy biographies, who 'did not mix with the professional classes depicted in Galsworthy's Forsyte Saga'. With unwavering determination Anita kept on buying Glaslough farm-land on Tarka's behalf, entering into such complicated transactions that her son protested that he felt as though his feet were stuck in cement. To no avail: his mother's method of dealing with dissent was to complain that 'it makes my head spin', or simply 'not noticing'. As the Northern Irish Troubles escalated in the 1970s and farming on the Irish borders became a dangerous occupation, she continued not to notice. Apart from her blindness where Glaslough was concerned, she held views on Northern Ireland that were radical for their time, recognizing that economic and social inequality in the province were the sources of discontent. She held the British governments of Edward Heath and Harold Wilson to blame for making no attempt at healing the fractured society over the water. This was from a very traditional woman who basked in what Trevor-Roper called 'the stifling, desiccating glow of boring royalty', to the point of genuinely admiring the late Queen Mother's plumed hats and tut-tutting when a television drama series showed Edwardian debutantes wearing the wrong kind of jewellery.

'When a writer is born into a family, the family is finished,' wrote the poet Czeslaw Milosz. But that's only true if the writer strips the family bare. Anita cast a rosy glow over the generations of Leslies, Jeromes and Churchills about whom she wrote. Although she had the run of the Glaslough attics with their collections of intimate letters and diaries – 'family twaddle' – she was wary of revelation. You will not learn from her biographies or from the sly memoirs written in old age that there were doubts about Winston's brother Jack's parentage or that the father of another illustrious Leslie cousin, the sculptor Clare Sheridan, was probably King Milan of Serbia. The truth is to be found in the letters she wrote to Rose, the one person to whom she could be 'as awful as I feel like'. She asked Rose to destroy her letters but they survived, to be given eventually by Rose's daughter to Anita's son. Reading them, I understood what Edmund de Waal meant when he wrote: 'And I have the clammy feeling of biography, the sense of living on the edges of other people's lives without their permission.' I can see why James Joyce called biographers 'biografiends'. The letters to Rose ended in the 1950s when Rose, having deserted her third husband and young daughter, descended into a haphazardly nomadic and druggy life. After that, although Anita wrote gossipy, interesting letters, sometimes ten a day, to many other people, she never again revealed her feelings so candidly in them.

Nor did she talk about the war. Tarka was taken by surprise when, casting about for a career, his mother was able to introduce him to many influential figures in the Intelligence Services, whom she had known in the Middle East during the war, leading one to suspect that what Anita did in that spy-ridden area was rather more than producing an English-language newspaper for the troops. Her editor at Hutchinson, her longtime publisher, was equally astonished when, in 1983, she wrote a wartime memoir, *A Story Half Told*. He had not imagined that his ditsy, charming author, who had never quite got the hang of spelling and punctuation and whose life seemed bound up with repairing draughty castles and driving horses around Ireland, had tended wounded men on wintry French battlefields under sniper fire, as the snow around them became flecked with blood. By that time, *Train to Nowhere* had been long out of print and completely forgotten. People took Anita at face value: a witty, horsy lady who wrote a bit. Even after the well-received publication of the memoir, Anita played down her heroism. Being a professional heroine wasn't her style.

But a heroine was what she was. Geoffrey Wheatcroft reviewing Winston's daughter Mary Soames' memoir (*A Daughter's Tale*, 2013) wrote: 'Sentimentality about "the greatest generation" is a besetting temptation. But damn it all, they were wonderful, and we who came after have not lived up to them.'

TELLING TALES

*The Fabulous Lives
of Anita Leslie*

I

Putting on a Show

It was a very deceptive wedding day. The 35-year-old bride, described by her cousin, the sculptor Clare Sheridan, as looking 'very *jeune fille*', was three months pregnant by a man whom she wasn't marrying that Wednesday, 12 January 1949. Her marriage certificate stated that she was a 'spinster and gentlewoman', which wasn't quite the case: after many years of pleading for a divorce she had recently disengaged herself from a previous husband. And gentlewoman seemed too mild a term for a woman who had published two books and been awarded the Croix de Guerre for her wartime service. So, radiantly flying her false colours, Anne Theodosia Leslie, known as Anita, married Commander William (Bill) Donald Aelian King, DSO and Bar, DSC, who was thirty-nine. The marriage was solemnized at the Catholic Chapel of Sisters of the Holy Ghost in the grounds of Anita's family home, Castle Leslie, Glaslough, County Monaghan. After the ceremony, bride and groom joined hands over 'that notable relic the Great Bell of Cappagh Abbey and in presence of Clan and County sworn troth accordingly', as Anita's father, Sir Shane

Leslie, put it in a typewritten declaration. He also wrote a lyric to mark the occasion, to be sung to the 'Londonderry Air':

> An Irish winter brings a sight surprising –
> A slice of silver Spring has seemed to bide:
> Though Summer's gold is gone, the flowers are rising
> To greet Anita Leslie as a bride.
> The old green lake is all a gentle glimmer,
> The forest firs have kept a bridal wreath:
> And though Demesne and fields are looking dimmer
> The buds of Spring are coming up beneath.
> So take each other now for worse or better
> And laugh at gains or losses in the game:
> Just take the sunny weather with the wetter
> For Irish rain and sunshine are the same.

This was the wedding for which everyone at Castle Leslie, seat of the Leslies since 1665, had been waiting. Anita wrote to her best friend Rose Gardner:

> I'll always be so glad I gave them [the estate workers] my wedding – the event of their lives! 40 or 50 old employees with gnarled hands and eyes shining with such sincere wishes for our happiness – the thrill for them of the conservatory full of flowers and downstairs cups of tea and cakes and pipers to dance to till midnight.

One wonders whether the *Irish Times* report of the wedding struck a deliberately cryptic note when it reported: 'Owing to the shortness of the notice over fifty guests were unable to come over from England, as well as many from America' – 'shortness of notice' suggesting a shotgun wedding.

Anita's son, Tarka, was born in Dublin on 26 June of that year, although his birth remained a secret until August, the month in which Anita declared he was born. This meant that the baby had two birth certificates with different dates. '*Cache ton jeu*' was a favourite admonition of Anita's American-born grandmother, Leonie Leslie, *née* Jerome, and Anita was also steeped in the traditional wiliness of the Leslies, a family that could then be described as thriving on secrets and lies.

Anita was born on 21 November 1914 at 10 Talbot Square in Bayswater, London, not far from Great Cumberland Place and a street known as Lower Jerome Terrace where Leonie and her two sisters, Jennie Churchill and Clara Frewen, Anita's great-aunts, lived when in London. Anita's parents were Shane and Marjorie, *née* Ide – 'two more disparate beings could hardly be imagined,' according to their daughter.

On Anita's birth certificate Shane's profession is given as 'journalist'. He was also a poet and, since the Leslies were Protestant landlords, an unlikely Irish nationalist who had converted to Catholicism in 1908 at the age of twenty-three. For a time, Shane had considered entering the priesthood and, when his cousin Clare Frewen, later Sheridan, a beloved confidante since their teenage years, suggested that it was a restrictive thing to do, he told her: 'I don't want spiritual independence. I want intellectual anchorage.' He eventually decided against the priesthood but changed his name from John Randolph to the more populist Shane and renounced ownership of the Leslie estates in favour of his younger brother Norman. The latter's death in the First World War resulted in the sort of financial chaos that was to become familiar to future generations of Leslies, including Anita.

The worldly Leslies, outwardly at least, accepted Shane's conversion. Embracing Catholicism was something of a fad among idealistic and spiritually delicate young men under the influence of the famous convert John Henry Newman. Not all Protestant families were as tolerant. After Gerard Manley Hopkins' conversion in 1866, his father wrote: 'The blow is so deadly and so great that we have not yet recovered from the first shock of it.' Marriage to the elegant American socialite Marjorie Ide on 12 June 1912 made Shane less austere. His younger brother Lionel noted: 'When I returned from India in 1927 I found that a very surprising metamorphosis had overtaken him [Shane] and instead of a moody introvert a talkative society loving extravert had emerged.' Shane himself was rather apologetic about this personality change. In his book *Long Shadows* (1966), he lamented the death of many of his male friends in the First World War since it had meant that 'Fate cast me in the arms and converse of women against my will.'

Marjorie Ide was the pampered, high-spirited daughter of a self-made lawyer from Vermont, Henry Ide, who had become a judge in the Vermont Supreme Court, Justice of Samoa, Governor of the Philippines and, most enjoyably, the American Minister in Madrid. He was widowed young and brought up three little daughters. Marjorie was the youngest: golden-haired and leggy, it was said that she had turned down a hundred marriage proposals before Shane Leslie, who was lecturing for the Gaelic League and turned up at her sister Anne's house, The Cedars, in Long Island. Anne was married to Bourke Cockran, the American politician who had schooled Shane's cousin Winston Churchill in the art of oratory. The 27-year-old Irish poet seemed more interesting than those rejected suitors; for one thing, he went around in a kilt, the traditional Leslie one in saffron yellow, or in St Patrick's Blue, either style probably a first for Long Island.

He was tall and handsome, moody and witty. In 1907 he had visited Russia and had stayed with Leo Nicolaevitch Tolstoy, who had urged him to become a vegetarian and learn how to plough. Shane was also prone to nervous collapses, which, along with the kilt and the Catholicism, didn't endear him to Henry Ide, who would have preferred Marjorie to marry someone less poetic and properly American.

Shane and Marjorie might have settled in London contentedly enough – it offered a literary life for Shane, a shiny society one for Marjorie and the *de rigeur* pram rides in Hyde Park with a uniformed nurse for their first-born, Anita – had not the First World War dimmed all the lights for the Leslies, as it did for the whole of Europe.

Captain Norman Leslie, owner of the family estates, was killed near Armentières in northern France only two months into the war. He had been the favourite son, conventional, good-natured, an excellent polo player and a captain in the Rifle Brigade. Shane set off for France to find his brother's body, which lay between the guns of two armies. He had it encoffined and cut a lock of Norman's hair for Leonie. Most unsuitably, since he was an appalling driver, Shane was put in charge of an ambulance, landing several wounded soldiers in ditches. After a short spell of rolling bandages Marjorie sailed back to America with Anita, a lady's maid and a nanny, where she stayed with the Bourke Cockrans in Long Island and Washington or with her father in Vermont. Shane, having given up the ambulance, went to the Dardanelles with a mule transport unit, where he had a nervous breakdown. His position as a loyal British subject and a committed Irish nationalist can't have been easy to reconcile and may have had something to do with his frequent nervous collapses. Recovering at a hospital in Malta, he wrote a mournful book of reminiscences, *The End of a Chapter* (published 1917), its theme 'the suicide of the civilisation called Christian'. Since he was of little use in the war effort, Leonie decided to take him to America to join his wife and his daughter.

There he turned out to be a convincing propagandist. He believed wholeheartedly that the war was just and England and her allies must win it, and that Ireland must be granted independence. In Washington he worked towards both aims, rightly feeling that there would be more chance of America entering the war on the Allied side if Irish-American disapproval of British policy in Ireland could be assuaged. He had excellent contacts on both sides: his cousin, Winston Churchill, who was First Lord of the Admiralty until his mismanagement of the Dardanelles offensive, his brother-in-law, Bourke Cockran, the British ambassador, Sir Cecil Spring-Rice, and John Redmond, the moderate leader of the Irish Nationalists. The Easter Rising of 1916 and the pitiless reprisals by the British caused Shane to despair but he was able to celebrate with Marjorie when America joined the war a year later.

He didn't spend much time with his family – Anita remembers seeing him only once during her early childhood – but a son, Jack, was born in New York in 1916. Jack's Leslie grandparents decided that he should be their heir and bonfires were lit at Glaslough to celebrate his birth. As with so many Leslie decisions, this one turned out badly.

Anita's American childhood was privileged but unpleasant. Every afternoon she would be put into one of the eighty-two exquisite dresses bought for her by her childless aunt Anne and taken down to tea where she might meet Alice Longworth, the daughter of President Theodore Roosevelt. Her grandfather Henry Ide let her ride on his foot and she was much petted. But she began to suffer from severe asthma. Jack was another sickly child: like his parents, he came down with the Spanish flu, which killed millions just as the war was ending, and then got pneumonia and a mastoid on his ear that needed an operation. Winston Churchill inherited the robust Jerome constitution from his lustrous mother, Jennie, but the equally healthy Leonie, Jennie's sister, doesn't seem to have passed on this hardy genetic inheritance to Shane or his offspring, although the children's fragility may also have been partly due to the stress of having Shane and Marjorie as parents.

Shane's grandfather Sir John Leslie, 1st Baronet of Glaslough since 1876, had died in 1916 and his widow, the bookish, dissatisfied Lady Constance, lived in London, so Leonie and her husband, another Sir John, were delighted when in the summer of 1919 Shane and Marjorie decided to move back to Ireland. Anita claimed that Shane didn't come near his children during the voyage; like his own father, he found children boring. At Liverpool they were met by Leonie, who was horrified by Jack's bandaged ears and the special mattress required for Anita's wheeziness. A train from Liverpool to Belfast, a smaller one, 'the train to nowhere', as Anita later called it, for the sixty-mile journey to Glaslough was followed by arrival in darkness at Castle Leslie to be fussed over by servants and carried upstairs to bed.

It was a strange time to be settling in Ireland, with the War of Independence raging, and many Protestant landlords fearing for their lives and the survival of their estates. The once-wealthy Leslies had unwisely invested their compensation money from the Wyndham Land Acts, which had transferred some of their land to their tenants, in Russian Railway Bonds and faced a problematic future. Yet there was a steely serenity about Jack and Leonie that allowed them to live peaceably with their Catholic tenants and with their fidgety son, the ardent nationalist. There is a story that in 1920, Sir John, quite deaf and short-sighted, inspected some armed troops in Glaslough village, thinking that they were loyalist Ulster Volunteers when they were in fact members of the Irish Republican Brotherhood (IRB). That summer Marjorie took her seven-year-old daughter to the Donegal resort of Bundoran for some sea air. Since the railway station was blown up while they were there, they had no means of getting away. Anita rather enjoyed the drama ('the atmosphere of vague danger seemed delicious') but Marjorie didn't. After several jittery days, a local man was able to drive them to a shooting box that the Leslies owned in the village of Pettigo in County Donegal. To Marjorie's surprise, she came across her father-in-law who, civil conflict notwithstanding, had come there for a spot of trout fishing. Soon afterwards the younger Leslies moved to London where Shane, by now an experienced nego-tiator, became involved in meetings which, the following year, resulted in the treaty that established the Irish Free State, of which more later. Anita hated London, its tamed, boring parks and the mindless routines inflicted by her governess Miss Butler, a bombazine-clad religious fanatic. She missed her grandparents and the wooded lakeside where wildlife and changing skies made every day an adventure. She determined to live in Ireland, although decades were to pass before she was able to do so.

Not everyone who knows Castle Leslic falls in love with it. Shane certainly didn't. His novel about the family seat, renamed Kelvey Hall but recognizably Castle Leslie because of its colony of rooks, woods and lake, was called *Doomsland* (1923) and dedicated to Marjorie. The Leslies had lived at Glaslough since 1665, when they bought the land with the £2000 given to the fighting bishop John Leslie by Charles ll. Their long tenure makes the Leslie motto 'Grip Fast' very appropriate. The castle in the Scottish baronial style was built in the 1870s for Anita's great-grand-father, the Sir John Leslie who had the distinction of having a picture hung in the Royal Academy in the same year that he won the Military Grand Steeplechase. It stands on the site of an earlier building, incor-porating part of it. Its dour and austere limestone façade surrounded by three miles of stone 'famine walls' was commented on by Shane: 'No one who has seen Glaslough in Monaghan could believe it was merely the residence of Irish Squires.'

The forbidding Victorian building was softened by an Italianate Renaissance cloister that linked the main house to a single-storey wing containing the library and billiard room, and was the original home of Sir John's impressive Italian art collection. Anita did not mind the dark cold of the castle. She loved the lake, said to be the finest specimen pike lake in Ireland, the ancient woods and terraces flanked by giant lime trees. She loved the scrambled Leslie ancestry of soldiering (the family could trace this back to Attila the Hun) and bookishness. Dean Swift had been a visitor and had written in the castle's guest book: 'Glaslough with rows of books/ Upon its shelves/Written by the Leslies/All about themselves.' The castle was not just full of books but of letters and journals relating to genera-tions of Leslies and, in the attics, clothes and jewellery and mementos of every kind. When Anita began to write about the lives of members of her interesting family, her research materials were all around her.

There was a Bechstein in the drawing room, chosen for Leonie by the famous concert pianist and Polish prime minister, Ignacy Jan Paderewski, and a Della Robbia fireplace that Sir John had spotted as the fifteenth-century sacristy in Florence that housed it was being pulled down. When Jennie Churchill visited with her third, much younger, husband Colonel Montagu Porch, she and Leonie, excellent pianists, played duets, enchanting Anita and Jack. How dull London seemed after that. Great-aunt Jennie lived at 8 Westbourne Street and Anita passed her door on the way to her monotonous daily walk in Kensington Gardens but Miss Butler seldom allowed her to visit. No wonder that Jennie was regarded as a treat. Determined to always look on the bright side, she painted all the light bulbs in her house yellow, to reproduce sunlight. She and Leonie thought that mopiness was ill-mannered and in bad taste. 'Smile dear, it costs nothing,' Leonie would urge her sulky granddaughter.

Desmond Leslie, Marjorie's third child, was born by Caesarian section in London on 9 June 1921 to very muted celebrations. Only days before-hand, Henry Ide had died in Vermont without either of his daughters by his side, since Anne Cockran had come to England to be with Marjorie. And then on the day of Desmond's birth, Jennie Churchill died suddenly, following complications after breaking her ankle. Marjorie took flight. With the new baby, a nanny and a personal maid, as well as Anita, she went to San Remo on the Italian Riviera, a spot chosen partly because the sun and sea air might cure the little girl's asthma. Anita went to school at the local convent where she played with the nuns' pet rabbits, picked up a few words of Italian and was prepared for her first Holy Communion in that language.

Back in London, Marjorie discovered that her eight-year-old daughter was unable to read. It was Miss Butler's fault. She had never conveyed to her pupil that letters represented sounds, so Anita just memorized the printed pages Miss Butler read aloud to her. In time, she knew *Alice in Wonderland* by heart and it was only when she was given the unfamiliar *Alice Through the Looking Glass* to read aloud that the game was up. It is hard to make excuses for Marjorie, a neglectful mother who saw her children as nuisances who cramped her style. 'Why has God given me such children,' she would complain when some naughtiness made her late for a dinner party.

Shane's time was taken up with the negotiations that led to the Anglo-Irish Treaty. He had no recognized status, unlike Winston Churchill, who was Secretary for the Colonies and an official delegate to the peace talks, and his role seemed mainly to persuade various interested parties of the benefits of Irish Home Rule. Lady Lavery, the beautiful wife of the artist Sir John Lavery, entertained the delegates at her house in Cromwell Place, opposite the Victoria and Albert Museum. At one of her dinner parties, Winston asked Michael Collins, President of the IRB and its Director of Intelligence, if he could make sure that Castle Leslie wasn't burnt down as his favourite aunt lived there.

Hazel Lavery was a femme fatale from central casting. During the treaty negotiations she was rumoured to have had affairs with both the charismatic and handsome Michael Collins and the Lord Chancellor, Lord Birkenhead. Her biographer, Sinéad McCoole, in *Hazel: A Life of Lady Lavery 1880–1935*, thinks that Shane wasn't included in her long list of lovers, in spite of penning her love poems, sending her roses and, years later, writing: 'She merely whistled to men and they obeyed as if it were a whip fashioned of her eyelashes.'

Shane was becoming an important literary figure. During the First World War a Catholic schoolmaster, Monsignor Cyril Fay, who had taught F. Scott Fitzgerald, gave Shane the manuscript of *This Side of Paradise*, which Shane recommended to the publisher Scribner. When Fitzgerald's first novel was published in 1920, he became instantly famous and so grateful to Shane that he dedicated his next novel to him, 'in appreciation of much literary help and encouragement'. The book, published in 1922, was called *The Beautiful and the Damned* and Marjorie asked her husband which he thought he was. She was no longer sure.

The aesthetic Irish nationalist was now intoxicated by the Jazz Age and attended wild parties with the actress Tallulah Bankhead who once, memorably, said: 'I tell you cocaine isn't habit-forming and I know because I've been taking it for years.' Shane, an unlikely Casanova, retained the prejudices of Catholic Ireland, writing scathingly of James Joyce's *Ulysses* in the *Dublin Review* (September 1922): 'In this work the spiritually offensive and the physically unclean are united. We speak advisedly when we say that though no formal condemnation has been pronounced, the Inquisition can only require its destruction or, at least, its removal from Catholic houses.'

Although, outwardly, Marjorie seemed like a typical product of the Roaring Twenties with her bobbed hair, short skirts that showed off her long legs, shaking cocktails or dancing at the Embassy Club, a favourite haunt of the Prince of Wales, she took an old-fashioned view of her husband's behaviour, referring to his conquests as his 'band of alley cats'. She thought of herself as an exciting woman. As a young girl she had gone on an official visit to China with her friend Alice Longworth and had been instructed in captivating sexual techniques at the court of the Dowager Empress. Marjorie is supposed to have passed on what she learned at the Chinese court to her friend Wallis Simpson, who had caught the eye of the Prince of Wales. Shane's lack of attention was insufferable and, although Marjorie had converted to Catholicism, she began to think about divorce.

Leonie was appalled. Her generation tolerated adultery if love affairs were conducted with tact, discretion and consideration but divorce was an upsetting experience for everyone, especially when the divorcing couple were parents. Shane and Marjorie were too absorbed in themselves to consider their children, leading to one of Marjorie's characteristic flits. In 1925 she took the three children to Paris, where she attracted a rich American suitor, Major Logan. He longed to marry her but her Catholicism made her indecisive.

It was an unhappy and unsettling time for Anita and Jack. Walks in the Parc Monçeau were even more disagreeable than in Kensington Gardens.

Anita's asthma got worse and she had three separate bouts of pneumonia, while Jack had painful recurrences of abscesses on his ear that required operations. Convalescence was pleasurable. Anita wrote later: 'Jack and I decided we liked being ill. Once the pain ended we preferred being in bed to out of it … It was safer.'

After some weeks, Shane appeared. He went down on one knee and offered his wife a bedraggled bunch of violets. The marriage was saved after a fashion and, within it, the children remained haphazardly parented.

2
An Education

Henry James called his formal education 'small, vague spasms of school'. Like Anita, he had unsettled parents who didn't attach much importance to steady routines. Marjorie Leslie regarded schools as useful establishments, like kennels, where you could plonk your children when you wanted to travel (she loved travelling) and where you could remove them when you thought that their company might be amusing for a while. One of Anita's obituarists calculated that Anita had been educated, or not, by fourteen governesses and at seven or eight schools. The most successful of the governesses followed the Parents' National Education Union (PNEU) syllabus, designed for home schooling, and Anita, after much frustrated sobbing, finally learned to connect letters with sounds.

When she was in her early teens she was sent to the Convent of the Sacred Heart in Roehampton, outside London, the school notoriously described in Antonia White's autobiographical novel *Frost in May* (1933) as 'The Convent of the Five Wounds'. Antonia had been expelled from this house of horror when she was fourteen after the nuns had found her reading a novel. Books other than text books were prohibited. In an undated letter to her father, Anita thanks him for sending her two books, *The Vicar of Wakefield* and *Hangman's House*:

> But, incredible as it may sound, they (Mother Ward) would not let me read
> either of them. I protested and showed her your letter ... but the old bug
> said that it was not a book for school. She was much shocked at [*sic*] Oliver
> Goldsmith and murmured 'Well of course if your father likes to let you read
> such books out of school.' Did you ever hear such bunk?

Resourcefully, Anita wrapped the books in a towel and hid them up the chimney. Another pupil at the convent during Anita's time was Vivien Leigh and Anita later wondered whether the tuberculosis with which the actress was diagnosed soon after making *Gone With the Wind* in 1939 was due to the damp, cold, starvation rations and lack of exercise that made up convent life.

In her memoir *The Gilt and the Gingerbread* (1981) Anita made light of the experience – 'I began to wonder what sort of lunatic asylum I had fallen into' – but her letters to Marjorie at the time were plaintive:

> Have a good time Mum and write to me a lot and don't worry about my
> being so unhappy ... the food is foul and occasionally gives even me violent
> indigestion but this week some mothers complained about it so that for a
> few days it was properly cooked ... I don't think three quarters of an hour a
> day out of doors is enough in the summer ... I may be able to stand another
> term but I should much rather be with you where I could swim and work
> hard by myself.

The suffering convent girl was always concerned about her mother's happiness: 'My Own Darlingest Mummy, I do hope you are having a good time. Getting up for lunch, spend the afternoon buying expensive clothes, go out to tea, rest till eight, dress for dinner go out and come home at 6.30 A.M laiden [*sic*] with flowers diamond necklaces ect [*sic*].' A fairly accurate account of Marjorie's life as she jaunted around Europe, seldom letting Anita know where she was or writing to her, except to complain about her own poor health. But Anita loved her and felt that, as far as her schooling was concerned, she and Marjorie were in it together and that the convent must be endured so that she was seen to be getting an education responsibly provided by her mother. She invented private endearments and nicknames for them both ('Bambipoo' and 'Mousita') and illustrated her letters with charming drawings of mice and veiled schoolgirls. This undated poem, with the original spelling, shows her adoration:

> O Mummy Darling
> You are soft as a starling
> And your sweet eyes
> Are just like the skys
> And your hair O your hair
> Could ever fine gold be so rare.
> And your feet O your feet
> Why to see them's a treat
> But your hands so white
> Are a wonderfull sight
> O your lips so red
> What sweet things they have said.

During her second term at the convent Anita worked hard and passed her Junior School Certificate. Marjorie, returning from a trip to Italy, paid her a visit and disapprovingly noticed the convent's insanitary practices, although Anita didn't tell her that the girls' hair was shampooed only once, at the beginning of term, when their heads were fine-combed for nits. Soon after that visit Anita became ill, with a temperature of 101°F and was neglected in the sanatorium. She could bear it no longer: 'O do bring me home, it's awful here.' A week later, an order arrived that she was to be sent home to the Leslies' London residence, 12 Westbourne Terrace, Bayswater, in a taxi.

Her next school, where she was dispatched in 1928, aged fifteen, was an improvement – 'a boarding school which actually possessed a library!' This was the brand new Westonbirt College, housed in the former home of a Victorian magnate, where there were welcoming rooms with brocade curtains and open fires, as many hot baths as you liked and no restrictions on reading and writing. 'You're a darling to have sent me,' Anita wrote gratefully to Marjorie, who was probably unimpressed that the staff were university graduates; she had chosen the school because it had featured in a magazine article. But she may have been relieved that her daughter would not have to wear the same navy serge dress every day for every activity, as had been the case at the convent and that Anita's friend Winifred (Pooh) Paget, who had been a day girl at the convent, was going to Westonbirt too.

A school photograph of the Westonbirt intake in September 1928 shows lumpy-looking girls in grey suits and red ties, and teachers in academic robes with hair coiled around their ears in bluestocking fashion. I haven't been able to identify Anita – the girls all look the same, squinting into the sun. She might have done well in this scholarly atmosphere had Marjorie, in need of a travelling companion, not taken her away after one term. One wonders what Anita's teachers thought about a woman like Marjorie, who deposited her daughter at various schools 'as if conferring a favour' as Anita put it. Anita would have liked more time at Westonbirt but released from the classroom she was 'now free to read and read and read' and, true Leslie that she was, 'to write and write and write'. The rare sightings of her razzle-dazzle parents, who were always somewhere else, turned her into an assiduous correspondent. Writing letters became a lifelong habit: she would often write six letters a day, repeating the same bits of gossip and news to friends and family, letters that were to prove useful when she began to write her memoirs. She was a haphazard diarist; telling herself about herself seemed like a waste of time, and experiences were for sharing. With little formal education, she had learnt to be observant: 'I perceived people's emotions and my memory became sharp,' she wrote later. These were helpful attributes for the nascent biographer.

Throughout her childhood and teenage years Anita's letters to Marjorie made it clear where she most wanted to be. From a letter written from Glaslough on 23 January 1929, to 'My Most Beloved Mummy':

> Glaslough when I came to it at the age of ten was the heaven of all my twisted narrow little dreams – I adored it and when I was taken away to Paris or London I nursed a most savage and injurious idea against my surrounding [*sic*] in particular and civilisation in general.

In the same letter she apologizes for being surly and sulky and, she suspects, a disappointment to Marjorie: 'I was selfish, I admit but only as a starving

man is selfish for Glaslough was my bread and I was ravenously hungry.'
She wrote that she had turned over a new leaf, spread her interests beyond
the woods and lake, dogs and horses, practises the piano ('nearly 3 hours
today') and reads the newspapers, although she rails against 'the world of
governesses, convention and schools that dragged my defiant body along
the foul byways of men'.

This letter, written when she was fifteen, is a more melodramatic
version of those she wrote to her mother when she was much younger:
'Please let me [stay at Glaslough]. It is so lovely and big and green here
and the lake and boat and everything compered [*sic*] to dark little London.'
A similar letter to Shane, written miserably from Westbourne Terrace,
tells him wistfully: 'I do wish I was at Glaslough, I love it better than
any other place.' But she realized that she had to face up to the demands
of the conventional world because the person she most admired insisted
on it. This was Anita's older cousin, Margaret Sheridan, the daughter of
Leonie's niece Clare, a woman so wild, and so neglectful a mother that
one of her admirers, the writer Axel Munthe, later told Margaret: 'The
children – whenever I hear of Clare I say to myself: "The children, *ach*,
the poor little children!"' Another of Clare's admirers, the great financier Bernard (Barney) Baruch, a scandalized witness to her escapades,
said of Margaret: 'I'd do anything for that poor kid.' In 1976 Anita wrote
an engrossing biography of Clare, an irresistible subject whose lovers
included Charlie Chaplin, Lord Birkenhead, the Lord Chancellor and Lev
Kamenev, Trotsky's brother-in-law and a high-ranking Soviet functionary.
Clare, a dauntless journalist and talented sculptor, was brought more
spikily to black-hearted life in Margaret's memoir *Morning Glory* (1961)
written under her pen name, Mary Motley.

Margaret, like Anita, had been dumped briefly and unhappily in a
convent ('the Kensington snakepit') and then inadequately cared for in
both Europe and America while her mother embarked on sensation-
seeking exploits. Her escape from her rackety childhood had been in
reading. From the time that Anita first met Margaret in 1923, Anita did her
best to catch up. From Westonbirt she sent Shane a list of the books that
she had read during the year. They included Clare's memoir *Nuda Veritas*,

an early version of the kiss-and-tell memoir, which had been published the previous year, 1927, and Shane's more respectable *Isle of Columbcille: A Pilgrimage and a Sketch* (1910), published by the Catholic Truth Society of Ireland. She told him: 'I do truly try to educate myself and it is so important to be well-read like Margaret.'

While Anita was at Westonbirt, Margaret was in Algeria, where Clare had exotically chosen to live. The two girls wrote each other long letters: 'Darling Margaret, Thank you so much for your last epistle of 23 pages' begins one of Anita's letters. The younger girl tried to persuade her cousin to become a Catholic: 'Christ is essential. It is foolish and ungrateful after what he went through for us not to believe in him.' They were two unhappy teenage souls. Anita to Margaret, from Glaslough: '*À quoi vivre?* you ask – the only answer is *pour mourir*. The climax of life is death.' But she was at Glaslough, where she could never be unhappy for long: 'O Margaret I am so happy here and it really is my home.'

On 25 January 1929 when Anita was fifteen, she wrote to Margaret, 'my dear I think I've only just noticed it but I've lost all my looks, it's quite extraordinary. I used to be so pretty and fresh.' She then gives out about the recently established Irish Free State, 'which forbids untenanted land being held by anyone'. This could prove a problem for the Leslies, who owned 35,000 acres of heather-covered hills and moors. She is furious when Margaret hasn't written for a while: 'You're spoilt, Margaret, disgustingly spoilt, you do just what you like.' But, although they are miles apart, the cousins founded a Hell Fire Club in June 1928. It had a proper UK-style cabinet, except with a President – A. Leslie. M. Sheridan is Secretary of State for Foreign Affairs and for India and for Air. Anita makes Westonbirt sound like an early version of St Trinian's, telling Margaret that one of the girls 'had some interesting experiences around India Dock Road etc. She bought a lovely little dagger for 1/6d.'

Sometimes, during Clare's long absences, Margaret stayed at Glaslough but she didn't share Anita's love of the place. Her letters to Clare belittle Leonie and Marjorie, who annoyed each other by moving ornaments about. For all her sophistication Leonie was very conventional and thought that the best choice for Margaret was to marry well, which meant wealthily. In *Morning Glory* Margaret wrote: 'Great-aunt Leonie offered to present me at Court but Mama would not hear of it ... It might be thought, with her Red reputation, that she was not being received!' It was typical of Clare to cause a scandal by going to Russia as a guest of the Soviets and then express concern that this might count against her in English aristocratic circles.

1929 was the year in which Marjorie and Anita went to Bab-El-M'Cid, near Bisra, to stay with Clare and Margaret, a trip that had been happily anticipated by Anita. The visit was a disaster. Predictably, Marjorie and Clare didn't get on. Marjorie was, at heart, a conventional matron. She travelled with her personal maid and complained that sitting cross-legged on the ground at mealtimes, in Clare's white house built among date gardens, laddered her silk stockings. Clare had given up maids – and probably silk stockings – years before although, Anita noticed, she was not self-sufficient, since everyone in her orbit became her willing slave, so that Clare herself never had to boil an egg or make a cup of tea. Worse than the friction between the two grown-ups was that Margaret had become intensely Arabized, fasting during Ramadan, wearing Arab robes and being eyed up by the local tribal leader, who would gladly have added her to his collection of wives. She had left Anita far behind; the latter's companion during this tense holiday was Margaret's younger brother Dick, with whom she rode and climbed sand dunes.

On their return, Marjorie sent Anita to yet another educational establishment. For the next year and a half, for three days a week, she would go to Miss Wolfe's school, just across the park from Westbourne Terrace, to study history, literature and French. Miss Wolfe was a former governess and her pupil-centred teaching methods were very advanced, with the focus on interesting books. 'We learned a lot because all our studies interested her personally,' Anita wrote approvingly. Jack fared less well: he was sent to Downside, the Benedictine monastery school, whose head was the terrifying and sadistic Father de Trafford.

Marjorie and Shane were settling down, although Shane's biographer, Otto Rauchbauer, wrote frostily: 'From the 1920s onward he [Shane] allowed himself sexual liberties in a society that was becoming ever more permissive.' But there was no more talk of divorce from Marjorie, who seemed happy enough to travel extensively with her sister Anne and buy dresses in Paris. Her children, as they got older, got used to her frequent absences; Anita didn't mind Marjorie spending Christmas in New York as long as she herself could spend it at Glaslough.

Anita, in her memoirs, describes herself and Jack as wild children, fighting until they drew blood and prone to dangerous japes such as creeping along the gutter, heedless of the forty-foot drop below, to pour jugfuls of water down the chimneys of the house next door. But at Glaslough they were well behaved. They loved and were loved by their grandparents, liked by the gamekeepers, foresters and dairymaids, and too engrossed in trawling for pike to get up to mischief, although Anita's habit of climbing to the top of a sixty-foot Douglas fir caused an anguished Marjorie to wail: 'Why have I such a daughter?'

When the older Leslies were away and Shane and Marjorie were in charge of Glaslough, exciting visitors arrived: W.B. Yeats, who walked around the lake declaiming his poetry, and a peer of the realm with his mistress who wore gold lamé trouser suits and drank cocktails. When Leonie was in charge, cocktails, mistresses and evening trousers were out of the question. Shane was now working for A.S.W. Rosenbach, the American bookseller known as 'the Napoleon of the book trade'. Shane's familiarity with Big House libraries and owners who were willing to sell them was an invaluable asset but helped to deplete the stock of rare books on this side of the Atlantic. He still wrote prolifically – novels, poetry, literary criticism – and continued his involvement with the Catholic Church and Irish politics.

Clare Sheridan, contentedly living near Bisra, at least for the moment, was not scandalizing her family as much as previously. Her 1920 visit to Moscow to sculpt the heads of the Soviet leaders had greatly embarrassed her cousin Winston Churchill, who was then Secretary of State for the Colonies, and had caused a temporary rift between him and Shane, who had known about Clare's plans. But Winston's cousins were soon forgiven, although MI5 remained convinced for some years that Clare was a Russian agent. Since she was scattily indiscreet, this seems unlikely.

Shane, hardly a family man, made this unfounded criticism of his mother and aunts: 'The Misses Jerome never entered into British family life.' It was Shane himself who didn't pass through that particular door. Anita wrote: 'I think we [Shane's children] realised fairly early that our own father did not exactly dislike us – he would merely have preferred us not to have been born.' To convey his boredom during rare family meal-times, he developed a trick of closing both the upper and lower lids over his eyes, like a weary tortoise, causing an enraged Marjorie to leave the table. Anita's two paternal uncles, Shane's younger brothers, were more amenable. Seymour, born in 1889, had spent ten years of his childhood bedridden with a tubercular hip and emerged from that decade in the sickroom as 'the best-read member of a hard-reading family'. He wrote books and a series of gossipy articles for *Vogue*, called 'Our Lives from Day to Day'. He abandoned his literary career to become a successful fundraiser for Queen Charlotte's Hospital. His younger brother, Lionel, only fourteen years older than Anita, had inherited from his mother the robust Jerome constitution. Having served as an officer in India at the end of the First World War, he decided to walk home, crossing the Himalayas en route. He then became an explorer in Labrador and wrote a book, *Wilderness Trails in Three Continents*, for which Winston Churchill supplied an introduction.

As well as these entertaining uncles, Anita was blessed with the kindest of great-aunts, Olive Guthrie, *née* Leslie, the owner of Torosay Castle in the Isle of Mull, where Anita and Jack were invited to stay when Marjorie was on her travels. The Leslies were well born and wealthy but their domestic arrangements, whereby they looked after each other's children and never doubted that blood was thicker than water, were not unlike those of traditional working-class families as depicted in Michael Young and Peter Willmott's superb study, *Family and Kinship in East London* (1954). Her unsatisfactory parents aside, Anita was taken up by her large extended family and, like her grandmother Leonie, kept them close throughout her life. The Leslies' attitude to their relations was one of staunch tolerance, so that the nationalist Shane could live under the same roof as his unionist father and indiscreetly promiscuous Clare was constantly forgiven, although she once noticed her aunt, Jennie Churchill, looking at her 'in a kind of overhauling way'.

Anita still did what she was told, and what was now prescribed was a period in Paris, the city where, it was hoped, poise and polish could be acquired by gauche aristocratic English girls. As important as these Parisian attributes was allure, although not so overtly on the 'finishing school' agenda. Anita was aware of her shortcomings in this department: 'An odd streak in me remained resentful of any attempt to cultivate the art of alluring the opposite sex. This was what all mothers hoped of their daughters — maximum sex appeal with the minimum of sex experience.' There had been previous attempts to make her prettier: 'Asthma and recurring pneumonia had rendered me thin and unattractive.' Her aunt Anne had taken her to Switzerland for animal gland injections. The result was that she grew two inches in a month and, inclined to sallowness, now had a sea-green complexion.

Lodged in the Rue de Longchamp, near the Eiffel tower, at the home of the Mesdemoiselles Armoury, with her friends Winifred (Pooh) Paget and Elizabeth Darrell, Anita's health and appearance soon began to cause concern. She had never eaten a lot, as heavy meals seemed to bring on asthma attacks, but now she and her two friends took to serious dieting: 'We all wanted to be thin and longed to look depraved.' Word got back to Marjorie and on 30 November 1930 Anita wrote protestingly to her mother:

> I DID NOT go three days on water in Paris … I am afraid that my bony legs must be an optical delusion [*sic*] as according to measurement they are exactly the same as for the last three year … I have no defence what so ever [*sic*] for my previous wish not to eat except that it was an interesting mental experience to see just how far my will controlled my body.

She ended by describing a visit to the Casino de Paris: 'I thought Josephine Baker the loveliest thing I had ever seen on stage … how could you be disgusted by that perfect brown body.'

Anita, bony legs notwithstanding, was lovely too, tall and slender with the clear Leslie brow and slightly slanted eyes, the type of looks that would become more fashionable as the slinky fashions of the 1930s took hold. In Paris she was held responsible for the dieting craze that resulted in Pooh and Liz coming down with pneumonia and influenza and being brought back to London. Anita was moved to the home of an aristocratic Russian emigrée, Madame Lermantov, and enrolled at the Sorbonne. And then the good times began. Her youngest uncle, Lionel, was studying animal sculpture in Paris while living with a nightclub dancer whose stage costume was a covering of gold paint: 'I had never met anyone like this. Nor for that matter have I done so since.'

She began to study French literature and, introduced by her Russian landlady to a very old French sculptor, Alfred Boucher, once an intimate friend of Auguste Rodin, she kept a diary in which she recalled Boucher's anecdotes. This later became the seedbed of her first biography, *Rodin: Immortal Peasant* (1939), a lively, if highly fanciful, book. In 1931 she was reluctantly dragged away from this exciting milieu to prepare for the following year's debutante Season: 'After all, it just means dull expense and lots of clothes and "amusement", which I don't want.' Meanwhile, there were country house parties, which she found distasteful if, as was often the case, they involved shooting: 'I found it repellent that the shooters' faces always looked so red!' But, coming from a literary family, it wasn't all ruddy-cheeked squires and tedium. She sat next to W.B. Yeats at a Dublin dinner party. At a house party in Oban, given by her great-aunt Olive Guthrie, she looked so leggy and dashing that the local people thought that she must be a film star.

She made some exotic new friends, among them the disreputable Tallulah Bankhead, whom she visited in Mayfair, 'feeling tiresomely undecadent amongst ladies whose eyelids glistened with incandescent violet grease'. Another unlikely acquaintance was the American Gladys Marlborough, a ruined beauty, miserably married to the Duke. When their ghastly marriage ended in 1933, 'I tried hard to appear sophisticated and one of my letters [to Gladys] ends, "Wishing you the best of luck in the divorce – with love – Anita".'

Every debutante's account of her Season tells a story of wretchedness and dismay. Even the flamboyant Clare Sheridan had been overawed by the weighty procedure of coming out. She wrote in *Nuda Veritas*: 'I stood in ballroom doorways longing to be hidden in the crowd, cursing my conspicuous height and shrinking from introductions.' During her own Season, being carelessly parented worked to Anita's advantage. Marjorie seldom chaperoned her because 'it bored her to see my sulks'. And Shane 'would only go to balls which took place in grand private houses'. Indifferently watched over, Anita could evade the dull young men in the ballroom, appalling dancers every one, and attach herself to a livelier lad, a well-born bad lot who, unknown to Anita's family, had been wiped off the high-society listings on account of, among other misdemeanours, having a drink-driving conviction and losing his licence. Anita became his evening chauffeur. She would sneak out of the ballroom and into the driving seat of his sports car. They headed for the Ace of Spades, a racy nightspot on the Great West Road. Then Anita would sneak back for the closing moments of the debutante dance. Clare's parties in her St John's Wood studio, where writers and artists dined on red wine and spaghetti and there wasn't a suitable boy in sight, provided another welcome distraction from the stuffy Season.

Leonie, too, came to the rescue. When she was in London she took her wilting granddaughter to receptions at Londonderry House, where the guests were eminent statesmen rather than callow striplings or, if a dance was obligatory, she introduced Anita to 'the most amusing people – never young however'. Every debutante was required to attend Royal Ascot: 'When my turn came, she [Marjorie] had left London and Pa disappeared.' Anita went by herself with two sandwiches in her handbag and got picked up by 'an olive-skinned gentleman with roving – very roving – eyes', who tempted her with several helpings of strawberries and cream. He was Aly Khan, son of the Aga Khan and the kindest and most courteous of men, but a potential source of scandal. At the end of the Season, thankful that 'one could not be a deb twice,' Anita reflected that 'if my ambition throughout had been to annoy Mama, I had succeeded wonderfully.'

Marrying off their daughter to a rich suitor was important to the upper classes, since a wealthy husband's money could alter the circumstances of an entire family. Clare Sheridan, daughter of the reckless Moreton Frewen, knew this well: 'My father regarded me as an investment. If I married well

I should have proved myself worthwhile.' To this end, she was forbidden to see the brilliant but poor Wilfred Sheridan for years. There was less pressure on Anita to marry well, perhaps because the Leslies' finances weren't as dire as those of the Frewens, but parents and girls were mindful of the fate of unmarried women at a time when there were no careers to provide an alternative to matrimony. In *The Gilt and the Gingerbread* Anita tells the story of the six unmarried sisters of Lord Belmore of Castle Coole, Enniskillen, thirty miles from Castle Leslie:

> Each girl had been given one London season and when she found no suitor of equal rank returned to the Irish demesne for ever ... Nothing ever happened. Nothing could happen. One of the six sisters drowned herself in the lake and when the butler announced the news at breakfast, her brother, Lord Belmore, reportedly said, 'Well, don't stand there, man. Bring in the porridge.'

In 2008 I visited an exhibition called 'The Last Debutantes' at Kensington Palace. The last debutantes to be presented at Court made their debut in 1958, nearly three decades after Anita's much-resented Season. By then a wider world than that offered by an early, wealthy marriage was on offer but you could still feel desperation in display stands of expensive frocks, walls papered with invitations, a film of girls being taught how to curtsey. Even the smiling debs photographed in their Dior and Balmain dresses seemed to be quivering from the ordeal.

I can't imagine Anita quivering. Although her family would have been delighted had she landed a duke, she wasn't seen as an investment. It was probably just as well since her recalcitrant personality would not have been suited to the narrowness of English aristocratic life, impressed as she was by titles. Anyway, she soon made it clear in a letter to Shane that she never wanted to marry, 'although I might make quite an intelligent mistress – I don't mind sacrificing my body but not my freedom'.

3

The Devil's Decade

Anita, despite her taste for unsuitable boys and her dislike of matrimony, was not the most outlandish debutante of the 1932 Season. That title belonged to Unity Mitford, younger sister of Diana, 'the most flawlessly beautiful woman I have ever seen' according to the diarist James Lees-Milne. Diana's triumphant debut in 1928 had culminated in her engagement to Bryan Guinness, heir to a great fortune. Unity, less beautiful than her older sister but more striking, seemed unlikely to repeat Diana's success. Nearly six feet tall, she attracted more notice by adding swirling capes and paste jewels to the regulation *jeune fille* wardrobe. In case attention was still lacking she took along her pet rat, Ratular, to dances, or wound her grass snake, Enid, around her neck instead of pearls. More sinister was her abiding interest in fascism: when she was fifteen she said that when she grew up she would go to Germany to meet Hitler.

In 1932 this didn't seem such a horrible idea as it would by the end of the decade. In Unity and Anita's debutante year, *Tatler* magazine photographed Adolf Hitler, the leader of the German National Socialist Party, as a man about town – just another ambitious politician hoping to triumph in troubled economic times. On 1 October in Great Britain another charismatic politician, Sir Oswald Mosley, launched the British Union of Fascists (BUF). Mosley was – this is James Lees-Milne again – 'a man of overweening egotism ... he had in him the stuff of which zealots are made'. Diana Guinness, after a long affair with Mosley, married him in secret in October 1936 in the drawing room of Joseph and Magda Goebbels' Berlin apartment, with both Hitler and Unity in attendance.

Almost until the outbreak of the Second World War, most British people regarded communism as a greater threat than fascism. In 1934 an early Gallup poll found that of its interviewees 70 per cent of those under thirty preferred fascism to communism, perhaps because living standards were improving in fascist Germany and Italy. It was estimated that the BUF had 30,000 non-active members and supporters. The Reichstag fire of 27 February 1933, which had brought the Nazi party to power the following month, had not inspired as much fear as the news from the Soviet Union: the Stalinist collectivization policies, which led to the famines of 1930–33 and the intentional starving to death of three million Soviet Ukrainians, an event known as the Holodomor – 'murder by hunger'. *The Brown Book of the Hitler Terror and the Burning of the Reichstag*, edited by Otto Katz (1895–1952), the mysterious and dashing Czech-born spy said to be the model for the heroic Victor Laszlo in the film *Casablanca*, and published by John Lane in 1933, listed the new German anti-Semitic laws but was widely thought to be communist inspired.

In her early twenties Anita shared the dreary, casual anti-Semitism of her insecure and arrogant class but probably didn't give the political situation much thought; young girls of her background seldom did. Nancy Mitford even said of her younger sister Unity, who is now regarded as having been a rabid fascist: 'With her the whole Nazi thing seemed to be a joke. She was great fun ... Unity was absolutely unpolitical. No one knew less about politics than she did.'

Later Anita described herself as having been 'an idiotic London debutante' and, in her 1981 memoir, describes a highly suspect scene which, supposedly, took place at Glaslough at the beginning of the 1930s. Leonie, seated at her dressing table, holds up a clipping from a German newspaper that showed 'an unhappy-looking man walking along a street in his under-pants with a large star pinned to his vest'. This so distressed Leonie that 'her trembling hands kept dropping her silver brushes'. This doesn't quite square with a letter that Anita wrote to her friend Rose Burgh, *née* Vincent, on 13 October 1938. In it, Anita complains that Ireland 'was swamped with Jews' and quotes a conversation between her grandmother and a customs official: '"What will you do about them?" Gran asked the Customs man to divert his attention. "Argh sure we'll send for Hitler to chase 'em."' No mention of trembling hands.

Shane, a devout Catholic as well as a world-class philanderer, felt more threatened by Russian communists than German Nazis. In 1922 Lenin had executed 4500 priests and monks and 3500 nuns, while fascists were notable only for silly uniforms and successful economic policies. Shane had a dubious acquaintance in Charles Maurras, the French royalist and founder of the extremely right-wing Action Française who, after the Second World War, was found guilty of collaboration. At this verdict, he shouted: 'It's the revenge of Dreyfus!'

The Leslies, like many of their friends, didn't take the rise of Nazism very seriously, unlike their cousin Winston Churchill. In September 1933 after she had lunched with Winston, Clare wrote to Shane, 'what impressed me most about Winston is his vibrant hatred of Hitler … He says Europe must unite to keep Hitler down – that he's the most dangerous thing that ever happened.' But the world was largely indifferent to the threat of Nazi domination, and the Anglo-Irish particularly so. The news from elsewhere hardly penetrated their days of hunting and picnics. In March 1932 in the Irish Free State, Éamon de Valera's Fianna Fáil party had been elected on a platform pledged to deliver 'social justice', with policies designed to show the Protestant ascendancy that it was no longer, in the words of the poet Patrick Kavanagh, 'part of the national consciousness'. This dimin-ished status wasn't felt at Glaslough, situated at the edge of the country. There, Sir John Leslie, Protestant landlord, lived on with his lively wife, cared for by devoted Catholic servants, who made sure that the flowers picked from the garden that day matched the dress that Leonie changed into for dinner.

Leonie was more concerned, as Anita's dismal London Season drew to a close, with what her granddaughter should do next. The granddaughter herself was delighted to return to Ireland and the country pursuits she loved. Hunting with the Ward Union, a prestigious stag hunt founded in 1854, she wrote to Shane: 'I have never had such fun, it's the grandest life and the one I'm made for. Sociaty [*sic*], clothes and complex intellectualism can all go to blages [*sic*] while there's this.' But perhaps bearing in mind the fate of the Belmore sisters, she seems to have realized that she couldn't stay on the family estate forever. On 28 September 1932 she wrote to Shane that she was about to start 'my Daily Express job'. This came to nothing, so Leonie, as she so often did, took things in hand. She wrote to her friend Noël Coward, with the result that Anita, who had been taking lessons in Spanish dancing, was auditioned by the impresario C.B. Cochran to be a dancing showgirl in his new musical *Nymph Errant*. Coward had turned down Cochran's offer to write the score and Cole Porter took over. He considered this show one of his best because of its worldliness and sophistication.

Anita in her memoir gives a false account of this episode: 'So I became a Cochran Young Lady. Granny Leonie was disgusted, Mama could not believe that I, who loved horses and country, should be ready to miss a summer in Ireland.' The truth was that Leonie had brought about the introduction to Cochran, Marjorie had encouraged the dancing lessons and even Shane was enthusiastic. He sent his daughter orchids on the opening night at the Opera House theatre, Manchester, and wrote to her: 'You looked so well and wiry and brilliant that I was overwhelmed with pride when I saw you again.' The vagabond, theatrical life suited Anita: living in digs, cadging baths from friends, greasy spoon suppers. She wrote to Shane in 1933: 'I feel that I have opened the doors of an entirely new world.' She admired the show's star, Gertrude Lawrence, for her hard work but not for her diva-ish behaviour: 'Anyone else who sings better than she gets turned out or their song cut which is not good for business.'

While Anita was hoofing in the provinces, her friends were, more traditionally, getting married. Betsan Horlick, a member of the malted milk dynasty, who had sat next to Anita in Miss Wolfe's classes, married John

Coats, a deceptively unconventional stockbroker. Soon after the wedding, the couple went to India as vegetarian lecturers for the Theosophical Society. In 1933 Anita became the godmother of their son, Christopher. Winifred Paget married Guy Carleton, 'a horsy young man with a quick wit' as described by Anita in print, but less favourably in her letters. The most spectacular of the weddings was that of eighteen-year-old Rose Vincent to Alexander Leigh Henry Leith, the 6th Lord Burgh, known as 'Alkie', on 6 June 1934. According to Rose's future daughter-in-law, the novelist Anita Burgh, Alkie's brother Jock was the man whom Rose really loved but Alkie's mother pushed her into marriage with the older brother. Alkie was on the verge of bankruptcy and Rose had been left a fortune by her American mother, whose grandfather had developed a Californian goldmine. Rose's childhood had been spent at Muckross in Killarney, an estate of 11,000 acres which, in 1933, was donated to the state by Rose's father, Senator Arthur Vincent, and became Ireland's first national park. Money as much as convention motivated these early marriages. Brides could get hold of their inheritance as soon as they married, instead of having to wait until they were twenty-one. Husbands were the key to the safe, although sometimes discarded a few years later, with scandalous divorces and custody battles. 'Matrimony represented their [the brides'] only mode of escape,' Anita wrote. The alternative to it was the restrictive gilded cage of the parental home.

Shane and Marjorie knew the Vincents and had stayed at Muckross at the same time as W.B. Yeats, that frequent and demanding guest of big-house owners. Anita and Rose became friends after their debutante Season and, for three decades, Rose remained the most important person in Anita's life, the soulmate to whom secrets were divulged in long, sometimes daily, letters, while lives and husbands changed. Unlike Rose, Anita was under no pressure to marry – there would have been no great fortune to inherit if she had – and she was now determined to become a writer. Shane showed her the way. During the 1930s he published prolifically: books on the Oxford Movement, *Poems and Ballads* and a book of brief biographies, *Studies in Sublime Failure*, whose subjects included his late uncle-by-marriage, the rascally Moreton Frewen. In authorship, as in life, Shane was overshadowed by his cousin Winston, whose wilderness years, outside of government, from 1929 to 1939, saw the publication of his magnificent, four-volume biography of his ancestor the first Duke of Marlborough.

If Shane resented living in Winston's shadow, he didn't show it. He praised Winston's books. Of the first volume of *Marlborough*, 'It is certainly the most remarkable perusal of history made in our time.' He kept his cousin up to date with family news: 'Dicky Sheridan [Clare's son] has signed on a wind jammer of Finnish extraction on which he sails for the Cape – Australia and the Horn – a very manly proceeding.' Shane asked for, and received from Winston, money for Hugh Frewen, Clare's brother who, like his father, had a talent for launching ruinous business ventures. And he made shameless use of his cousinage to seek introductions for his cronies, such as an American, Mrs Eustis, who wanted Winston to write an article for *Today* magazine, which Shane offered to write for him. Shane also solicited invitations for Winston to give lectures: 'Would you care to lecture to the admirals and captains at Greenwich? ... If you go I would like to go with you.'

In May 1934 Anita was back in Paris, being entertained by Lionel and the gold-painted dancer and getting on with her book on Rodin, which she went back to Glaslough to finish. On 25 February 1935 she sent the manuscript to Shane, who was in New York: 'I do do do hope you think it good enough – if it isn't I shall just die of rage, exhaustion and humiliation and never take up a pen again ...' She says that she has too many 'alternative satisfactions' in her life to be good at any one thing – writing, acting, riding: 'The result is I never get anywhere or will I get everywhere in time.' She was twenty-five. At Glaslough she rode and stayed with friends with whom she hunted. She borrowed 'Paul's saddle' and it is clear from her letter that Shane knew who Paul was. Then she went back to Paris, discovering, as all biographers do, that just when you think that you've exhausted every line of enquiry, more information comes your way. She wrote to Marjorie: 'Now I have pages to insert in my nice clean typescript.' Marjorie helpfully tried to interest the publisher M.M. Short in her daughter's book.

Paris was no longer the frolicksome city that Anita had loved: 'The French are all very gloomy … take war with Germany for granted.' Her family encouraged her to travel; widowed Aunt Anne took her to St Moritz, which Anita found 'too civilised', although she enjoyed excursions in the 'super Rolls Royce' belonging to the Granville Barkers. But it was dull for her: 'Lady Ashley and Douglas Fairbanks are the only hotel excitement. They are generally to be found in the bar.'

The following month there was a more enlightening trip: to the estate of Count Larvich, an old friend of Leonie's, at Solza, Karviná, in Poland. Anita, an admirer of people whom the writer Edward Upward labelled 'poshocrats', sent Marjorie the guest list, which included the Duke of Alba and the Austrian Count Kinsky, cousin of the Count Charles Kinsky who had been Jennie Churchill's great love. It was a lavish house party: 'We had a sumptuous picnic lunch in the woods – wooden table, bonfire and butler included! In Poland!' But the mood was sombre: '[P]olitical feeling is very strong here. One cannot discuss Hitler openly even in a private drawing room.' Her host was examining his cellar in case of future air raids. The Poles didn't seem to be panicking like the French but were taking 'calm, mechanical precautions as the cloud of disturbance and war looms nearer and gloomier'. Anita didn't mention this visit in any of her published writings. In this atmosphere of unrest, Margaret Sheridan married a much older man, Comte Guy de Renéville, at the time an admirer of Hitler and later described by General de Lattre de Tassigny as 'the most likeable lunatic in the French army'. The marriage was not a success.

Quite suddenly, in 1936, Anita's own marriage prospects became a subject of interest to her family, for reasons which would later become clear. In February Marjorie took her daughter to New York, 'where she and aunt Anne wished me to marry a rather nice American of their choosing'. Anita and the said young man, Ben, got on well but neither wished to marry someone who had been shoved at them 'with the tact of a sledgehammer hitting you on the head'. While staying at her aunt's Fifth Avenue penthouse apartment, Anita had one of her frequent changes of career-plan and took acting lessons at a drama school run by émigré Russians from the Moscow Arts Theatre: 'I have decided I want to try to get into the Old

Vic when I return,' she wrote to Shane. After New York she stayed with the Baruchs at their South Carolina plantation. Barney gave her a useful lesson: 'There's only one thing worth studying – human nature.'

The year 1936 was besmirched with shabby events as well as tragic ones. It was the year when Diana Guinness, *née* Mitford, secretly married Sir Oswald Mosley in Berlin. A new Public Order Act had banned BUF uniforms and Sir Oswald was no longer able to appear in his menacing fascist regalia. Another notorious marriage was being discussed: that of King Edward VIII and the American divorcée Wallis Simpson. Both Leonie and Marjorie knew the leading players in the abdication crisis that followed the King's decision to marry the woman he loved. Marjorie played bridge with Wallis and admired her beautifully shaped eyebrows and quiet manners, neither of which cut any ice with Queen Mary, the Queen Mother, who suggested that Leonie, a devoted Royalist, and the Duke of Connaught visit the King at Fort Belvedere, his country house in Berkshire, to judge how serious the affair was. After the royal party had returned from a walk, Wallis ordered the King to take off her muddy shoes, which he did. Leonie knew then that all was lost. The King abdicated in December and married Wallis in 1937.

In the spring of 1936 Italy annexed Abyssinia and Hitler's army marched into the Rhineland. In July the Spanish Civil War began, a harbinger of the wider conflict to come. Even then, invading dictators were not taken very seriously. At the Ideal Home Exhibition in London, a fashion display posed the question: 'If England had a dictator what would women wear?' and Diana Vreeland, in her *Harper's Bazaar* column 'Why Don't You?' suggested: 'Why don't you wear bare knees and long white knitted socks, as Unity Mitford does when she takes tea with Hitler at the Carlton in Munich?' But perhaps she was joking.

There was a death in Anita's family. Dick Sheridan, the seafaring young man of whom Shane had written so admiringly to Winston, had turned twenty-one on 20 September of that year. This was a matter of great apprehension to his mother, Clare, because he now became the owner of Frampton Court, the Sheridan family estate in Dorset, whose lands carried a curse: 'No first-born son had ever survived to inherit those lands from which Henry VIII had evicted the monks.' Dick sold Frampton, to Clare's relief, but he didn't tell her that he had retained a single acre, which contained his grandfather's grave. Dick, reckless survivor of storms and mishaps at sea, decided that he wanted to be a playwright, like his famous ancestor and namesake, and set off with a girlfriend to drive to Bab-El-M'Cid, where he could write in peace. It didn't seem particularly worrying when he needed an operation on his appendix and was flown to the French hospital in Constantine. Then Clare, now living in London, received a telegram: 'Peritonitis developed, come quickly.' She went at once to Paris, from where she could get the evening train to Marseilles, and there found another telegram telling her that her son was dead.

Anita's family had always known that she looked upon Glaslough as her home and that the sporting life she enjoyed there was good for her health; Leonie, suspicious of her granddaughter's rosy cheeks, once accused her of wearing rouge. However, in 1936 she was urged to go anywhere but the place she most loved and, since she seemed disinclined to marry nice young men who were pushed towards her, her ever-changing ambitions to act, write and travel were encouraged. There was a reason for this: his name was Colonel Paul Rodzianko CMG and it was clear that he meant trouble.

4

Married to the North Wind

In 1981 after *The Gilt and the Gingerbread* was published, Harold Harris, Anita's editor at Hutchinson, asked her why Paul Rodzianko, to whom she had once been married for more than a decade, had been only sketchily mentioned in her memoir, with no reason given as to why Anita married this penniless Russian, thirty years her senior. Anita told Harold: 'I found it very difficult to blow him up or explain why I married him. I don't know.'

Nobody else knew either. When he first visited Anita at Glaslough in 1935, having met her at another Irish country house where he was training steeplechasers, Leonie referred to him as 'that NHB', the letters standing for 'noisy, hungry bore'. Lionel's daughter, Leonie de Barros, told me that Lionel had thought that Paul had given Anita the idea that the Russian Revolution would one day be overturned and that he and Anita would return to the land of his birth and resume his former aristocratic, landed life, with one hundred horses in the stables, where wolves were hunted with borzoi dogs and where, for a fancy-dress court ball, Paul's mother had all her diamonds made into a glittering breastplate. Or, perhaps, having known other émigré Russians in both Paris and New York, Anita had admired the resilient and courageous way they coped with the loss of their fortunes and estates and adapted to new, much harder lives. Annoying Marjorie, who did not see Paul as suitable husband material, also had something to do with it, as Anita admitted. During the years of maternal neglect Anita had adored her mother but when Marjorie began to take more of an interest in her, Anita resented her interference.

Of all the riches-to-rags émigré lives that Anita encountered, Paul's was the most extraordinary. Born in 1880, he was the son of Princess Marie Galitzine and General Paul Rodzianko, whose lands were in the Ukraine and who composed military marches including 'Cassez Tout', which became known as the 'Rodzianko March'. The family estates were about the same size as the British Isles. After a privileged childhood, the younger Paul joined the Chevalier Guards and married Tamara Novosiloff, a maid of honour to the Russian Empress. During the First World War, Paul was an officer in the Tsar's Imperial Guard but was, luckily, on a riding course at the Italian Cavalry School at Tor di Quinto when the Revolution broke out in 1917. He had placed his children in English boarding schools earlier in the year but his wife disappears from the story about this time – they may have been divorced by then. The rest of Paul's family, after much hardship, managed to get out of Russia. His mother, who had been imprisoned and condemned to death, was rescued by the departing Swiss ambassador.

Paul went to London, somehow managed to enlist in the Royal Fusiliers, and, later, because of his friendship with the British general Sir Alfred Knox, received a commission in the 10th Hussars. For a few years, from 1928, he was the instructor of the Irish Equitation School, which had been set up in 1926, both to advertise the new state and to promote the Irish horse. 'Having found it in a state of depression, Rodzianko left the Equitation School with the capability of taking on the world,' runs one testimonial. After six months of Paul's training sessions, the Irish show jumping team won the Aga Khan trophy for the first time. Paul was, indisputably, the greatest riding instructor of the twentieth century and had himself been taught by two masters in horsemanship: the Englishman

James Fillis, who could make a horse canter backwards on three legs, and the Italian Captain Caprilli, who invented the 'forward seat'.

As a fifteen-year-old Paul had seen the first, chaotic production of *The Seagull* at the state theatre of St Petersburg, in 1895. He had discovered the remains of a wedding party in Siberia, eaten by bears down to the last bridesmaid. He had walked the battlefields after the Battle of Tannenberg in 1915 and found a whole division of corpses; the six-feet tall, snub-nosed descendants of soldiers recruited by the then Tsar because they resembled him. He had identified the bones of the last Tsar's pet dog in the blood-stained cellar of Ekaterinberg and had been summoned to lunch with King George V at Windsor Castle to give his account of the murder of the Imperial Family, cousins of the British king.

Leonie may have thought him a noisy, hungry bore but Anita found him entrancing. On 4 February 1935, she wrote to Shane: 'Paul Rodzianko stayed here [Glaslough] nearly three weeks and trained all the horses. He is delightful but so temperamental and Russian – thinks he can't live without me and all that so I will be terribly nice to him till I come to U.S.A and that will be a good chance for it to die out. Don't tell Ma or any one.' It didn't die out. Just over a year later Anita wrote to Shane: 'Paul Rodyanko [*sic*] has improved my riding and also goes to church and prays on the days I hunt so what with his training and his celestial influence I have been lucky! Mum does not want me to go to Clare's [who was then in Bisra] but I must. I am determined to – otherwise I will marry Paul just to annoy her.' Then, on 17 May 1936, another alert: 'As soon as Rodin is settled, I'm going to write Paul's life.'

Paul was not deterred by the Leslies' disapproval. Glaslough must have seemed to him like a kind of homecoming. There was something Chekhovian about the dark woods and gleaming lake, the greenhouses and log fires, the elegant formality made possible by devoted servants and, best of all, a susceptible young woman who loved horses as much as he did and, unlike her grandmother, who preferred the witty gossip of London dinner parties, listened attentively to his dramatic life story. Anita admired his exuberance: the way he sliced off champagne corks with his sword or walked on his hands while singing Russian songs.

Paul started to take over Anita's life. She wrote his life story, which became the book *Tattered Banners* (1939), and collaborated on another title, *Modern Horsemanship*, posing for photographs in immaculate riding gear to show the correct position of hands and body. It's a wonderful book; you feel that Paul knows exactly what it's like to be a horse – he was a horse whisperer before the term was invented. But she knew that her involvement with Paul was playing with fire. In *The Gilt and the Gingerbread*, she wrote: 'Mama's efforts to halt what she regarded as an appalling match goaded me into it.' When she tells Marjorie that she isn't going to marry Paul, her mother says: 'How could you be so cruel as to torture me about that man for nothing,' and refuses Anita's request to be allowed to travel around the world. So, two weeks later, in April 1937, Anita married Paul at the Harrow Road register office, with her friends Rose and Winifred as reluctant witnesses. Her account of her wedding day is bleak – 'My heart had turned to lead at the word "wife"' – but the letter she wrote to Marjorie from the Isle of Wight, where she and Paul were spending their honeymoon, paints a cheerier picture and suggests that the wedding, instead of being decided on the spur of the moment, out of spite, had been some time in preparation:

> Darling Mum, My marriage day was perfectly lovely – it went beautifully – thanks to you ... I think both our costumes were extremely successful – and the flowers went so well with them. You looked lovely. I thought the party 'went' excellently – the room was always full never crowded. Everyone seemed to enjoy themselves much more than at a formal wedding reception ...

and more in this happy vein. These conflicting accounts call to mind E.L. Doctorow's opinion that 'I am led to the proposition that there is no fiction or nonfiction as we commonly understand the distinction; there is only narrative.'

A perfect example of Anita's ambivalence towards her bizarre marriage: in spite of writing in the 1980s to Harold Harris of how 'hellish Paul' had ruined her young life, in April 1965, learning of Paul's death, she wrote in her diary:

> What a character he was. I am glad I could write his book [*Tattered Banners*] and give him some happiness – tho very little for our penniless, garret life

was such a strain. It was like being married to a bear – or to the North Wind! … How much more worthwhile he was than any of the people I met at 12 Westbourne Terrace. I wish I had possessed a little money or a house or anything to help him during our marriage – I had not seen him for so long but now a loneliness fills me that he is not in the world.

In her memoir, descriptions of her marriage continue miserably. She wrote of the Leslies: 'Having brought me up to be as impractical as possible, the family blithely turned me adrift without any allowance when I married a penniless man.' One wonders. Even on her honeymoon, Anita is instructing Shane to promote Rodin, which is doing the round of publishers, and it's clear from this letter that Marjorie is preparing Anita and Paul's first home, a flat at 154 The Grampians in Shepherd's Bush, west London. Back from their honeymoon, the Rodziankos ate often at Westbourne Terrace – Marjorie had an excellent cook, Mrs Young – or at the homes of richer friends, so Anita's domestic hopelessness wasn't much of a problem. They went to exciting parties, many of them given by Rose Burgh, now separated from her husband. 'She saw me struggling in the coils of a thoughtless matrimonial muddle and she sorrowed at my plight.'

To outsiders, her plight looked like a rather interesting literary collaboration. In the acknowledgments in *Tattered Banners*, Paul wrote: 'My thanks are due to 'Anita Leslie', my wife, for her invaluable help in writing this book', the single quotation marks around her name making Anita seem rather ghostlike. Marjorie had no illusions about the book's true authorship; in her copy, next to her own signature, she wrote 'written by her daughter', which it undoubtedly was. Anita's girly fingerprints are all over it: the liberal use of exclamation marks, the small, fascinating details that brought the Tsarist era alive, such as boys having to sleep 'in knobbly curl-papers till a few years before we started military training!' It's a story of revolution, regicide and exile, of life at Court and on the battlefield. That it was published during what came to be known as The Great Terror, 1937–8, in Stalin's Russia added to the book's poignancy.

To Paul, wretchedly dispossessed, communists were synonymous with Jews. Thus his account of the murder of the Imperial Family: 'Then the guard, headed by three Jews, began to shoot, somewhat wildly, as they

were probably drunk.' This is conjecture, although there is little doubt
that the murder was particularly brutal. Paul's impassioned anti-Semitism
was transferred to his young wife. As well as jointly authoring books, the
Rodziankos were training horses and, while on a visit to Glaslough, Anita
sent Rose notice of another enterprise: 'Here is one of my lingerie cards –
give it to anyone who might be interested.' She enclosed a green business
card for 'Olita Exquisite Lingerie' with the name and address of a Miss
Walker at 8 Lyndale Avenue. I have not been able to find any more information about this project.

Anita's uncle Lionel could see that Anita was unhappy when he and
his future wife, Barbara Enever, visited the Shepherd's Bush flat soon
after Anita's marriage. Although the visit had been previously arranged,
Paul and Anita were out when Lionel and Barbara arrived. According to
Barbara, who related the incident to her daughter, Leonie de Barros, when
the Rodziankos did turn up, Anita tried to prepare a meal. Finding the
meat safe empty, Paul shouted, 'The Jews have stolen the meat.' Supper
consisted of gritty leeks. Anita looked bored. Barbara wasn't impressed
by the appearance of Rose Burgh, who claimed not to be able to open her
front door on account of her long fingernails and needed help. Barbara
thought that she overdid the effusiveness.

Cousin Winston completed the final volume of *Marlborough* in 1938
and Shane continued to pester him to meet his protégés, one of whom
was an air force pilot with concerns about the War Office. Like Winston,
Shane now thought war with Germany inevitable. The Rodziankos, on
the other hand, wanted only to extend the hand of friendship to Nazi
Germany, in the belief that Hitler would restore Russia and, more particularly, Paul's homeland, Ukraine, to a land fit for the poshocracy. To this
purpose, Anita became involved with an old friend of Clare's, Vladimir
Korostovetz, a Russian exile who was now a naturalized British citizen
and the author of several books on Europe. In the 1920s he had been the
New York World correspondent in Berlin, where he had met and fallen in
love with Clare. Although he constantly left bouquets of red roses at her
bedroom door, Clare saw him merely as a useful translator and arranger
of journalistic assignments.

In 1939 Korostovetz became the UK representative of the exiled Hetman (leader) of the Ukraine, Pavlo Petrovich Skoropadskyi, the German-born former Imperial Army General, and Paul's commanding officer, who had been toppled from power in November 1918 and was now living in Potsdam. It was probably through the Hetman that Korostovetz became friendly with the Rodziankos. On 13 March 1938 he wrote excitedly to Anita of his admiration for Hitler: 'Yes indeed Hitler does not talk he acts and that is the single way to get on isn't it? The stabilisation of Central Europe will go on now apace and then other parts of the world will need a strong hand to get things brought in order.' Then, more sinisterly, referring to Paul: 'I hope soon he will be of greater use for our common cause.'

Enclosed with this letter is another one to Rose, with whom, like most men, he was besotted. This letter ends: 'I kiss your hand', whereas Anita gets only, 'Yours very sincerely'. In Rose's letter, written the day after Germany occupied Austria, on 12 March 1938, he is exultant: 'Hitler is a great man ... it is one step further towards clearing out the nests of international intrigues – his Austrian move!' He believes that the 'Red Plague' will be wiped out everywhere: 'You ask about Spain. Things there are going most excellently.' He is convinced that Ukraine will soon regain its independence. In *The Gilt and the Gingerbread*, Anita makes a delicate reference to these unsavoury pre-war circumstances. She and Paul were touring Europe and met with two of Paul's former commanding officers, the aforementioned Hetman and General Mannerheim, who was now Finland's leader. Anita wrote of these visits: 'I returned to England drugged with political issues I had never heard of before.' This is hard to believe; married to Paul, she must have encountered his pro-Nazi views from morning till night. That spring, she had written to Rose about her life with Paul: 'I feel his heavy mind and fuddled ideas simply clog my mental equipment.'

Rose herself, now involved with a man referred to as 'Pops' was in Amsterdam having a yacht built, named *Leprechaun*. Years later she told her then daughter-in-law, Anita Burgh why she had left her first husband, Alkie Burgh. When they married, Alkie, having lost his fortune, had sold

Northcourt, his estate on the Isle of Wight. Rose had bought it back, as well as much of the former contents, which she had tracked down, and given it to him as a wedding present. Three years later she was reading the newspaper in bed when she saw an advertisement for the sale of Northcourt and its contents. It was the last straw; she got out of bed and left. Walking out of a marriage was something she was to do more than once. It was Anita who should have considered leaving. On 15 July she wrote dispiritedly to Rose: 'Having injections for exhaustion as all insides have gone wrong.' But she and Paul were making more travel plans. On 3 August she told Rose: 'We may go to Nuremberg as Hitler's guests on September 5th but Paul is supposed to be back at work. Rather fun to meet all the Nazis.' Her mental equipment was quite definitely clogged.

On 29 September the Munich Agreement forced Czechoslovakia to cede the Sudetenland to Nazi Germany, which occupied the rump of the country the following year. Avishai Margalit wrote of the Agreement in *On Compromise and Rotten Compromises* (2010) that it was 'a pact with radical evil, evil as an assault on morality itself'. Anita took a different view. A week after the signing of the Agreement, she wrote to Rose from Glaslough that war had been averted and 'Mothers whose hearts ached with terror are going back to their bridge and scolding the cook.' Korostovetz's book, *Europe in the Melting Pot*, came out that month and Rose sent a copy to Anita who 'read every word of it with ease', since the peacefulness of Glaslough was conducive to serious reading, as well as outdoor pursuits. She told Rose: 'I ride and chop trees all day – am getting quite subtle with an axe.' Paul came to join her, and his loathsome influence may explain the shrill tone of her next letter: 'Ireland was swamped with Jews during the crisis.' Korostovetz's book has made her dwell on 'the evil genius – Lenin ... to what extremes the human mind stretches'. She goes on: 'Of course Germany is going to dominate Europe but as we can't stop it for God's sake let's be her powerful friend – not her weak enemy!'

At the time, this view was not an unusual one. Oswald Mosley's party had adopted the slogan 'Mind Britain's Business', which presumably, meant take no notice of what's going on elsewhere. As far back as 1933 Winston

Churchill had raged against the Oxford Union for voting for the motion 'This house would not fight for king and country'; he called it 'this abject, squalid avowal', but he was still swimming against the tide. In 2009 Derek Malcolm, reviewing Stephen Poliakoff's film *Glorious 39* for the *Evening Standard*, recalled 'my own well-born mother [who] strode around London with a placard reading "Hands Off Hitler". My father simply went on hunting.' And a Secret Service report from 1936 on Sidney Bernstein, then a cinema magnate, later the creator of Granada Television and a member of the House of Lords, divulged: 'He always cuts the news films in his cinemas so that Fascist scenes etc. which might make a favourable impression are removed. Items about Russia are given prominence.' The future peer of the realm was 'reliably reported to be an active secret communist'.

Anita still imagined that Paul's fortunes could be restored. She wrote to Rose: 'Korotovetz and Paul are very excited in London and keep hinting at action! We'll ride in a troika yet darling.' On the following day, 13 October 1938, she wrote to Rose:

> If there is a war I am going to work at propaganda behind the lines – Anti-Jew stuff – just like the Bolshies in Russia only vice versa. Try to organise an anti-Jew Revolution and make a sort of Brest-Litovsk treaty with Germany! What do you think? Will you be my Mata Hari?

The Brest-Litovsk treaty of 9 February 1918, initiated by the Ukranian-born Leon Trotsky and the Soviet government, recognized the sovereignty of the Ukrainian Peoples' Republic. It must have been anathema to Paul.

The rest of this chilling letter is devoted to one of Anita's constant themes: the foulness of cities and the need to return to nature. 'That is why it is so good for a man to have a "country place" and the earth is the best of masters.' It was the twenty-fourth anniversary of her uncle Norman's death: 'The gardener who's been here 35 years has just brought a laurel wreath to put on his cross in the church. Again one thanks God that war slipped by.' The letter crossed with one from Rose, who is mopey and suffering from asthma in Amsterdam. She is getting *Leprechaun* ready for trials and regaling unreceptive Dutch listeners with tales of the little people of the hills, leprechauns, banshees, fairies and elves. Rose takes it for granted that 'Germany will have all that Middle Europe' and, like

Anita, thinks that 'we should go back to the land and simplicity while there is still time – it was our first heritage and so many have forsaken it for things utterly false, transitory, and of no depth or purpose'. She is advocating this way of life while waiting for furnishings for her yacht to arrive from England. She has harsh words for Anita, who is obviously 'at cross purposes with the world, which is the expression of God's will – for when you have achieved harmony with that force, the world will not hurt you any more'.

It is difficult to excuse anti-Semitism, as Hermione Lee acknowledged in her biography of Edith Wharton:

> Her [Edith's] attitudes were commonplace among upper-class Anglo-Americans, and the French, in pre-Holocaust times. But comparisons, historical tolerance, and recognition of the licence we all take in private correspondence do not make good excuses here.

I share this opinion with regard to Anita, an upper-class Anglo-Irishwoman, although I recognize that during her marriage to the bullying Paul it was hard for her not to be influenced by his rancid ideas. Once she had, with great difficulty, extricated herself from his orbit, she became less prejudiced. Like Edith Wharton, she belonged to a class that prized a light-hearted giddiness in its young women and didn't encourage them to think deeply. Even intelligent Leonie was worried that the beautiful Margaret Sheridan might put off young men because of her obvious erudition. This is not to say that Anita was ever comfortable with Jews; she envied them for being cleverer than her and better at making money. On her 1935 trip to the USA, when she had stayed with Barney Baruch, he had told her that no good school would accept his daughter because he was a Jew. Anita told him that there had been Jewish girls at her English schools and added: 'I did not much like them because they were so clever. Lessons seemed so easy to them.' She insisted that Barney 'guffawed' at this honest remark. At the time, Anita was very young and naive but, in his book *Blood Kindred*, W. J. McCormack observes: 'One should recognise naiveté as amongst the most dangerous attributes the innocent might possess.'

The night of 9 November was Kristallnacht, evidence of the slide towards genocide as German Jews were arrested, imprisoned and their property looted or destroyed. On 26 November Anita wrote to Rose from The Grampians: 'Unity Mitford is dining with us and Paul is all prepared to like someone who really likes Hitler as much as he does. I've asked Des [her 16-year-old brother] as he'll do funny sketches of it.' There is also a brief mention of Paul's son – she doesn't give his name – who has arrived in England 'run down and seedy ... We are terrified of a return to T.B.' On 15 December the *Evening Standard* ran a story that the 21-year-old Grand Duke Vladimir, pretender to the throne of all the Russias, was leaving Paris for a meeting with Herr Hitler to discuss the Ukraine. Anita commented: 'Utter fiction – according to Korostovetz. Invented by Jews and Soviet White Russians to befuddle everyone of the real Ukrainian problem.'

The day after the *Evening Standard* article appeared, the real Ukrainian problem and everything else was put out of Anita's mind when her five-year-old godson, Christopher Coats, fell down a lift shaft outside his parents' Belgravia flat. Betsan and John (Jackie) faced the loss of their son with a courage that Anita marvelled at. They were sustained by their faith – 'They believe that it happened deliberately because it had to – but Why?' an anguished Anita wrote to Rose. Betsan had asked everyone to wear bright colours at the little boy's funeral at Golders Green crematorium and Anita described the mourners' pretty hats 'perched over faces that looked as if they'd been scrubbed with a floor brush!' Even Paul, 'who has seen so much of death said he has never been so shocked – that boy was adorable, unique.' 'Icy and exhausted with nerve strain' Paul and Anita went to spend an uneasy Christmas with the Coats at their house in Somerset. The loss of this small godson, the sight of his Christmas stocking and the memory of his tiny coffin sliding through the crematorium doors while his stoic parents watched arm in arm, put Anita's own problems to the back of her mind, at least for a time.

5

Things Fall Apart

In the last year of that devilish decade, Winston Churchill castigated world leaders: 'They go on in strange paradox, decided only to be undecided, resolved to be irresolute, adamant for drift, solid for fluidity, all-powerful to be important.' The mood in Great Britain was one of tension, unease and wariness, artistic types being particularly suspect. The theatre director Joan Littlewood and her husband, the singer Ewan MacColl, were placed under MI5 surveillance early in 1939, when they lived in Hyde, Cheshire, where it was reported: 'A number of young men who have the appearance of communist Jews are known to visit Oak Cottage.' Politicians came under suspicion too. The year before, W.H. Auden had written to his brother John: 'The central committee of the Conservative Party [is] already refusing, in the nicest possible way, all Jewish candidates,' while 'the military engineered the dismissal of the Jewish secretary of state for war, Leslie Hore-Belisha, on thinly disguised anti-Semitic grounds.'

In February 1939 Anita went skiing in Chamonix with her brother Desmond. The short holiday had to be extended when Des had a bad accident on the slopes. Hospital arrangements were primitive. Anita wrote to

Rose: 'Yesterday, I had a battle royal with the surgeon who wanted to take the pin out of his knee without anesthetic [*sic*].' When Des was finally put under, Anita tried to clean up his bed, 'which was a miniature "Western Front" blood and other things mixed'. She kept these grisly details from Marjorie and asked her to send Irish bacon for Desmond's breakfast. She told her mother: 'Des takes a French newspaper and we both delight in the recognition of Franco!' The victorious Spanish dictator had destroyed the town of Guernica, killing 2000 people in 1937, during his country's civil war.

Sitting around in a hospital gave her time to think about her marriage. Her reason for coming to Chamonix had been to escape, for a time, her husband's growly presence. *Tattered Banners* had gone into a second edition, having received 'quite good but stupid reviews'. When Des was well enough to be left, Anita told Rose, she planned to return to London 'and write & write & write & try to make some pennies to pension Paul with'. She thought that if Paul had enough money she would be able to leave him: 'One of my few beliefs is that one can do what one likes in life as long as it does not cause other people suffering – And behold here I am trapped, unable to kick off the shackles and live because it would hurt Paul.'

Shepherd's Bush was a prison:

> Oh I am so bored, and caged and unhappy there ... for nearly 5 years he has bound me down to material worry and struggle! I have learnt to do accounts and cook and put up quite a good little conventional bourgois [*sic*] show but oh the inner weariness and boredom. ... One can't struggle for ever between pity and irritation! I am glad he is being so pompous and silly as it makes it easier to loosen the shackles. If he was 'little boy' and weepy it would be far worse.

From Chamonix, she wrote to Rose every day, signing off 'Love, Nita'. They understood each other's

> uncomfortable souls ...we can't fit into a respectable little nitch [*sic*] and like it ... For the moment I am living – it is like cold water thrown in one's face, icy water that makes one's blood feel like thin fire – I like snow and rocky crags and inaccessible summits and I hate ordering vegetables in Shepherd's

Bush. Have just heard Desmond's doctor broke his leg ski-ing this afternoon!!! Such a nice young man!! Don't tell Mummy!

By early March Des was able to have the plaster cast on his leg
removed. Anita could have returned to London. But she didn't, writing
to Rose: 'I am a new person – out of the rut, rebellious, not at all inclined
to drudge any more.' Her daily schedule obviously included a liaison, 'go
out ski-ing with lunch at 11 (private please) and come back at 4'. As for
Paul: 'I can't cope with him. I have only tried to help him and I have dug
that book [*Tattered Banners*] out of him. It sounds so brutal but to me that
book was the kernel of Paul and now only the husk remains.' She went
back to London in April, following Rose's advice not to make a hasty decision to leave Paul because 'it may be just the beginning of dawn and one
should wait till the light comes'.

On 14 April Anita wrote to Rose from Shepherd's Bush:

> I believe Paul must have intercepted a letter from my friend in Chamonix.
> He gnashed his teeth and wanted to strangle me with a belt. I got to the stairs
> and shrieked. He clouted me and then broke down in hysterical weeping, lay
> on the floor and sobbed wildly. ... If Paul continues raving I'll have to leave
> or my nerves will break up too.

But she stayed, explaining that she was sorry for Paul and didn't want to
upset Marjorie or cause a scandal.

At some stage during that last pre-war spring Anita made another
attempt to leave. An undated letter to Rose, written from Dover, en route
to Calais, describes how she hid in the train lavatory while Paul prowled the
station platform looking for her. He didn't have his passport with him, so
went back home, where he found a letter from Rose explaining the point of
Anita's journey – whatever it was. She seemed to be planning a permanent
move, partly because of the favourable exchange rate – 'it is mad to live out
of France!' – but, predictably, she returned to Shepherd's Bush.

Everyone had opinions about the likelihood of war. Korostovetz's
view was that 'Roosevelt's plea ... was just a Jewish machination to put
all the blame for war on the dictators.' Writing to Rose on 4 April, before
her short-lived flit to France, Anita returns to her domestic dramas:
'Thank goodness the sun helps one to laugh things off ... Oh – it's all so

opera comique!' Paul is delighted by Anita's suggestion that they write 'a Ukrainian book entitled "We Wait for Hitler". He is such a maddening child – I am like a mother with an awful baby that I can't leave just because it is so awful and no one else would look after it.' 'We Wait for Hitler' seems to have been accepted by Longmans Green but not published. Other titles had more success. Anita helped her husband write *Just Hacking* and, at the end of April, her life of Rodin was published in America where it was well reviewed and earned her one hundred dollars. Thoughts of war returned in her letters to Rose. On Easter Sunday: 'Some day England will just have to put a stop and then it will be war and then … ???' A few weeks later, on 29 April: 'I thought Hitler's speech brilliant, sane and dignified, the best he has ever made.' She was dismissive of her cousin Winston – 'his head is like an angry beehive of ideas'.

Anita hoped that she and Paul could travel to Central Europe together as foreign correspondents or, should war come and with it communist domination, 'go so peasant that you won't recognise me'. But she was being facetious. For the foreseeable future, life was about writing books on Paul's behalf, stabling and exercising other people's horses and trying to calm down Marjorie, who dreaded Jack being called to arms. With the bad timing that was Anita's speciality, *Rodin, Immortal Peasant* was published in England by Herbert Joseph in July.

Sir John Lavery RA, who had known Rodin well and painted his portrait, wrote the introduction, and the Duke of Westminster and Lord Howard de Walden were among the notables acknowledged by the author for their 'invaluable assistance'. Sir John noted Anita's family connections – daughter of Shane, cousin of Winston and Clare – and declared that 'Rodin himself would have asked for no greater tribute to his memory than that his biography should be written by a girl.' This is perhaps a sly reference to the sculptor's womanizing ways. The book is decidedly girlish in its unfettered admiration for Rodin, who Anita admitted was a wife-beater and unable to feel affection for anybody but who had a lumbering innocence and a love of nature.

In his lifetime Rodin had been called 'The Zola of sculpture'. He was an anti-heroic realist who ignored the Victorian fashion for vapid stonework.

His *Burghers of Calais* (1889) shows a group of wretched, vulnerable men stumbling towards their expected execution rather than righteous martyrs. He was a man, Anita wrote, 'for whom life was anything but dainty'. Nevertheless, she gave him a Mills & Boon makeover: 'He saw her coming, starlit and virgin, flowing in loveliness to the arms of the mysterious city … Autumn swept in, scarlet-cloaked and frosty-fingered.' There is quite a lot of this. As was the case in all her biographies, Anita knew more than she was telling. What she didn't divulge about Rodin was that he used women to further his career and then discarded them. So Rodin's affair with Camille Claudel, whose surname is withheld by Anita, ends because of the jealousy of his permanent mistress Rose Beuret. Not a word about Camille's reluctant abortion, her conviction that Rodin was appropriating her work and even conspiring to have her murdered, nor that she spent the last thirty years of her life in a mental asylum, where she was committed by her appalled family. This is Anita's version of the end of the affair: 'They did not meet again, but Rodin knew that he would never forget the appeal in those brown eyes, the deep brooding eyes of his Venus of Villeneuve.'

Anita is determined to present a love story between Rodin and the long-suffering Rose, a peasant woman whom Rodin married in 1917, the year they both died. The other women in his life get short shrift: the American-born Claire de Choiseul, again not named, is the villainess of the book, a blowsy, tipsy harridan, although, in fact, she introduced the sculptor to rich American investors. The English artist Gwen John, who was twenty-seven when she began an affair with the 67-year-old sculptor, isn't mentioned at all. These evasions and omissions may have been because, in 1939, when the book was published, Camille and Gwen were still alive. Even so, twenty-two years after Rodin's death, it was questionable to depict him as an unassuming innocent; he was a man who pushed for and received multiple public honours and appointments, including the presidency of the International Society of Painters, Sculptors and Engravers. The book is undeniably fun to read and shows a fine understanding of Rodin's work and how he transformed sculpture into something more painterly. But in a country edging towards war, there was little interest in a sculptor no longer as admired as Jacob Epstein, whose work was more massive, more controversial and more fitting for the stark times. *Rodin Immortal Peasant* received good reviews in *Punch*, *Tatler* and *The Northern Echo*, which, unhelpfully, didn't appear on the news stands until 5 September, two days after war was declared.

On 23 August the Nazi-Soviet Pact, sometimes called the Molotov-Ribbentrop Pact, was signed by the two thus-named foreign ministers. It specified a non-aggression policy between Germany and Russia. On signing, Molotov suavely remarked to the journalists present that 'fascism is a matter of taste!' The exiled Trotsky called it 'the midnight of the century'. Anita found the news 'glumly depressing'. Paul feared that Russia and Germany would form a permanent alliance and mourned the loss of Ukrainian independence, which might have held Russia in check. But sitting out in the sunshine at Marjorie's cottage in Hertfordshire improved Anita's mood. After all, Leonie had told her that the Duke of Connaught's secret scouts had assured him that there would be no war.

When war was declared two days after Hitler's invasion of Poland, it was something of an anticlimax. Anita was more concerned with the reception of her book: 'Paul innocently says everyone will read it in the trenches.' Shane had a new book out too: *Mrs Fitzherbert: A Life Chiefly from Unpublished Sources*, was published by Burns Oates, as was a second volume: *The Letters of Mrs Fitzherbert and Connected Papers*. Neither made much impact. Shane and Desmond became citizens of the Irish Free State, although both took part in the British war effort. During that first wartime autumn, the Leslies, like many other scattered families, were deciding where best to wait out the conflict, which Shane predicted would be over by Christmas. Marjorie, with ten pieces of luggage, went back to Glaslough. Shane applied for a teaching post at his old school, Eton, so as to be near Jack, who was stationed at Chelsea Barracks. In Somerset, Betsan Coats, assisted by a Buddhist monk, took in twenty-four evacuated children and their minders. They left after three weeks, as they thought that the countryside was 'utter desolation'. In London Paul was fretful as he had no success in finding a job at the War Office and Rose decided to rent Marjorie's cottage.

'It would take a war to give Paul a rest and me a good time,' Anita wrote to Rose in November. There were fewer horses to train, no point in writing books, which hardly anyone would notice or buy. She went cubbing in Northamptonshire, justifying this larking about to Leonie: 'I feel I am "helping the war effort" much more by having as pleasant a time as possible which is just what he [Hitler] doesn't want.' She had no intention of doing any war work since women who had volunteered for service, she told Rose, 'have resigned in futile rage and disgust at the petty jealousies that ruined all their efforts.' She didn't listen to Winston's stirring speeches, writing to Marjorie in Ireland: 'You can't imagine how bored people are with the war here. No one wants to listen to fancy speeches. They are just entirely occupied with the way it hits agriculture or finance in their particular business.' In this letter, she gives an account of her birthday party, for which Marjorie paid, which she held at Quaglino's restaurant. 'It was packed with Jewesses in mink coats and the newest ultra hats over one eye.' The following month Anita and Paul moved into Marjorie's London flat in South Lodge, St John's Wood, assuring her that they would keep the flat tidy. They had no qualms about buying clothes on Marjorie's accounts at Harrods and Simpsons. Their main inconveniences were the blackout, which meant they had to stumble through dark streets en route to a restaurant, and Paul's failure to find a job – 'the Intelligence is packed with Jews and I don't think there is much chance'. This was Anita at her most unpleasant. On Christmas Day, in spite of petrol rationing, she and Paul were able to drive to Hertfordshire and eat a delicious turkey with Rose.

At the beginning of 1940 Anita had earned £15 from Rodin, which had, so far, sold 140 copies. In May *Finland's Saviour*, Paul's book on Field Marshall Mannerheim, was published by Jarrolds. It claimed to be 'recorded by Anita Leslie' and, like Paul's previous books, was obviously written by her, her tinkly style recognizable from her own biographies: 'Until he was three years old little Gustaf Mannerheim never spoke a word … Petrograd, where the 'Nineties were as naughty and infinitely more glamorous than elsewhere! … There were blushes and lowered lashes as he passed at a Court ball.' An early hint that the naughty and glamorous 1890s were the years that Anita would make her own in her later writing.

On the publication of *Finland's Saviour*, the Rodziankos were featured in a *Tatler* article. At the South Lodge flat, Paul is seen popping a champagne cork with his sword, while Anita, exquisitely dressed and made up, sits decoratively on an antique chest making a telephone call. Nothing about the article gives any intimation that a war was going on. The photographs had been taken some weeks before the issue appeared. By the time the magazine went on sale nobody felt much like popping champagne corks.

The German blitzkrieg on western Europe began on 10 May, when the Netherlands and Belgium fell to the Nazis. Anita didn't seem particularly disturbed. She wrote to Rose: 'Have just heard news of invasion of Holland and Belgium – a pretty pair! I doubt if Jack will get his weekend with Grania Guinness.' She was more interested in getting some kind of foot treatment, which involved putting her feet in plaster and staying in bed for a week. There was no mention in her letter of that day's other main news story: Winston Churchill, whose opinions Anita had derided, had become prime minister.

6

Enormous Changes at
the Last Minute

What happened next meant that Anita could no longer ignore what was going on beyond the world of hunting and foot treatments. In the same month that her cousin was chosen to lead Great Britain, her brother Jack's regiment was sent to Boulogne and Jack was almost immediately reported missing in action while commanding a forward post. On 15 June, after weeks of not knowing whether Jack was still alive, Anita received a postcard from Second Lieutenant John Leslie Prisoner 400, in Oflag V11 B, in Eichstratt, Bavaria, Germany. Jack asked her to send him thirty Gillette razor blades, brown shoes, size 9 ½, bootlaces, handkerchiefs, face towel and soap, and wanted her to get the hat-maker, Edward Smith Ltd, Cork Street, to post him an Irish Guards brown service dress cap. It was inevitable that the regiment would fare badly. In contrast to the efficiently equipped Germans, Anita was told, 'the Guards had so much equipment they could hardly walk – blankets, saucepans, picnic accessories and only a few rounds of ammunition'.

This was the month that France fell and Britain stood alone, threatened with invasion. Winston Churchill made a speech that inspired a generation:

> We shall fight on the seas and oceans, we shall fight with growing confidence and growing strength in the air, we shall defend our Island, whatever the cost may be, we shall fight on the beaches, we shall fight on the landing grounds, we shall fight in the fields and in the streets, we shall fight in the hills; we shall never surrender.

The country was stirred by Churchill's language and what his biographer, Roy Jenkins, called 'a euphoria of irrational belief in ultimate victory'. General Alan Brooke, Winston's chief military adviser throughout the war, wrote: 'Without him England was lost for a certainty, with him England has been on the verge of disaster again and again.'

Anita seemed to be the only person in the country who wasn't inspired by her cousin. She didn't mention him in her letters, or express any loyalty towards him, until she herself became a soldier. Instead, she returned to her petty obsessions. On 26 June, the day that the Battle of Britain began, she complained to Marjorie that 'All the Jews are buying uncut diamonds and good pictures.' In July she began to focus on her own mortality, not altogether seriously. On 9 July she wrote to Marjorie: 'In my legacy – Gemma and Ham [her dogs] go to Rose, Bully [another dog] to Olive Walker, Bestobel [her horse] AND Paul to you, and my clothes to the Nation!' In her 1981 memoir, Anita reflected on the deaths of several friends in the early summer of 1940: 'How lucky I was to be husbandless, childless, unloving, unloved.' A beautifully written sentence, if not quite factual.

Inspired or not by Winston's rhetoric, by August she had decided to do some war work. This wasn't a completely altruistic or patriotic gesture: it had dawned on her that enrolling in one of the women's services might be a way to escape from Paul. Both the WRNS, Women's Royal Naval Service, and the WRAF, Women's Royal Air Force, turned her down – 'on account of my American mother and Russian husband', she informed the aforementioned American mother. On 28 August she learned that she had been selected to train as an ambulance driver for the Mechanised Transport Corps (MTC). On 7 September she wrote to Marjorie:

I am very fond of Paul but he does get on my nerves. For six years his financial difficulties have kept me in a mental rut of worry … You know how I
have always longed to explore and never been able to … I feel this is my only
chance ever. Now don't get upset because I won't go if you really can't bear
to let me but the time has come to try to make something of my life and I
must make a decision soon.

During her last few weeks in England, her letters to her mother were
light-hearted, the way they had been when she was a schoolgirl, and she
did her best to reassure Marjorie that all was well. She doesn't mention
her imminent departure to Africa with No. 11 Coy. of the MTC, nor
the effect on London of the Blitz, which began on 7 September, when
German bombers crossed the English Channel into British airspace, filling
800 square miles of sky and killing 430 Londoners in a single night. Forty
thousand people were to die as a result of the German air raids. Anita
reported only the comical: a captured German pilot's pockets contain
photographs of beautiful women, 'an English half crown and three birth
control appliances!! An odd idea for a bombing expedition.' She enlists
Marjorie's help in trying to track down missing jewellery: 'Did I give you
the diamond and ruby bracelet Olive gave me for my wedding to put in
your jewel box for Glaslough? I think so. It is in a small pink leather case.
Do you remember?'

In September she went back to Glaslough for embarkation leave. Of
Leonie's three surviving sons, Shane and Seymour were in the thick of the
London bombing while the youngest, Lionel, in kilt and sporran, was in
the Cameron Highlanders. Of her grandchildren, Jack was a prisoner of
war, Desmond had joined the RAF and now Anita was about to set sail on a
troopship. But there were no tears. Marjorie's only advice to her daughter
was: 'Don't get sunburnt in Africa – men hate it,' while Grandpa Jack
pressed a pound into her hand as he saw Anita off in the family brougham
and told her, 'Take this, my dear and be careful of yourself.'

The MTC was a fairly bizarre organization; 'a voluntary unit of considerable renown' was how Anita put it. Officers were addressed as 'Madam'
and recruits paid for their training and the attractive uniforms designed
by Hardy Amies. But these well-heeled girls knew how to take a car apart

and put it together again. Soon they would learn how to cope in the desert and help wounded men to survive. In her memoirs, Anita doesn't tell the half about the MTC but her letters are more revealing. In 1981 she wrote to Harold Harris, her editor at Hutchinson:

> We regarded ourselves somewhat snobbishly as a sort of Guards Brigade, ready to rush forward into any breach. BUT were pernickety about our uniforms and what we wore!!! Unlike the ATS who hated us and waged a war-long battle against our smart leather belts and becoming caps. We had a certain CHOICE as to where we went & what we did – as long as you bought your own uniform and did the training one could volunteer to drive ambulances at ARP posts or go abroad as in my Unit or use one's own car for VIPs at War Office!! Hence the ghastly entanglement of Colonel [*sic*] Eisenhower and Kay Summersby – she drove him in her own car to start with … it was all a scream.

Harold Harris's successor at Hutchinson was Anthony Whittome and, on 27 January 1983, just before the publication of her memoir, *A Story Half Told*, Anita wrote to him about her MTC commandant Maria Newall, including facts that couldn't be published because Mrs Newall, now in her eighties, was 'still being unutterable in Portugal – I wouldn't put anything past her'. In her letter Anita wrote:

> After being forced out of the MTC, she [Maria Newall] ruined Walter Monckton's career – he was to be Minister of State Middle East but she settled herself in his office (still in MTC uniform with pistol on her belt!) … Eventually, she went too far – shocked a desert Arab chief by attending Walter's lunch for him and eventually was SENT home against her will by the Military Police!! He had his job taken away and was flown back to England and she got on his plane and was picked off it in West Africa by the authorities, then had to wait six weeks for a slow boat from Lagos – and when Lady M did agree to a divorce, lost him to Biddy Carlisle! So there!

Since all the principals in this story are dead, it's not possible to verify Anita's account of scandalous goings-on in the desert.

Anita had told Marjorie that she had always wanted to explore but escaping her marriage was the main reason why she was glad to board the liner *Arundel Castle* on 15 October and sail away from the Glasgow docks. From the ship, she wrote to Rose: 'Only I could invent this way of running away from a husband.' She wrote 'PRIVATE' in the margin. Rose was now involved with someone called Tony. 'Don't consider his feelings,' Anita advised her. 'That is the worst thing to do with men – they immediately start inventing feelings designed to keep you attached to them.' On 7 November, as the ship neared Pretoria, she wrote again to Rose: 'Never again am I going to live a dull domesticated existence – I'm just going to be naughtier and naughtier! He he.' She had left Paul and his smothering routines in London, pestering the War Office for a job. Heady with the idea of freedom, it didn't occur to her that Paul would follow her to Africa and stalk her wherever she went.

The *Arundel Castle* sailed on through U-boat-infested waters. On board were squadrons of the Free French Air Force, including the writer Romain Gary, on their way to reclaim North African states from the Vichy French. Also among the passengers were Lord and Lady Dunsany, sent by the British Council to read poetry to the troops in Crete, a visit that had to be curtailed as Greece was shortly captured by the Germans. Anita knew the Dunsanys well: 'How often had I seen the great poet astride his horse when the hounds met at Dunsany Castle in Ireland!' Throughout the war, Anita met people she knew: old playmates, ex-debs, childhood neighbours who had since become generals. And, of course, the war was directed by her cousin Winston, her grandmother Leonie's favourite nephew. Max Hastings wrote of Churchill: 'He wanted war, like life, to be fun.' So did Anita. In all but the most horrifying moments, she made the war sound like an amusing cocktail party with sudden death attached.

7
Sunburn Is So Unbecoming

Anita's bid for freedom was soon compromised by Paul's arrival in Pretoria, her unit's first posting. Forty years later, when she was writing her memoirs, she decided not to mention the frequent and unwelcome appearances of her husband. To Harold Harris she explained, in 1981:

> I somehow cannot bear to go on and on about him – explaining how for years I was running like a hare and he was following and swearing he'd give me a divorce 'as soon as war ended' ... He kept turning up to annoy me – BUT when he produced nice horses I did ride them! – And we thought one of us would be killed – we weren't – ! My own mental hysteria makes a book on its own – a psychological trauma. He RUINED my youth but it was my own fault – if that is any comfort.

But in those first weeks in Pretoria, in November, with no inkling that Paul had tracked her down, Anita reverted to carefree, giggling girlishness. It turned out that the MTC wasn't needed in Kenya, so it was attached to the South African army. This was an unpopular decision but had the unit refused to be sent to Durban, the girls would have been denied wages, shoes, socks, knickers and breakfast. While waiting for their new posting, Anita wrote to Marjorie (26 November):

We have nothing to do but drill, polish our belts, march about and be taken
out to tea by charitable societies – the Synagog [*sic*] soc. And the Mothers of
Sons of England!!! Even the 6000 men who clamour to take us out every day
are getting monotonous.

The hooting cars encircling the MTC barracks were 'like Piccadilly Circus'.
Picnics, swimming, sunshine, the veldt and mountains and Anita's 'gang'
of three like-minded girls, Anita, Betty Holberton and Susan Southby –
'we stick together as we're all frail, foolish and lazy and we all go out
together always' – began to wipe out the unsatisfactory past. 'We feel
already we could never settle down to a normal existence again! We'll just
wander round the world in search of war and adventure.'

And then, in February, Paul arrived in Pretoria, staying at Polley's
Hotel, where Anita joined him during a 48-hour leave. He had somehow
obtained the command of the 3rd Remount Detachment, training and
supervising English and Irish horses. She made a second escape thanks
to the redoubtable Maria Newall who had flown to Kenya, seen people
in high places and arranged for her girls to join the advance MTC unit
driving the wounded in the East African campaign. They sailed from
Durban aboard the Dutch ship *Nieuw Holland*, in a military, and wageless,
limbo since the MTC was no longer part of the South African army and
not yet part of the British one. During the uncomfortably hot two-week
voyage, the commandant became increasingly tyrannical, holding daily
court-martials. Betty Holberton, a diplomat's daughter who knew only
'that it was imperative never to wear a ball dress twice without sending
it to the cleaners' was made to be Mrs Newall's batman and launder her
khaki shirts. The MTC recruits were now unsuitably dressed in collars,
ties, corduroy trousers and blue chiffon scarves. They were issued with
tropical kit that included 'jungle outfits, mosquito veils and mittens and
anti-insect gaiters. None of this could be used except the topees, in which
it was so difficult to salute.'

On 3 March, after a delay caused by mines dropped by Italian planes,
which had blocked the Suez Canal, the *Nieuw Holland* docked at Suez,
where a fleet of Dodge ambulances, a gift from the USA, was waiting for
them. When, tired and hungry, they arrived in Cairo, they were made

to listen to a lecture from the High Command on the perils of flirting. Wherever they went, the girls caused consternation mixed with amusement, partly because they were women doing what was regarded as men's work and partly because nobody had been expecting the arrival of uniformed females. These females could strip engines and drive all night but were instructed: 'Now girls! Even though you wear trousers you must always sit as though you were in skirts.' This insistence on ladylike behavior was understandable. Even wearing trousers, the MTC girls were alluring. Anita herself, slender, tall and leggy with large, moony eyes was lovely, as was the equally tall Betty Holberton. Regarding these willowy creatures, an Egyptian general, Aziz-el-Masri, sighed, 'Magnificent girls. All giraffe stock.'

Based at Helmieh camp, outside Cairo, 'a horrible entanglement of barbed wire and petrol tins in the sand', where the heat in the huts led them to drag their beds outside, the girls were on duty three days and three nights running, working in heavy, sand-filled air and the hot wind called *khamsin*. In the first week of April, Benghazi fell to the Germans and Anita, driving wounded men back from the battlefield, felt part of the desert war and its 'maddening discomfort'. Among the casualties transported in her ambulance were, she wrote to Marjorie, a sergeant with venereal disease and a soldier knocked out by a cricket ball. 'So English!! Imagine coming 12,000 miles for v.d. and cricket casualties.' In this letter of 5 April she discussed her finances – always a concern. Marjorie had put £150 in Anita's bank account but Anita was managing to live on her army pay of fourteen shillings a week, 'which none of the other girls managed to do'. Bizarrely, in the middle of the gruelling desert war, her expenses included taxis, laundry, shoes, stockings and hairdressers. She asked her mother to send her a pair of brown suede shoes and jodhpurs. About the work, she wrote: 'Though most of it is hell and one's entire life is ruined by petty rules and regulations, I would not have missed it for anything and hope to write a comic book about it some day.'

While her troops were eating hard meat, cabbage and rice pudding in the noonday heat, Mrs Newall was living luxuriously in Cairo, meeting de Gaulle, General Spears and other notables and lunching at various embassies before inspecting her dungareed ambulance drivers. She had put Anita, Betty and Susan in different units because they were 'too cliquey'. These mindless regulations reminded Anita 'of a convent rule that girls must never walk in twos or the devil will make a mischievous third'. Most of the girls in the MTC shared something of Anita's background: careless parenting, bad experiences in dubious educational establishments and the expectation that they would make the best of things – 'Smile dear, it costs nothing,' to quote Leonie once again.

That April, after the triple occupation of Greece by Germany, Italy and Bulgaria, the MTC ambulances met the wounded who had been evacuated from Athens. The summer of 1941 was Egypt's hottest for fifty years. In her diary of 1 June Anita wrote: 'We love the starlit nights and hate the blazing day, hate even the pink dawn that is its herald.' The fifty MTC drivers were doing the work of the hundred men who, with their ambulances, had gone missing in Greece. The MTC vehicles were loaded with British, Australian and New Zealand wounded, patients and drivers exhausted by heat, flies and lack of sleep. Every sixth day off-duty drivers entered the dream world of Cairo, where they had the sand washed out of their hair, sipped iced drinks at the Gizera Club and watched officers on leave play polo. Then the officers went back to the desert to fight, some-times to die, and the MTC drivers went back to their hot huts and suppers of black tea and beans. From Glaslough, Marjorie wrote to her daughter, reminding her: 'Be sure to wear a hat, this modern craze for sunburn is so unbecoming!'

In her memoir, Anita wrote about the ten days' leave in June 1941, spent with Betty Holberton in Jerusalem, during which they were driven the three hundred miles from Cairo by Father Blount, the Roman Catholic chaplain. An intriguing cast of characters scurried around the King David Hotel: Generals Wavell, Maitland Wilson, de Gaulle and Catroux, and Prince Aly Khan, who had once treated Anita to strawberries at Ascot and was now a soldier in the Warwickshire Yeomanry. He drove a peacock-blue sports car and was the lover of the beautiful Emira of the Druzes. The reason for so much activity around Jerusalem was that the invasion of Syria by Allied forces was taking place. After bitter fighting, Damascus fell to the allies on 21 June and Damour, just twenty-four kilometres south of Beirut and a strategic crossing point, a month later. 'It was indeed the oddest week of sight-seeing that two girls and a priest could have known,' Anita recorded.

There was something, or rather someone, she left out. Paul had arrived in the Middle East and, in an insinuating letter to Shane, made it clear that he was still part of Anita's life: 'General Alex [Alexander] and I had lunch together in Cairo the other day. He is in very good form! We talked for hours and I nearly missed my train!' He was now in Jerusalem, where he and Anita 'ride around the same places where our Lord Jesus Christ walked, preached, suffered, and eventually was crucified ... From the hill to the west, a mile outside the Old City we admire the beautiful and most impressive view of the sacred town.' These excursions with Paul may have been the reason behind Anita's request for jodhpurs. Her wartime photograph albums contain several pictures of Paul on horseback.

Mrs Newall, whose uniform was now made even more alluring by 'the addition of large naval epaulettes embroidered with the mysterious golden rose which designated her rank', developed duodenal ulcers, which she endured in VIP conditions in a private room with telephone in a Cairo military hospital, wearing a pink turban, 'a vision which no military hospital had seen before'. Mrs Newall continued her machinations. She found a secretary for Winston's son Randolph, now a lieutenant-colonel and head of a propaganda department in Cairo. She made him return the favour by using his influence with his father to obtain a command for Colonel Orde Wingate, who had been suffering from post-traumatic stress in the room next to Mrs Newall. The posting that followed led, in time, to Wingate's famous mission to Burma.

Anita, less influential than her cousin Randolph, was under orders to bring her Commandant 'special food in a bucket' prepared by Mrs Newall's Egyptian cook but soon, like many other overworked MTC drivers, she got ill herself, with laryngitis, and was sent to the same military hospital but in a ward and without a turban.

On 22 June 1941 Germany had invaded Russia, producing different reactions from two of Anita's cousins. On the day of the invasion, Winston, justifying the new alliance with Russia, said:

The Nazi regime is indistinguishable from the worst features of Communism. It is devoid of all theme and principle except appetite and racial domination. It excels all forms of human wickedness in the efficiency of its cruelty and ferocious aggression. No one has been a more consistent opponent of Communism than I have for the past twenty-five years. I will unsay no word that I have spoken about it. But all this fades away before the spectacle which is now unfolding. The past, with its crimes, its follies, and its tragedies, flashes away.

Clare Sheridan, writing to Anita on 12 September, took another view: 'God couldn't leave the future of the world in the hands of the U.S. – Think of it! Jewish international finance. Pray God Russia triumphs and has the big final word to say, that will spare us being a vassal of the U.S.' She wrote this before the attack on Pearl Harbor, at a time when Winston, like Clare, half-American, was doing his best to bring the USA into the war. It says something about Winston's affectionate nature that he was loyal to his family, many of whose members, particularly Clare, held outrageously foolish views, and, while constantly wheedling favours from him when he was in power, had no respect for his opinions.

In October, a year after the MTC had left England, the decision was taken to disband the unit, since the official perception was that it was frivolous. The girls in No. 11 Coy. were now free to take other military jobs or, if they wanted to remain as ambulance drivers, join the regular British Women's Army – the ATS (Auxiliary Territorial Service). Anita wanted to go on driving an ambulance but the ATS didn't appeal. Apart from the grim senior officers and ugly hats, the Service wasn't allowed in fighting zones. She could not bear 'the ignominy of being a base ambulance driver ... The British authorities made it such a handicap to be a woman that I decided when the time came I would seek a new job as far away as possible from Headquarters.' The time duly came; Sir Walter Monckton, head of the Ministry of Information, as well as Mrs Newall's unfortunate love interest, needed someone to go to Beirut and start up the first English language newspaper – the *Eastern Times* – to serve the troops, stationed in distant camps, from the Mediterranean to the Euphrates. Anita wrote, 'Prince Peter of Greece, hearing Sir Walter tell me to take the first transport available, kindly offered me a lift in his car.'

Shortage of newsprint meant that the *Eastern Times* was a single sheet of paper but at the newspaper's Beirut office there was a large Lebanese staff, working under the direction of Major Roselli, the British press liaison officer. It seems to have been a very suspicious outfit. It was odd that Prince Peter was instantly available to drive Anita across the Sinai Desert, as far as Jerusalem, lunching on caviar and chocolate en route and that, from there, she was picked up in a car belonging to General Maitland Wilson, the army commander in the Middle East. The paper's print run would have, perhaps deliberately, revealed the number of troops in Syria and Lebanon. There were also the taxis 'laden with strange passengers' that arrived at the newspaper office after midnight to transport copies of the following day's edition – and, possibly, more secretive cargoes.

Anita described her job as 'seeing that it [the newspaper] reached the farthest isolated camps quickly, and that as little news as possible should be printed upside down'. This was difficult since nobody else on the staff could read English. She writes as though she were taking part in a zany farce: the time she inadvertently took lodgings in a brothel; the time she rode a non-stop galloping female camel in Palmyra. In the wartime memoir published in the 1980s, she mentions that the 23-year-old Princess Priscilla Bibesco, granddaughter of the former British prime minister, H.H. Asquith, was given a cover job on the *Eastern Times* while working rather erratically for the secret service, having hitchhiked from Romania to Beirut to offer her assistance. I suspect that the newspaper also provided Anita with a cover job. The wartime Middle East was a place where German and Vichy French sympathizers congregated. Anita, driving all over Syria and Lebanon delivering newspapers, would have noticed who was where and what they were doing. She was good at keeping secrets, a prerequisite for successful espionage; her life and her books are both exercises in non-revelation. What she did reveal was her love of Lebanon: 'Damascus was so beautiful that I felt a slice of my heart must be cut out and left there.'

That winter, driving as far as Aleppo, a city three hundred miles from Beirut and bustling with spies and spy-catchers, Anita, coping with cold, discomfort and muddy or snow-blocked roads, doesn't seem to have noticed news of the attack on the US naval base at Pearl Harbor, Hawaii, by Japan's Imperial Navy on 7 December, a date that President Franklin D. Roosevelt proclaimed 'will live in infamy'. The following day America declared war on Japan and, by 11 December, it was at war with Germany and Italy. On Christmas Day, having helped to entertain several hundred Australian soldiers at a tea party hosted by the wife of Sheik el-Khoury, a future president of Lebanon (a social event that was not an unqualified success because the guests got drunk on the four dozen bottles of whiskey generously provided by Madame Khoury), Anita went to Major Roselli's house for dinner. The major observed, as he always did, that her tie was crooked.

8
Laughter Among the Skulls

In 1942 the *Eastern Times* recruited a new editor, a lieutenant who had been a journalist in Fleet Street, so Anita had more time to ride in the mountains of Lebanon, which in early spring were covered with wild flowers. She recorded that 'Our horses [were] the last of the Cavalry Division sent out in 1940,' which means that Paul was with her, since he was training those horses, but, as usual, she doesn't mention him. She made an interesting new friend: the famous singer Amal al-Atrash, Emira of the Druzes, better known by her stage name Asmahan, with whom Aly Khan and every Allied officer who met her became smitten. The only man she loved had been banished to England, where she was not allowed to follow him, and so was contemplating a return to her previous career. She told Anita: 'What does it matter where I go? I am destroyed. I have nothing to care about. I will make films again.' According to Simon Sebag Montefiore in his book *Jerusalem: The Biography* (2011), the Emira was 'an Eastern Mata Hari who allegedly spied for all sides during the war and met a mysterious death in a car accident in 1944'.

Another visitor to Anita's flat in Beirut was Miranda Lampson, the former femme fatale of the MTC, renowned for leaving a yellow cotton mop in her bed to simulate her blonde hair, while she crawled under the barbed wire for an evening's forbidden entertainment, telltale shreds of silver lamé fluttering behind her. She said that her uncle, the US ambassador to Egypt, had forced the abdication of King Farouk. Anita could be as ditsy as Miranda: assigned to cover a visit to the Middle East by the Duke of Gloucester, she managed to be in the wrong place at the wrong time wherever she went but was appreciated by the ranks lined up for inspection: 'Hey there … look at the Dook's girlfriend. We 'ad to leave ours behind.'

But this year was far from light-hearted. Later, Anita wrote to Rose that 1942 was 'the most emotional of my life … it was frankly the first time I've ever loved with my whole heart and mind without any doubt or hesitation.' The man in question was Colonel Philip Parbury, an Australian whose division was fighting in the Middle East. They had met in Syria, where Philip was attending a course at the Staff College, only ninety miles from Beirut. 'During four long months we met every weekend – such luck during a war,' she wrote to Rose. In the best romantic tradition, Anita and Philip 'waded knee-deep through a sea of wild larkspur and hollyhock and saw the snow-covered mountains of Persia, and explored great ruins that were the first cities of the world.' And then Philip failed to get a posting in Egypt and had to go back to Australia. Before that he had a week's leave and Anita 'tore down to Palestine in the hottest khamsin of the year to say goodbye to him – broiling nerve-racked days'. They parted in Gaza – 'a queer Arab town where Samson and Delilah hung out – and I returned dazed and heartbroken to Beirut.'

June was a wicked month. On the 21st, Tobruk fell to General Rommel's forces, after two years in British hands, and German forces reached the outskirts of Alexandria. At the British Embassy in Cairo there began a burning of secret papers. Most of Anita's French friends were killed on the battlefield and – a farcical element among the slaughter – Paul turned up again.

Anita had moved from her flat to a villa outside Beirut, beside the French military prison, which – the flat, not the prison – had 'several palatial unfurnished rooms and a bar'. Her housemates were Patsy O'Kane, recently escaped from China on the diplomatic ship, along with a trunkful of glamorous frocks, and Anita's cousin, Lilah Fortescue. Anita was delighted when Betty Holberton visited, less so when Paul did, although his visit was inevitable since the exuberant Russian couple who owned the villa were his friends. With Anita's help, he had been given the job of training the local Syrian cavalry with the Free French but soon lost it because the Russian ambassador to London had told General de Gaulle that employing Paul was 'considered an unfriendly act to the Soviet'. A year later (6 July 1943), Anita wrote to Rose:

> It was a pretty situation – Paul stranded, disappointed, pathetic, helpless, getting on my nerves, penniless, jobless, fell into a stupor. The moment he arrived I asked for a divorce. He wept and then promised one at the end of the war – this predicament made it impossible to force things.

The same old story.

The damp summer heat of Beirut along with Paul's irritating presence made Anita determined to leave. She took up an invitation to join the Trans-Jordan Frontier Force as an ambulance driver. The Frontier Force, which was set to replace British forces in the lands over the Jordan, was in the command of a man whom Anita described as 'a tremendous friend of mine', Colonel Peter Wilson of the Royal Dragoons. Anita was not another Emira of the Druzes but several men were in love with her, Peter Wilson among them. There is an old adage that war consists of long stretches of boredom punctuated by terror. Courting Anita, almost under the eye of her jealous husband, kept boredom at bay. It was a thrilling game, something between a lark and a challenge, which sometimes involved lovers, or would-be lovers, having to jump from hotel balconies.

Anita loved her time in the Frontier Force; driving through the wilderness, sleeping out under the stars. It made her realize that 'as well as being mad as a coot, I'm wild as a desert fox!' She noted the sombre sadness of the Jews, who found it difficult to settle on the land and – something she was more responsive to – the Arabs' 'merry, irresponsible outlook on life', which reminded her of the Irish. She recruited ten Arab girls as clerks, an experiment that failed because, as she wrote in *Train to Nowhere* (1948), 'the Palestinian HQ would not authorise them unless they joined the ATS, which they refused to do for fear of their "reputation".' Anita's published account notes: 'In the autumn of 1942 I had to leave Transjordan and resume working with the *Eastern Times* in Beirut.' But a letter to Rose tells a different story. 'The whole venture ended on account of malicious old women gossiping in Jerusalem about me and the ATS pounced on the Arab girls.' What with her relationship with the Commanding Officer and lovers jumping off balconies, there was a lot to gossip about.

Another visitor to the villa was the Leslies' friend and neighbour General the Hon. Sir Harold R.L.G. Alexander, who had been brought up at Calendon, only three miles to the north of Castle Leslie but situated in the Six Counties. Winston's favourite general, he was now Commander-in-Chief in the Mediterranean. To his colleagues, 'Alex' was not considered too bright: 'bone from the neck up' according to one of them. In those dark days, with German forces pushing eastwards towards the Suez Canal and the Axis taking control of most of western Europe and Russia, Alex remained unflustered, looking, according to one commentator, 'as if he had just had a steam bath, a massage, a good breakfast and a letter from home.' Not so General Montgomery, the man in charge of the Eighth Army, which was about to take on Rommel's Afrika Korps. Unlike the charming Alex, Bernard Montgomery was said to be 'as quick as a ferret and about as likeable'.

The battle of El Alamein, fought one hundred and fifty miles west of Cairo, began on 23 November. Before it, Montgomery sent a message to all his men: 'Everyone must be imbued with the desire to kill Germans, even the padres – one for weekdays and two on Sundays.' After ten days of fighting and forty-three thousand casualties, Rommel's army was decisively beaten. Winston said: 'Before Alamein we never had a victory. After Alamein, we never had a defeat.'

Winston wrote in *Closing the Ring*, the fifth volume of his history of the Second World War: 'Who in war will not have his laugh amid the skulls.' He could not abide joylessness, neither could his cousin Anita. Although she loved Philip – 'I wonder if I will see him again – it will be a hurtful lonely world for me if I don't,' she wrote to Rose – there were pleasant distractions. Even Paul occasionally forgot his woes and, divertingly, walked around on his hands while singing the Rodzianko March. Among Anita's suitors was one who referred to himself as 'number four admirer'. His name was Bill King, a submarine commander who had taken charge of his first submarine at the outbreak of war, when he was twenty-nine, and, by the spring of 1940, had sunk four transport and supply ships during the Norwegian campaign, for which he had been awarded seven medals for 'daring, endurance and resource in the conduct of hazardous and successful operations in His Majesty's Submarines against the enemy'. He wrote later:

> I did not know that I was beginning a routine life which would go on week after week for six years; that my world would be bounded by the chart-table, the periscope and the bridge during almost all that time; that the smell of diesel oil, chlorine and unwashed bodies would be continuous and that our every day was to be passed below water in a damp fug that would be cold in N. Europe, warm in the Mediterranean and an inferno in the Tropics.

He could have added that he slept in his oilskins so as to be ready for an emergency and nibbled bismuth powder to cure his duodenal ulcers.

Bill had emerged from the steel coffin of his submarine in the early spring of 1943 and was spending his leave in Beirut because his Commanding Officer, Captain Philip Ruck-Keene – 'Ruckers', had based his submarine flotilla there. Ruckers thought that making the exhausted submariners ski from one end of Lebanon to the other would do them good. And an even better cure for Bill would be to introduce him to Anita. Ruckers explained:

> She's an ambulance driver whose unit got dissolved for insubordination or something and now she's up here in charge of a troops' newspaper – obviously makes a glorious muddle of everything she touches and is the most undisciplined, disorganised person I've ever seen in my life. I would like you to meet her ... she is such a contrast to the Navy.

Bill later commented, 'These were the first words I ever heard concerning my future wife.' Bill and Anita were fine and fearless skiers. Anita learnt that Bill could be depended on to look after her safety and Bill discovered something admirable about his skiing companion: 'She had really reduced doing what you want, against any odds, to a fine art.' At the end of his leave, he wrote to her: 'I did not realise that I was in love with you until the day I left ... All my love and many kisses (even if they are not wanted).' Cured of his ulcers but with a bad case of heartache, Bill left Beirut to find a third submarine to command, claiming that his enemies were 'the sea, the Admiralty and the Germans, in that order'. He would not see Anita again until the end of the war.

In May Anita stayed in Jerusalem with Paul, who was organizing a horse show. He was now training mules for General Alexander. Mules are ideal wartime pack animals; they can carry as much as three hundred pounds seven hours a day, for twenty days. They are committed to self-preservation, snacking instead of over-eating, so that they remain nimble enough to climb mountain roads. They are still used by today's armies. Although absent, Philip was still classed as Anita's number one admirer, Paul number two and Bill number four but it was admirer number three, Peter Wilson, who was the most important to her in the summer of 1943. Her grandmother Leonie had died in August and she was at a low ebb, writing to Rose: 'I and my girl friends here are sick of just falling in and out of love – we want to do something heroic like capturing a tank.' Instead, she gave in to Peter's demands to get pregnant. 'P [Peter] wants me to marry Philip but begs me to give him a daughter to bring up first. It's all such a clamour!' An extraordinary plan, even if she wanted to repay Peter for his many kindnesses. I suspect that this was an example of akrasia, being alarmingly against her better judgement. She did get pregnant but, in September, lost the baby, which she had referred to as 'my little gift scheme':

> Incredible complications followed ... and every sort of horror was envis-
> aged from tumours to complete removal of machinery. Don't let anyone
> know as Ma would drop dead if she heard ... There is nothing radically
> wrong – just weakness.

That November there were riots in Beirut, with the French arresting the popular President Khoury in a brutal manner. Sentries were posted in the garden of Anita's villa and soldiers from the Rifle Brigade drove her to the office of the *Eastern Times* 'in a command car bristling with guns'. Rose was having a different kind of war, working as a VAD (non-registered nurse) while based luxuriously in her Belgravia house. In 1943 she married for the second time, to a fighter pilot called Michael Bell-Syer, but it soon became clear that she had not really settled down.

Anita wanted to leave the *Eastern Times* for good. She found a job in the Red Cross, assisting Pamela Wavell, whose father was about to become Viceroy of India. The two girls drove supplies to isolated field hospitals in Lebanon and Syria, Pamela's Red Cross uniform being a snowy white dress and white picture hat. These journeys were probably spying missions. On 23 March 1944 Patsy O'Kane married George Jellicoe who, at the age of twenty-five, had won a DSO, MC and the Croix de Guerre as a Commando. Before the wedding, Patsy had had to disengage herself from another attachment in Egypt – 'poor Peter Wilson, who was flying to Cairo, has had to take back the ring and dismissal letters,' Anita wrote to Marjorie. The wedding was held in the Italian chapel in Beirut, the reception at the villa, its garden scented with orange blossom, and the honeymoon in Cyprus, where Richard Coeur de Lion and Berengaria had honeymooned.

After three years in the Middle East, Anita asked the Red Cross HQ in Cairo to be sent to Italy. In May she boarded a hospital ship at Alexandria, travelling light, since all she owned were 'my uniforms, some Damascus sandals, Aleppo sheepskins and a hoard of memories'. This was the published account of her departure but she told Rose the real story. She had become pregnant again and 'in the end one did the brutal sensible thing – Peter minded terribly and so did I … it was a really ghastly goodbye'.

9
A Cobweb of Affection

There was a problem with the Italian assignment: Paul was in Italy, heading long treks with horses and mules. Anita wrote to Betsan: 'I am demanding a divorce from Paul all the more urgently as the Red Cross has a mobile canteen for me to drive in Italy but I can't if I have a husband in the same command. If I can't fix that I go off to Tunisia to drive with the French.' Somehow, she fixed it. She told Betsan how much she wanted to be in 'the fight that lies ahead in Europe', not least because of the personal problems she was leaving behind in the Middle East:

> I am in such a tangle really as I so want to marry two men and cannot decide between them. One of them begs me to give him a child to bring up if I don't marry him and altogether it is getting most complicated and I feel like buzzing off into the desert again and leading a clean soldier's life.

Peter Wilson, who was in his forties, was closer to hand than Philip Parbury but was, nonetheless, a distant marital prospect. He was already married, as irksomely as Anita was, and had a teenage son. Anita never noticed obstacles. To Rose: 'I want to have several cakes and eat them too.' She tried to shake herself free of Paul by heading her letters 'A Rodzianko

Leslie'. 'I am gradually changing my name back to Leslie as I'm just sick of being a Ukrainian!!' She could drop Paul's name but the man himself refused to let her leave him. Before she left for Italy she wrote to Rose:

> I told the old boy that if he does not give me a divorce I will never speak or write to him again. Have had no answer to this! O Rose I so nearly did not marry him but was in such a state of nervous exhaustion and so weak-willed in consequence. He is such a bore, loathes Peter who wasted a whole hot afternoon trying to be nice to him and is just as selfish as he can be. Peter is so terribly nice about Philip. O Rose I am longing to get back to some nice tough desert work and out of this cobweb of affection.

Bill King was part of the same snarly cobweb. While on leave in London, he had visited Rose and Anita wrote to her: 'O I grew so fond of Bill – he takes ages to know.' At times, Anita thought that the only way out of the tangle was to 'never marry again but just be ME and perhaps breed a few more to please my friends'. Italy provided the perfect exit. From Naples, she told Rose:

> And now here I am, with a job after my own heart - a mobile canteen to drive to meet the wounded in ships and trains and the guns booming some 40 miles away and our workers having a thrilling time and doing such wonderful work up near the front and nothing else to think about but work work work!

But there was something else to think about: how to end her marriage. Her latest scheme was to try to get a nullity decree 'on non-consumation [*sic*] grounds'. This sounds far-fetched although when Rose wondered whether Anita's miscarried baby might have been Paul's, Anita responded: 'You don't imagine there's ever been anything between us!!! What a horrid idea.' Yet another facet of this strange marriage, during which so much had been done jointly – writing books, training horses – was that it may not have been consummated.

General Alexander was Commander-in-Chief of the Italian offensive, and Anita's youngest uncle, Lionel, now married and father of a new baby, had been seconded from the Cameron Highlanders to the Independent Mountain Brigade, which helped escaping prisoners of war make their way over the mountains. Casualties from Anzio and Cassino streamed into Naples. Anita felt that it was like trying to run a canteen in Dante's

Inferno. Peter Wilson was in Syria where his life was stagnant, boring and unpleasant. He envied Anita for being in the thick of battle, which he thought, correctly, would improve her health. He still wanted Anita to have his child, telling her that if she would bear him a daughter, he could let her go. On the other hand, he didn't want her to go through the hell of pregnancy again or to jeopardize her future; rather irreconcilable demands. He told her loftily that he was worried that she would never 'reincarnate' herself, leaving future generations to be born to stupid women, who would produce stupid children.

On 5 June 1944 Rome fell to the Allies, the event overshadowed by D-Day in Normandy, the beginning of the end of the war. Peter's letters to Anita were increasingly discontented. He was forty-seven that month and, although he was performing a thankless task in the desert, had been turned down for promotion. He wanted the war to be over so that he and Anita could be together although he suspected, with reason, that Marjorie would think him too old and too poor. In the middle of June, a new order regarding the Middle East made it compulsory for anyone who had been in service abroad for more than five years to go home after 1 September. Peter saw this as an opportunity to get his affairs in order and try to get a divorce.

Anita was no longer euphoric about her escape to Italy. On 5 July she wrote to Betsan:

> My own life is interesting but unhappy. My world is a tent where in clouds of dust the wounded are laid on stretchers while being sorted for various hospitals … It is extraordinary how quickly one gets shock proof with the wounded – it took me just 6 hours! I do so love the British Tommy. They tug at one's heart as no other wounded do – isn't it curious? Somehow it is their humour and courage that no one else seems to have when blown to bits.

Patsy and George Jellicoe, in their married bliss, were concerned about Anita. George wrote to her: 'If I am sure of anything it is that someone so alive and perceptive and subtle as you is not destined for permanent depression. Please for our sakes get out of the dumps.' But she was lonely and frustrated and regretted the abortion. To Rose, 4 July 1944: 'I did so want just what Peter wanted only it seemed such a hopelessly bad time.

Now I kick myself for having taken the decision … ' She was doing

> wonderful work grappling with the mental state of men blown to bits and
> how one gets to love them … such courage and humour [but] I am restless
> and discontented and long to join the French Ambulance Corps which are at
> the front and have a wilder freer time.

Of the men she loved the best, Philip was fighting the Japanese in New Guinea and would soon be evacuated to Australia, ill and skeletally thin. Peter was trying to get sent to Yugoslavia – 'I just can't think how I am going to keep them both and I love them so much.' Paul, whom she didn't love at all, 'writes jauntily from Sardinia that he lives in planes and cars and swoops from Sicily to Rome as he wishes, doing very important work that he cannot tell me about'. Bill King, now the captain of the submarine *HMS Telemachus*, during that same restless July, wrote Anita a poem, 'Sonnet to a Lady weary of lovers'. It ended: 'O beautiful, lovely passionless lady / Someday you'll have to bear somebody's baby.' Aware that he was ranked only admirer number four, Bill thought that he had lost Anita although 'you will always be an angel to me'. Then along came the pleasant distraction of admirer number five. Anita had known Bill Cunningham for a long time before he turned up in Italy as General Alexander's military assistant and gave her the chance to know him much better. An undated letter from him: 'So nice to find that someone one always thought would be rather sweet … is actually so much sweeter than one could possibly have imagined! Dammit.'

There was a feeling that the war would soon be over but the mood was sombre, as the horrors of what had been happening away from the battlefields became more widely known. Winston Churchill wrote to Anthony Eden in July 1944, on the Nazis' murder of the Jews:

> There is no doubt that this is probably the greatest and most horrible crime
> ever committed in the history of the world … It is clear that all concerned
> in this crime who fall into our hands, including the people who only obeyed
> orders in carrying out the butcheries, should be put to death.

Anita wrote in *Train to Nowhere*: 'I had a faint selfish hope that war would not end before I had time for some startling achievement.' So far, she had done nothing that was, by her own standards, extraordinary. Her old MTC unit, now incorporated in the ATS, had never left Alexandria, although the fighting had moved elsewhere. In all, 200,000 British serving women had scarcely seen the front. Other countries deployed their female troops more usefully. Soviet China engaged 800,000 servicewomen, 70 per cent of whom were in close combat. The Poles, Americans and, more pertinently for Anita, the French divisions, allowed women at the front line, the French deploying female ambulance drivers when its forces were attacking. Anita was determined to be one of them.

On 15 August Allied landings in southern France began. The Red Cross handed over Anita to the French army, which demanded a dossier, to include 'a certificate stating the British Government did not mind what was done to me ... there were unpleasant clauses about deserters getting shot'. Reading these clauses, Anita's friend, Comtesse Elizabeth de Breteuil, conveniently in charge of all female personnel in Italy, reassured Anita that she could always manage to '*te débrouiller*' – meaning to wriggle out of impossible situations. Once the dossier was approved, Anita became *un simple soldat de 2ème classe*, attached to an ambulance company that was due to sail to Marseilles. During her last days in Naples she dined glamorously at the Allied Officers' Club and met Lady Dorothy Macmillan and Lady Diana Cooper, both dressed in satin evening gowns. In Siena she had a farewell breakfast with General Alexander. As he left her, to tour the front with Winston, he said, 'Don't falter, Anita.'

In October the landing of a French ambulance unit at Marseilles began with a triumphal march through the streets – 'Women put down their baskets in the roadway to blow kisses.' But when the march was over, it was apparent that there was great suffering. People in the countryside were starving. On D-Day, an old man told Anita, a false alarm from the BBC had led the local Resistance to believe that landings in the south of France were imminent. But it had been another two months before the French army landed, by which time the Resistance had revealed itself in attacks on munitions dumps and acts of sabotage. The old man said: 'I saw the finest young men of my region go to the carnage pits.' 'Everywhere the same tales damped one's spirit,' Anita recorded.

After much chaotic travelling northward, she caught up with Combat Command 1 of the 1st Armoured Division, which was fighting in the mountains north of Besançon:

> Everyone congratulated me on being an ambulanciere divisionnaire. I had as yet no idea what these words signified nor could I imagine that from hence-forth Combat Command 1 with its Cuirassiers in their Sherman tanks and its Zouaves in their muddy boots was to be my entire world ... a small, intimate world of lovable human beings and good friends.

A world where 'some startling achievement' was possible.

It was also a world where Paul couldn't find her. Not for want of trying. He pestered Lionel in Italy and then tried to prise information from Shane in a letter dated 29 August. Most of the letter describes a visit to the Pope – Paul still held the belief that professing Catholic piety was the way to Shane's heart: 'I left the Vatican strongly impressed and somehow very happy,' he wrote before, as though as an afterthought, he added, 'I still have no news from Anita. I know she is somewhere in France! Hope she's well.' He had already asked Marjorie for Anita's address but, although she wrote back sympathizing over the death of his mother, she refused to reveal her daughter's whereabouts.

Anita too was taking a sturdy attitude, telling Rose that she had made it clear to Paul that he could keep her officer's wife's allowance but

> must save it as when he is demobilised neither I nor my family can help him ... I've told him frankly he can't finish his days sponging on my family ... I'm never going to smile nicely and pander to that man again ... My only bond is that of British law – my signature in the registry that day binds me to a contract which I can only terminate if he gives me evidence of his adultery. A legal annulment is infinitely more complicated and expensive. In the eyes of the Church I am not married.

And then, casually, in brackets, '(as his 2 other wives alive)'. This was a revelation. In *Tattered Banners*, only his first wife, Tamara Novosilzoff, is mentioned, very briefly. Other members of Paul's family and friends who made perilous escapes after the revolution are also mentioned, but not a second wife and I have been unable to find out anything about her. These dispossessed aristocrats were extraordinary survivors. Penniless, they opened dress-shops, painted decorative glassware, served behind the counter at Selfridges, trained horses. Perhaps Paul's elusive second wife was among their number.

Peter, on leave in London, had found a sympathetic listener in Rose, a great believer in marriage, who was about to embark on her third. She thought that Peter was the right man for her friend but Anita capriciously disagreed. 'We'd be the most awful couple if we were man and wife – we'd just huddle together reading books and cooking each other glorious messes and snigger at the world.' This is rather a change from a few months back when she claimed to want to marry both Peter and Philip, and the reason was that she'd received a long letter from Philip, which restored him to being her heart's love. 'Peter will tell you what a wonderful person he thought him – I know they'd get on together.' An unlikely scenario but Anita didn't dwell on it for long; she was caught up in the excitement of battle.

10
The Woods Are Full of Germans

During a cold October, Anita described events to Marjorie, who she knew suffered 'terribly from her overwrought imagination', that were bound to cause alarm:

> This is the most interesting work imaginable, as one goes forward with the regiments … we park our ambulances in any field or orchard where there are not mines and are ready to move at any time at any hour of the day or night … One drives in the pitch dark at night as there is a complete blackout within 8 miles of the front and that is no fun – especially as the woods are full of Germans! Anyway, I don't think any other Div uses women so far forward.

There had been a particularly tragic civilian casualty:

> He was the bravest nicest little lad and it was heartbreaking when he died … Alas I can't see how one can avoid killing civilian children now as we advance through smashed up villages – they can't evacuate to the hills as they did in Italy and they can't retreat – to Germany.

She had no pity for the ill-looking German prisoners, captured as the Allied forces fought their way northward. By now, Germans were 'barbarians lacking in judgement, pompous white savages with a power complex'.

Cold, wet and muddy, sleeping in her ambulance, dressed in men's trousers and underwear – courtesy of the Americans – instead of the well-tailored uniform of the MTC in which she'd left England four years ago, Anita told her mother, 'I've never enjoyed life more.' The cause of much of this enjoyment was her commanding officer, a remarkable woman called Jeanne de l'Espée. While on her way to join her unit, Anita had been assured by many people that several Englishmen '*très bien connus*' had been in love with Jeanne. The daughter of a famous general, she had nursed at the front during the Great War, driving through the lines in the middle of a bombardment to translate for the French wounded – she spoke perfect English – and had been awarded the American Medal of Merit. In that long weekend between the wars, she had run the couture house of Jean Patou and was admired for her enchanting personality and chic. An early instruction to Anita was: 'Whatever happens, remember to use lipstick because it cheers up the wounded.' Scarlet-mouthed, Jeanne drove out one nightfall to rescue wounded parachutists from a mountain top where they had lain for three days, surrounded by Germans. She brought them down, uninjured, driving through heavy shellfire. She was rather different from the histrionic Maria Newall.

The fighting in the Vosges went on for two months, as Allied forces drove north eastwards towards the Rhine, with heavy casualties on both sides. In *Train to Nowhere*, Anita told of one incident that encapsulated the grimness of war. The Germans had dragged out a sick boy and shot him a few days before the Allied troops arrived. The boy's mother asked to shoot two Germans – any Germans – in revenge. A French officer gave her a revolver. Two German prisoners were produced, 'too tired even to lift their hands. Whatever they saw in her face they were beyond caring and she was expressionless as she shot them.'

This was nothing like Anita's previous wartime life in the Middle East, where, miles away from the fighting, she had become too close to men whose shattered nerves made them dangerous lovers. Anita and her colleagues, when not sleeping in their ambulances, were sometimes allotted a room in a recently bombed-out village to dry their clothes. She learnt to differentiate the sound of a German shell from the less shrill sound of Allied guns. 'This was the world in which I found myself', she wrote. 'I who had once been an idiotic London debutante.' The *ambulancières*, after a day at the front, sat around in their muddy clothes discussing the perfect wardrobe. Jeanne told them: 'Only shoes, stockings and gloves really matter. For the rest, *mes petites*, you cannot dress too plainly, and black is better than navy blue – a well-cut black *tailleur* will take you from breakfast to midnight, and the hat is of great importance.' Shortly after this useful advice had been imparted, a large shell landed nearby and Anita fled for cover, snatching a tin washbasin in lieu of a helmet.

On 12 November 1944, Anita wrote in her diary: 'My twenty-ninth birthday! Reached the Rhine.' It was, in fact, her thirtieth. Peter Wilson, still on leave in London, wrote to her with plans for their future. Peter would stay on in London for a while to see something of his son Roddy, who was an apprentice at Rolls Royce. Then Peter wanted to become an agricultural labourer, living in a shack where wild creatures would come for sanctuary and Anita would visit whenever she wanted to meet the 'furry babies'. Just before Christmas, the battle of Strasbourg began in freezing weather. The *ambulancières*, billeted in Alsace villages, tried to reassure the nervous inhabitants that the Allied armies would not pull out, leaving them exposed to Nazi reprisals. They didn't know that General Eisenhower had, in fact, threatened to withdraw American troops from Alsace, since he considered the Germans to be solidly entrenched around Colmar. Only when Winston flew to France on 3 January to support General de Lattre, Commander of the French army, and General de Gaulle did Eisenhower change his mind, on condition that the French took full responsibility for the defence of Strasbourg.

The snow made the battlefields as horrific as the trenches of the Great War. Anita wrote: 'In all directions, men advancing through the fields were suddenly blown up in a fountain of scarlet snow and their comrades would drag them back, themselves sinking above the knees at every step.' The battle of Colmar lasted three weeks, ending on 9 February, the last battle of the war to be fought on French soil. 'The sound of guns, that had not ceased for three months, died away with the first breath of spring.'

While Anita, now admired as '*une Anglaise formidable*' was rescuing the wounded on the battlefield, Peter, in London, had found a job in Whitehall, running Winston's bombproof underground map room. He saw a lot of both Rose and Anita's brother Desmond, who had just become engaged, to Anita's disapproval, to Agnes Bernelle, a lusciously beautiful actress and the daughter of a Jewish-Hungarian theatre impresario, now exiled in London. In 1996 Agnes wrote a very appealing memoir, *The Fun Palace*, in which she revealed that, during the war, under the code name 'Vicky', she had been recruited to make anti-Nazi broadcasts to Germany, where she had been born. Peter's grumpy letters to Anita list how expensive clothes are – 39/6d for a shirt – and his distaste for ATS girls. Anita, living on disgusting soup, washing in a tin basin of cold water and sleeping in her ambulance was, perhaps, not too sympathetic.

The Germans did not retreat easily, returning by night to newly conquered villages to kill any of their countrymen who dared to put out a white flag. In March 1945 the Kreisleiter of Welzlar was hanged for defeatism, two days before US troops arrived, for putting up a sign proclaiming 'Welcome to our liberators'. That month Anita was given compassionate leave because Marjorie, whom her daughter had not seen for five years, was dangerously ill with pneumonia in Dublin. By the time Anita arrived at St Vincent's nursing home, Marjorie had recovered enough to criticize her shoes, so Anita went on to Castle Leslie, where Shane was living alone. The house was freezing but Shane was waited on by six servants. Anita travelled back to her division via London where, on Good Friday, the prime minister's car brought her to Chequers. When she left, Winston said: 'Give my love to the French … I think they are rather fond of me.'

Anita had just returned to Mulhouse when the Division prepared to cross the Rhine. After a special mass at Obernai, a medieval village just outside Strasbourg, to mark the quitting of French soil, the *ambulancières* were given a short lecture on 'how to behave *chez les boches*'. Anita thought it should be the other way round. The year before she had written to Betsan: 'How can one teach them [the Germans] how unattractive they are!' On 20 April Anita wrote to Winston the kind of letter, full of personal detail and sharply observed vignettes, that great leaders, concerned with great events, don't often receive and must find welcome. 'We're simply smacking through Germany,' Anita told him, and went on to describe terrified old farmers and their wives ingratiating themselves with their conquerors by bringing them delicious food:

> One feels so uncomfortable when they lick your boots. It's obvious they are damned frightened yet when driving back alone with wounded through the dark forests one doesn't feel quite at ease either! ... I suppose these are the most interesting days of my life – of any life – to be in at the kill at the end of this long long fight. Thank goodness we had you – it would have been so much harder and duller without.

She took up the letter again the following day: '10 villages later – gosh what a sight – the departing SS men shot at all civilians here they saw hanging out white flags – one man has three revolver bullets in his face.'

She decided that Peter was the most central point to distribute her letters 'to share my news with everyone' and put him in charge of copying and distribution. A letter dated 26 April, neatly typed by Peter, tells of Anita's excitement at taking over the Hohenzollern castle at Sigmaringen, where Laval and Pétain had recently been kept in semi-imprisonment before being hastily evacuated that very morning. The *ambulancières* splashed about in Maréchal Pétain's bathtub and, that evening, drank his delicious wine. There was a more sombre event to recount: the murder of two *ambulancières*, the sisters Lucette and Odette Le Coq. Their ambulance had been ambushed by retreating Germans, who shot the girls at point blank range, in spite of the Red Cross flag on the bonnet of their van. Anita wrote: 'Though we've taken risks under bombardment and quite a number of girls have been killed, we never expected to be attacked in the ambulance by daylight or shot like that.'

Her opinion of the Germans hardened: 'If you don't boot them morning noon and night then some tramp like Hitler comes along and takes over.' She was revolted by their obsequiousness – 'the women wave and smile under the white flags while the German soldiers lie dead along the road'. She and her colleagues went on tending the German wounded: '[O]ne does not know how to stop being kind to a suffering man – it seems so natural to do one's utmost for them.' In spite of the occasional bombardment, life was easier. The *ambulancières* lodged in houses, slept in proper beds and ordered their meals from eager-to-please householders – 'I've never eaten so much butter in my life – butter and eggs and milk.'

POWs were armed and put on guard duty, German policemen were ordered to pick up dying German soldiers: 'It's a queer sensation to work with Germans – it's like modelling with butter when you are used to hewing granite.' A German policeman, bullied by Anita into saving the wounded, presented her with a swastika-decorated dagger, engraved with the words 'to you I surrender my oath'. This event-filled letter ended, '2 armoured cars have just gone by laden with young German soldiers captured in the next wood – they fought hard aged 12 to 15'. The age of these schoolboy conscripts was a clear sign that the war was near its end.

On 2 May Peter, in his Whitehall office, aware that victory was imminent, ignored the general excitement and spent the afternoon watching the ducklings on the lake in St James's Park and hoping, he wrote to Anita, that they would spend the next hatching season together. Although almost the entire German army had surrendered, he suspected that Anita's regiment might still be fighting and remarked delicately, referring to her abortion, that, in the circumstances, it had, perhaps, been a wise decision. He wrote to her almost daily, trying to convince her that they must live close to the earth and forswear worldly belongings. He scoffed at those in 'the social world' who were planning VE day celebrations, feeling that such rejoicings were not yet in order. His wife had decided not to give him a divorce but he was going to talk to her about it. Anita had made it clear to Rose that she would never marry Peter but perhaps she hadn't made it clear to him. On VE day itself, 8 May, Peter spent the day in Kew Gardens, communing with nature and critical of the formal flower beds. He wanted to get away from the human race, especially 'so-called sophisticated humans'.

On 11 May Peter was able to write to Anita that her brother Jack, imprisoned since 1940 in Oflag VII B in Bavaria, had been released and was on his way to Dublin. Oflags were restricted to officer-prisoners; they had preferential treatment and weren't required to work but conditions were grim and very cold. At the outbreak of war, Anita had knitted Jack a balaclava cap in khaki angora wool and he'd slept in it every night during five freezing winters. As well as the good news about Jack, Peter also mentioned that General Knox, Paul's commanding officer in the Great War, had sent a minion to Peter's office to ask for Anita's address. It was clear that Paul was still on the prowl.

On 22 May Anita wrote to 'Dear Cousin Winston', a six-page letter full of criticism of the Germans, who left their dying in the sunlit fields to be tended by the occupying forces in makeshift surgeries set up in barns. Anita's brigade had taken 25,000 prisoners – 'I took dozens myself (slight exaggeration – dozens begged me to take them) … pleasant, kindly honest people, they are so tolerant they'll let children be tortured if someone in authority says so.' How unlike the 'outrageous prying old spinsters of England who show their disapproval of cruelty towards man or beast by whacking the perpetrator with an umbrella'. Fraternization was frowned on but, Anita told Winston, the 'acquiescent husbandless blond beauties' in vanquished Germany were so 'amiable, indifferent and ready' as to be irresistible to the French soldiers. Or so Anita believed. In his book *Liberation: The Bitter Road to Freedom, Europe 1944–1945*, William Hitchcock describes widespread rape in the Rhineland, as well as theft and looting by the occupying troops: 'The Red Army was the most culpable but was by no means alone in abusing the power of the victor.'

Peter was meanwhile ingratiating himself with Anita's family and friends. Clare Sheridan now called him 'Pete' and found him 'sweet, and so understanding'. When he visited her at Brede, she listed his support for what she told Anita (23 May 1945) was 'a community future … I'll tell you all about it when you come'. This was to be set up at Brede, although details were yet to be worked out. Clare ended her letter: 'If you were my daughter I'd be madly proud of you', which was perhaps a dig at Marjorie, with her instructions against getting tanned and her criticism of Anita's shoes. Peter had also become Rose's intimate friend. The two would spend evenings together, neither wearing much in the way of clothes during that sultry summer. Rose gave Peter the keys to her flat, although he had to give them back when her gentleman-caller situation became unusually complicated. Peter was also close to Agnes, who confided in him that Lord Tredegar, a friend of Desmond's, had given her a valuable jade necklace.

Peter was still intent on some sort of getaway when Anita came home; anywhere where he could forget what he called the sordid remains of humanity would do. The sordid remains were a worry. In a letter to Anita on 4 June, he lashed out at de Gaulle for being stubborn over Syria, the Jews in Palestine, whom he thought cowardly and, for some unexplained reason, Chicago newspapers. He had heard that France was swinging back to Pétain, although, at the same time, he feared that there might be a communist revolution there and was anxious lest Anita got mixed up in it. A general election – dubbed the 'khaki election' – had been called for 5 July. Like many other people, and most newspapers, Peter thought it inconceivable that Winston wouldn't form the next government, in spite of food shortages and social unrest. Sensing a reluctance on Anita's part to be demobilized, he tells her rather plaintively that he has all her clothes in the room he is renting at 75 Knightsbridge for a remarkably cheap £2 a week.

It was true that Anita didn't want to leave the army. She knew that if she did, she would be called upon to cope with a problem that concerned Jack. It had been hoped that, having recovered his health, Jack would take over the running of Glaslough. Instead he decided to relinquish it, apply for US citizenship and start a new life in America, his country of birth. Desmond's engagement to Agnes had initially met with opposition but when Desmond brought her to Glaslough, Marjorie liked her immediately and offered the couple her St John's Wood flat. Anita was not won over by her future sister-in-law. During her Easter leave, she wrote to Marjorie: 'I definitely disliked her and will not like her any more simply because she is Desmond's wife.' She disapproved of the pair's VE-day antics, when, or so she had been told, 'Desmond in slacks and open neck shirt bicycled Aggie to 10 Downing Street and went in asking to present our cousin with a bottle of whisky from some Jew.' In fact, as Agnes made clear in her memoir, the bottle, which had been handed over to Mary Churchill, was 'a litre of vintage wine, which a distinguished refugee, a Dr Wittkowsky, had kept all through the war, to be given to Winston when victory was declared.' Another dubious story, which got back to Marjorie, was 'that her son Desmond and his actress friend had held up the Victory Parade.'

Ungracious and sulky, Anita told her mother that she had decided not to see Desmond and Agnes for a few years. Anita had been the most caring of sisters, a Wendy to her two lost boys, who had suffered more than she had from their slapdash parenting. Now Desmond no longer needed her. He was loved by a beautiful and talented woman and, perhaps more painful to his sister, was regarded as the family success story. He had been a Spitfire pilot for two years of the war but, in 1943, a medical check had revealed a damaged heart. Invalided out of the RAF on a pension of 7/6d a week, he found a desk job, which gave him enough free time to write his first novel, *Careless Lives*, based on his own dashing wartime exploits. Dedicated to 'My brother John, a Prisoner of War', it became a bestseller when it was published in 1945.

The war was over but Anita and her ambulance were still needed in Germany. There were no more wounded soldiers to be rescued from the battlefield but, instead, the French survivors of Nordhausen labour camp who had been moved to a makeshift sanatorium when the camp had been liberated in April. Three ambulances, including Anita's, set out to make the 300-mile journey eastwards across Germany to Nordhausen in the Hartz mountains, now in the American zone. The *ambulancières* had thought that Nordhausen 'might be a hospital where French workers too ill to travel would be waiting for transport'. Only when they saw 'a kind of huge football goal' and were told that it was the gibbet from which forty corpses used to dangle at a time did they realize what had gone on there. Anita described Nordhausen as an extermination camp but, although people starved to death there or died because of horrific experiments carried out on them, it was in fact a forced labour camp. Ill or dying prisoners were often sent to camps such as Buchenwald to be slaughtered en masse. At Nordhausen the prisoners, who included French political deportees, had made parts for the infamous V-2s. Every month one thousand of the workers died from starvation and exhaustion. 'This suited the Nazis,' Anita wrote bitterly. 'They didn't want too many people who were not quite of their own sort.' This sentence seems to be an oblique reference to Jews but Jews would probably have been sent directly to the crematoria. The 'shivering, exhausted wretches' whom Anita saw in what was by then a transit camp were Dutch, Italian and Polish prisoners.

The ambulances were to bring fifteen patients back to France, although these men had only a few weeks to live. The American officer in charge of the operation said: 'I'd rather see men dead than looking like that.' During the two-day journey back across the Rhine, Anita and her colleagues, with great tenderness, dealt with the blood and diarrhoea, which made the ambulances smell intolerably. This was much worse than digging wounded men out of the snow in Colmar under the eye of German tanks. At the end of that terrible journey, on a night glowing with golden light, Anita wrote, 'better if the whole earth remained desolate as the moon if this is all mankind can make of it'. Geneviève, her co-driver, said: 'Nothing could ever matter again after this, could it?'

11

The War Heroine

The French army granted leave to those in its service who had a relative released from German imprisonment, so Anita was able to go home to see Jack. En route to Glaslough, she stayed with Rose, who was working her way steadily – or, perhaps, unsteadily – through a phalanx of fighter pilots. The latest one was Pete Gardner. He had escaped from a prison camp and, on meeting Rose at one of her favourite nightclubs said, immediately, 'You're going to marry me.' Unlike Anita, Rose seemed able to get divorced at whim. She and Pete married before the end of the year.

The RAF, 'always at Rose's beck and call', flew Anita to Belfast, where Jack met her and drove her to Glaslough in the familiar horse-drawn brougham. After this reunion Anita made her way to Berlin by an adventurous route, which included a stopover, near Frankfurt, at Schloss Friedrichshof, once the home of Queen Victoria's favourite daughter, Vicky. Army discipline was unravelling. Nobody seemed to know where anyone else was or how they got there, which led to some surprising encounters and equally surprising absences. On 19 July Peter Wilson, having had no news of Anita for a while, wrote to her, asking where she was. Peter was part of the British delegation in Potsdam, the last of the Second World War conferences, held from 16 July until 2 August and attended by Churchill (whose place was taken by Attlee after the British General Election), Truman and Stalin. The conference was held at Cecilienhof, the home of Crown Prince Hohenzollern, in Potsdam, a suburb of Berlin, nine weeks after the German surrender. Its aim was to impose order on the new post-war world. What was to become East Germany was given to Russia; the south of the country became the American zone, and the north was given to Great Britain. After some deliberation, France was given part of west Germany, carved out of the US and British zones. In popular parlance, the US got the scenery, the French the wine and the Brits the ruins.

And Anita? She was in Potsdam too. On the same day that Peter was writing to her, she was writing to Winston, boasting at having arrived there: 'My division – General Soudre's first armoured – is the only one here.' Somehow, the other *ambulancières* had been left behind. Peter found her a day or so later and they explored the smashed Tiergarten and the ruins of Berlin. Peter had a new plan for their future, one that didn't involve a gypsy life in the wild. He had been sounded out about the job of military adviser to the Syrian government and was convinced that Anita would be prepared to leave Europe and go back to the Middle East, perhaps forgetting that she hated the climate, had been wild with misery for much of her time there and thankful to have been posted to Italy.

From Berlin, on 22 July, Anita wrote to Marjorie on writing paper headed with a swastika and eagle, filched from Hitler's bombed-out chancellery. A Russian officer had plied her with souvenirs from the building: a piece of brocade from Hitler's chair and a bronze Motherhood Cross of the kind awarded to mothers of four children. Silver crosses were given to mothers of six and gold ones to mothers of eight. The crosses had been awarded every year on 8 August, the birthday of Hitler's mother. Anita was very excited: 'Darling Ma! The climax of my military career has now arrived!' She had lodged with her beloved 11th Hussars, the reconnaissance regiment of the Desert Rats. She had taken part in a grand parade watched by Winston, Alex, Monty and other wartime leaders. She had lunched with Winston and his daughter Mary at their villa in Potsdam, where she had sat between Winston and Anthony Eden. Her friends in the 11th Hussars had sent Winston 'a huge red Iron Cross decoration which he fancied greatly'. In a few days' time she would have to trek back to the Rhine to rejoin her ambulance unit but meanwhile, 'I've certainly had the most spectacular end of a war.'

But it wasn't quite the end. On 11 August, the day that the war in Japan ended, Anita travelled to Wittlich, the Rhineland city on the Moselle, where, a few days later, she and Geneviève were told to be ready at 6 am in ironed skirts (cut out of GI trousers), polished boots, neatly turned-down white socks and white gloves to join a parade at which decorations were to be presented. A band played the Marseillaise as a general pinned the Croix de Guerre on Anita's shirt. She had been awarded it for dragging wounded men out of the snow on the battlefields of Colmar. It was 15 August, the Feast of the Assumption, Napoleon's birthday and the anniversary of the Marseilles landing; a perfect day to have one's valour recognized and to experience the ecstasy of achievement.

The result of the British general election had been declared on 26 July, showing a Labour landslide with a majority of 145 seats. Labour's campaign slogan had been 'Let us face the future', an appealing exhortation to a people longing to forget the nightmare of the recent past. Anita wrote to Winston: 'We were all wild the Socialists got in till news came that you were in terrific form and going to lead the Opposition.' She then painted a picture of a drab, dull Britain of 'hideous little tin houses', which would be no fun at all to govern. A comforting letter for an old warhorse. Shane also wrote to his defeated cousin, in his usual mixture of pomposity and supplication. He asked Winston if he would have Jack down for a day at Chartwell: 'He was the only soldier a blood relation of yours in German power and they never found out!' Jack was staying at the Guards Club in London, while having 'medical treatments', which Shane doesn't specify.

In September Anita was demobilized via Paris. Thereafter things get a bit confused. *Train to Nowhere* ends in London where, thanks to Peter, although she doesn't mention him, she manages to get hold of the pink wool from Winston's map room, which had been used for marking the advance of armies, to send to her friend Monique in France, who was expecting a baby. *A Story Half Told*, the later version of her wartime life, ends at Glaslough, where Bill King proposes to her. She gives the impression that Bill's lakeside proposal took place in 1946 but, in fact, Anita suffered some years of emotional turbulence before Bill rescued her from chaos. Agnes's memoir describes things differently:

> Whenever my sister-in-law, Anita came to town, it was like a minor invasion of a major army. She was about to be demobbed and would arrive at South Lodge with kitbags, army boots, horse-blankets and gentlemen whom she referred to as her beaux. Beaux A and B [Philip and Peter] were semi-demobbed by then and, uncertain of their future whereabouts, they too brought their army gear and dumped it with us. Beau C [Bill] had not yet been released from his submarine duty and did not appear on the scene until much later, with spectacular results.

That Christmas, Desmond, Agnes and Anita were all at Glaslough. 'Anita looked incredibly beautiful in a tea-gown of cream-coloured lace,' Agnes wrote. At Castle Leslie, there were still eight indoor servants, four gardeners, meals served by a footman in livery and, if you so desired, breakfast in bed. But it wasn't enough.

12
The Unbearable Peace

'People don't recover from a war.' Kurt Vonnegut wrote that sentence from personal experience: he had been a POW in Germany, and witnessed the fire bombing and destruction of Dresden in 1945. In her book *Edwardians in Love*, Anita quoted from Cynthia Asquith's diary for 1918: 'I am beginning to rub my eyes at the prospect of peace. I think it will require more courage than anything that has gone before.' Or, to quote a German wartime joke: 'Better enjoy the war – the peace will be terrible.' The war had used up most people's supply of courage. In 1946, the first full year of peace, Anita and Peter's letters reveal a nervy, irritable couple, damped-down and disconsolate, while Jack was heading towards a nervous break-down. Bill King remained undaunted. At the end of the war he was put in charge of the surrender of German U-boats which, on Russian orders, had to be sunk in the Atlantic. Bill planned a post-war life of skiing, sailing and, if possible, marrying Anita although, in 1946, that last intention looked hopeless.

Anita decided that she wanted to live in the west of Ireland. Marjorie, always generous and now the beneficiary of her sister Anne's will – the childless Anne had died in 1945 – bought her discontented daughter a castle in County Galway. Oranmore Castle was on the site of a romantic Norman keep beside Galway Bay. Dating from the fifteenth century, it may have been on the site of an older castle. From the seventeenth century it had been part of the estate of one of Galway's twelve tribes, the Blakes, an extravagant clan who, over the centuries, left the tower and the adjoining house in a ruinous state. Marjorie, after a spot of house-hunting with her friend the writer and lawyer Oliver St John Gogarty, bought house, castle, tower, the keep and a nearby field for £200 and started to repair the roofs. Meanwhile, Anita and Peter lived in the village of Craughwell, a few miles from Oranmore. It was a strange household.

According to Peter, Anita wanted to live with both him and Philip Parbury. He wrote plaintively to Rose that as he and Anita still shared a bed, he didn't know how Philip would react when Anita invited him to stay, as she was determined to do. Peter told Rose that Anita had no idea he would be hurt by her invitation to Philip. Ten days later Peter wrote to Rose again. Philip was now at Craughwell and things were worse than Peter had feared. Anita had taken Philip to see Oranmore Castle and he had offered to pay for it. Peter regarded the castle as his and Anita's future home and had ambitious plans for its rebuilding, so he threatened to leave. This astonished Anita, who burst into tears. She insisted to Peter that Philip never made love to her, and she continued to sleep with Peter. Hard as it is to believe, Philip apparently had no idea about her relationship with Peter.

Seemingly oblivious to Peter's feelings, Anita asked him to arrange a picnic for herself and Philip. She then booked a suite at the Shelbourne Hotel in Dublin for herself and Philip, which she had shared with Peter six weeks before. When Philip went back to England the following week, Anita fully expected Peter to go to Glaslough with her, which he did.

Peter had convinced himself that he was far more important to Anita than Philip. His conviction was so strong that, even if he had known about the letter that Anita wrote to Winston on 24 June, he would probably not have believed it. This letter was posted from South Lodge, St John's Wood, where Anita was staying with Desmond and Agnes. She used Agnes's writing paper, headed by the initials 'ABL', Agnes Bernelle Leslie, which, in a curly and complicated typeface, could have been taken for Anita's own. The letter begins: 'I have a young man.' This was Lt Colonel Philip Parbury and Anita asked her cousin whether she could bring Philip to see him before the former flew to Australia in a week's time. She stressed Philip's love of Empire – a love that Winston shared – and went on: 'We have been sort of engaged for years but I hesitate to dampen the fire of his spirit with matrimony.' She also wrote, knowing how fond Winston was of Clare, that it was Clare who had encouraged her to suggest this meeting. Sometimes Winston scrawled a comment on letters he received but he didn't on this one, so there is no record of the meeting taking place. What could Anita have been thinking? She was living with one man and was still married to another, so could not have been even 'sort of engaged' to a third. Like Peter, and perhaps most other people exhausted by the war, she couldn't think straight.

During that hurdy-gurdy of a year, she visited Paul at his military camp in Scotland 'to beg for a divorce'. It would be another two years before she obtained it, in the nick of time, as it subsequently turned out. She sounded blithe enough when she wrote to Rose on 1 October, congratulating her on the birth of a daughter, Fleur. Since it was assumed that Rose was still married to Michael Bell-Syer, Anita suggested that she tell people that 'you'd divorced and married a fellow called Pete Gardner whenever anyone asks – and it will be simple just to announce how clever you are [for having Fleur] some other time!!' She wrote this letter from the Shelbourne Hotel, where she was expecting Peter to join her that night. The hotel staff must have been intrigued by Anita's frequent changes of escort.

In the 1950s Anita wrote to Rose that the years 1947 and 1948 had been the most cruel of her life. The book she had written about the war, *Train to Nowhere*, was rejected by several publishers, one of whom said that it was 'flung together and must be rewritten', before being accepted by Hutchinson, who offered her £100 on delivery and 10 per cent on the sales price on the first 5000 copies sold. When it was published in 1948 it was widely considered to be the best book about the war to have been written by a woman – a dubious compliment. But people were not yet ready to revisit the war, especially in a grisly account written by a woman, illustrated by the author's photographs of dead Germans, ruined cities and gibbets – for Anita had managed to take her camera and a supply of film everywhere. They preferred women in a keep-the-home-fires-burning role and, in 1948, both the government and women's magazines were putting pressure on women to leave their wartime employment and become full-time homemakers, so that men released from the armed services could take their place on the factory floor. After she published *Train to Nowhere*, Anita didn't write or talk about the war for another forty years, when she wrote *A Story Half Told*, a rather jauntier account of her soldiering. By that time she had found fame as a biographer of various Edwardian sexpots, including her great-aunt Jennie Churchill, and had a devoted readership. Also, by the 1980s there was an insatiable appetite for books about the war. *A Story Half Told* was more successful than its soberer predecessor.

Philip was still in England. Anita, living with Peter at Oranmore, wrote to Marjorie in an undated letter from 1948 that she had been operated on (possibly for an ulcer) by the remarkable Dr Bethel Solomons, Master of the Rotunda Hospital in Dublin. Dr Solomons had forbidden any fried food, given her glucose pills and planned to put her on a vitamin regime. She wrote that Peter would look after her at Oranmore and Philip in Croydon. She wanted to bring Philip to Glaslough: 'He is a terrific person and VERY MANLY!' Her legal escape from Paul was proceeding at the pace of a very slow snail. In the same letter to Marjorie: 'I have URGENT letter from my solicitor that my annulment petition has gone to Counsel and got a good report but I must rewrite it before it can be put forward and the quicker the better.' Then, on 28 July, to Marjorie: 'Paul is returning to England and has employed a lawyer to fight the case.' And in an undated letter to Rose: 'I got a letter from Paul's solicitors enclosing a bill for £47 and saying he had told them I'd pay all his legal expenses (to back the divorce!) and he'd just called on them to announce he was "without means". That dear little divorce had already cost me £200.' The plan for an annulment seems to have got nowhere, in spite of the two previous, and perhaps still living, Mrs Rodziankos. While waiting for her freedom, Anita changed her surname back to Leslie by deed poll. At the time, deed polls were enrolled in the Supreme Court and had to be advertised in *The London Gazette*.

In 1947 George and Patsy Jellicoe had paid their first visit to Oranmore Castle. For George, the visit had not been a success. 'The sea came in through the windows, nobody could cook and it was freezing cold,' the late Lady Jellicoe told me in 2007, when I interviewed her in London. She thought that Anita's poor housekeeping skills were a reaction against Marjorie, a domestic goddess: 'There were always white sheets and towels and good food. Anita was a free spirit.' The conditions at Oranmore didn't stop Patsy from visiting again, but her husband stayed away.

Shane's literary career had had a bit of a setback. He had planned to publish a biography of Leonard Jerome, grandfather of Shane and Winston, but, Anita wrote to Marjorie: 'Winston sent for him [Shane] and asked him not to put in ANY indiscreet bits or mention the three sisters' [Leonard's daughters] love affairs etc so he might let me work at it in the autumn but I am sick of writing books.' In 1954 Anita was to bring out *The Fabulous Leonard Jerome* with Winston's approval. Meanwhile, in wretched spirits, she told Rose: 'I don't know what to do with myself – it's time I rejoined some army.' She knew that she should be grateful to Marjorie, who had hoped that her generous gifts of a castle, a diamond bracelet and an allowance would dispel Anita's churning despair but, as Anita wrote to Rose, the one person to whom she could be 'as awful as I feel like':

> It just doesn't work like that. I don't know how to turn the wheels inside myself any more. They are so deep and out of one's control ... I know that I long for the feeling of life and comradeship that I had during the war and have now lost ... and that I am terribly tired and the last three years have been exhausting disillusion so that I don't even know what to grasp at any more ... and that I who used to have something to give to others now have nothing. It's the mental depression that gets me down now ... the utter futility and nerviness of everything.

The letter ends 'I am so sorry to go on being in such a bad state like a lead weight to my friends ... I just got all broken up and am bad at mending.'

Anita, in the early post-war years, sounds very like Susan Traherne, the heroine of David Hare's stirring play *Plenty* (1978). Susan had been a seventeen-year-old resistance fighter behind enemy lines and now finds the peace mundane and frustrating. 'I want to move on. I do so desperately want to move on,' Susan says. But she can't stop wishing for a return to the years of excitement, danger and valour and becomes increasingly unstable. Edmund Wilson, visiting England in 1945, understood this kind of self-pitying misery. He wrote: 'How empty, how sickish, how senseless everything suddenly seems the moment the war is over.' Anita's great-aunt Mary Crawshay, *née* Leslie, always said that self-pity was 'like sitting in wet shoes'. Anita couldn't take her feet out of sopping footwear.

Thinking about new clothes cheered her up for a while. She wrote to Rose: 'The stiff red dress sounds heavenly ... all I really badly need now is a black velvet ... I think Mme. Lavande could copy your navy blue.' But little else could cure her despair. Neither Marthe Bibesco's praise for *Train to Nowhere* nor the prospect of Bill King coming to Oranmore for a week's hunting worked to lift her spirits. The castle was eating money: 'I feel the whole project is getting beyond me and swamping me. I just long to go away and forget about it. But Peter thinks that he's there for keeps. Dear kind affectionate loyal Peter but oh what a muddler.'

No wonder that she was physically ill. Other people seemed to have mended better than she had. Rose was happily married at last, or so it seemed, with a baby daughter and homes in Paris and the ski resort of Megève; Desmond had Agnes and a baby son, Sean, born that June. With a successful novel behind him, he now had a film project, *Stranger at my Door*, which starred Agnes and was about to start shooting in Dublin. His shoes were perfectly dry.

13
The Burden of the Day

Nineteen forty-eight had started out hopefully enough. At the beginning of the year Anita had written to Marjorie: 'I won my case yesterday and have a decree.' Within two weeks of her divorce Anita left Oranmore and Peter Wilson, and sailed to America with Marjorie and Jack, then met Philip in San Francisco, 'on the express written understanding', or so she wrote to Rose, that 'it was to decide the course of our lives'. The couple visited Rose's brother Bill Vincent in San Francisco and confirmed their engagement to him, but it wasn't that simple. Philip had managed to become engaged to another girl at the same time, Eileen Sybil Phipps, a niece of the Duchess of Gloucester. Anita supposed, reasonably enough, that the other engagement had been broken off, since Philip showed her the plans of his house in Australia and wanted her to decide which walls to knock down. However, at the same time, the other fiancée was buying her trousseau.

Anita, looking forward to getting married and a new life in Australia, flew back to London. Philip arrived in England soon afterwards and insisted that she stay with Rose at a house she was renting at Frensham, a small town near Guildford in Surrey, since, if it were known that Anita was in London, there would be a scandal. Philip then came to Frensham and told Anita he could only think of one way of 'playing it now', which was to gain time by shamming a broken leg. Rose's doctor, Teddy Sugden, obligingly set Philip's leg in plaster. Philip then urged Anita to fly back to New York, where he would join her later.

'I still never doubt he would follow but get rather jumbled,' Anita wrote to Bill Vincent, in a mournful account of the proceedings. Too jumbled to follow Philip's instructions, she stayed in England. Philip took his bogus broken leg to Hermione Ranfurly's house and she agreed to let him stay on condition he told her the whole truth. In fact he told her that Anita was in America, and then fetched Eileen for inspection. On reading his engagement announcement to Eileen in *The Times*, Hermione called Philip 'a sneaking shit who has never loved anyone in his life' and turned him out of her house. Anita, at Frensham, collapsed with nervous frustration. Rose went to London to confront Philip, who told her that he thought he must go through with the marriage to Eileen. He wrote Anita 'a footling epistle', which said that he loved both Anita and Eileen equally.

Although Anita mentioned some of the consequences of this extraordinary jilting to Bill Vincent — collapsing in hysterics in the Ruck-Keenes' London flat and having to be given morphine by the ever-obliging Dr Sugden, being carried to a nursing home where the Duchess of Gloucester's ladies-in-waiting came to question her about Philip — she didn't tell Bill the whole story. At Frensham she had tried to slit her wrists. When she was back in Ireland, devotedly looked after by Peter Wilson, she wrote to Rose: 'I could have sworn that at least I was in my own clothes but find Rosie's dear little white angora jacket ruined! That is the final straw — in Rose's jacket!' She tried to analyze what she had done, writing to Rose:

> It was the fact that I had idolised Philip and idol to unbelievable trickster was a mighty fall — I had for 6 years selected him as the chevalier sans peur et sans reproche — to find a schzophrenic [*sic*] and the basest kind of liar was more than my reeling brain could stand.

Philip's behaviour is arguably harder to understand. What was the point of proposing marriage to two girls when, sooner or later, leg in plaster or not, he was bound to be found out? Philip had had a particularly tough war, returning to Australia from the fighting in New Guinea ill and skeletally thin. Perhaps suffering had affected his sanity, as it did so often to those who had to survive the peace somehow.

While Anita was still recovering in London, Rose left the UK to avoid paying £20,000 income tax. Peter Wilson was sent for to bring the addled Anita back to Oranmore, a labour of love willingly undertaken. Back in Ireland, Anita insisted that she had made a complete recovery. She wrote to Shane: 'Just a line to tell you I am completely over my breakdown and off to Glaslough ... the moment I could BEAR to face the fact of Parbury's baseness I could laugh it off.' And to Rose: 'I'm over it over it over it ... Once I could force myself to realise coldly he was everything I did not want him to be than [*sic*] suddenly I began to laugh at myself for being "had" – so completely unutterably "had" – led up the garden path of history.' She delighted in her surroundings, or said that she did: 'The castle is lovelier than ever – what lights – what flowers – baby seals – kittens – gorgeous vegetables to eat.' And, above all: 'The reality of dear Peter ... one person with one mind – a straight gaze, eyes 2 inches apart.' She was about to go to Glaslough where 'with enormous pleasure I am going to give the cowboy chaps I had made in Wyoming for Philip to Peter instead!!!'

Peter's way of celebrating Anita's recovery was to frantically socialize, something that he usually tried to avoid. He and Anita called on neighbours, planned a lunch out, a trip to the Balinrobe races and a dance where Anita would wear a spectacular American evening dress. They were both deluded in thinking that all was now well. How could a woman who had expected to fly to Australia and begin married life with the man she had loved and yearned for for six years, settle down contentedly in the mouldering Irish castle she had longed to escape – and with a man she didn't love? It was beyond endurance.

Philip Parbury's wedding took place on 7 July 1948, an occasion that Anita marked by swallowing a bottle of aspirins and other tablets, washed down with half a bottle of whiskey. By the time Peter found her, she was going cold. Peter made her vomit to bring up all the drugs. He was convinced that she hadn't meant to kill herself but wanted a few hours of oblivion to get her through the day. By that stage he was as exhausted as she was. He hired a nurse for a few days and realized that it would be a long time before Anita was over it, over it, over it. But the Leslie way was to make light of things. Anita told Rose: 'Mummy has written a really funny letter: "Her needs were so modest – one Australian bounder with hookworm – not a peer or millionaire …"'

Peter stayed at Oranmore when Anita went to Glaslough and, once away from him, she appreciated him less. To Rose:

> I realised 2 years ago we could never share life – he likes so much that I don't and to share a home with him drives me nearly mad – not to mention the complications of his wife and son … see I can't marry him and settle – he is too old – it wouldn't work – it doesn't work now! … I am the destruction of his happiness … So once again I have got to organise a cleavage and desert poor faithful Pete.

Another man was causing her problems too. Her brother Jack, who had cracked up in the prison camp, was again nearing breakdown and Anita felt that she was 'the only bolster that poor conflicting mind has between him and the world'. She took him to see 'a famous doctor' and resigned herself to looking after him indefinitely. These were not ideal circumstances for a woman recovering from a suicide attempt.

So much happened during July that Anita didn't mention the August publication of *Train to Nowhere*. It is hard to know when she wrote the book while restoring a castle, losing a lover and coping with family problems. The book was subtitled 'An ambulance driver's adventures on four fronts', carried a foreword by Alex, now Field-Marshall the Viscount Alexander of Tunis and was dedicated to Jeanne de L'Espée and the *ambulancières* of the 1st Armoured Division, and to the memory of Lucette and Odette Le Coq.

It is an extraordinary, unforgettable book and reviewers recognized Anita's 'impersonal integrity' and her unique point of view – 'a terse, keen reticence and the summing up of deadly situations in a line or two …' (*The Times*). It sold out quickly, was reprinted twice and then went out of print. For some years after the war, people wanted to read only about situations with which they were already familiar: Dunkirk, the D-Day landings, the death of Hitler. It was too soon to offer new revelations. In 1949 Elizabeth Taylor's fine novel *A Wreath of Roses* was published. In it, a man admits to a woman whom he has just met that he is writing a book about the war. Her reaction is this: '"The war and his experience in it", she thought. "Unreadable!"'

Viscount Alexander expected as much. In his foreword, he wrote: 'Our gallant French allies' ... contribution to the war is too little known by the world at large.' Even now, after a spate of books and films about the war, few of us are familiar with the 1944 Allied invasion of southern France, the exotic and slightly crazy Zouave troops who served in the French infantry, or the suffering of French civilians under German bombardment, stumbling out of their bombed houses, carrying dead babies in their arms. It is telling that when Anita revised her wartime memoir in 1983, she left out the episode of the exhausted French woman shooting two German prisoners, realizing that even forty or so years later, it was too distressing to read about. As Christopher Hitchens wrote: 'Real history is more pitiless even than you had been told it was.'

Train to Nowhere is lightened by the appearances of the *ambulancières* in their red lipstick, their hair somehow styled in complicated rolls even when there was hardly any water to wash in, turning up on parade with their legs browned with tanning lotion to give a boost to dispirited soldiers. Twenty years after Anita's book was published, another book by a female soldier appeared: the Israeli Yael Dayan's *A Soldier's Diary*. Yael, daughter of a general, shares Anita's view that women in the front line are a gladdening and civilizing influence – the way they hang bits of mirrors on trees to fix their make-up distracts from the shock of war. The French female soldiers of the 1st Armoured Division, many of whom, like Anita, were awarded the Croix de Guerre, did not even have the right to vote. That came in 1945, long years after the overprotected British service-women had been part of the electorate.

It would appear that there were no publication celebrations. The Leslies were concerned about Jack, who was now having sleep treatment for his nerves. At the end of August Anita removed him from a nursing home as his treatment there sounded alarming: '10 days unconscious and 4 of hallucinations caused by some drug that sweeps debris out of the mind!' It had been a bad idea to expect Jack to settle down to managing

Glaslough straight from a prison camp. 'It's been the ruin of him and now we are going to have a long tricky time to get him balanced mentally.'

Shane was now 'running (?)' as Anita put it, the estate, while Marjorie spent a lot of time in America, her arrivals and departures causing disruption. Anita wished that she would make up her mind where she wanted to live, although she herself was as indecisive as her mother. She wrote to Rose: 'I don't know what to do with myself. I can't bog down at Glaslough – can't spend another winter here [Oranmore] with Peter – it's too futile. The alternative is to try to get some sort of job.' And then, not for the first time: 'Peter does worry me – he is so irresponsible and unreliable about his own affairs.' He was now farming at Oranmore in a small, and loss-making, way, devoting all his time and energy to four bullocks and seventeen acres. 'There is a constant fuss on,' Anita complained to Rose, begging her to come and stay.

Instead, in November, Anita went to stay with Rose in Paris, in Rose's suite at the Hôtel de Vendôme. She attended a reunion with some of her wartime colleagues, and went with Rose to the couture shows. Rose paid all of Anita's expenses and bought her a coat that cost seventy pounds. It should have been a happy escape from the blustery west of Ireland but it wasn't because Rose looked so ill, which was the way that Anita felt. But she wasn't ill; she was pregnant.

14
Charades at Castle Leslie

Everything comes to him who waits, Bill King must have thought. He had loved Anita for five years. An early, undated, letter of his declared: 'Anita, dear heart, oh the awful gloom of leaving you again. I fell so in love with you in a week it's just unbelievable.' And now he was going to marry her. He didn't mind that she was carrying Peter Wilson's baby. From another undated letter: 'I want your happiness but we must think mostly for the baby. What are you going to call him? I think Eton is a good idea. All the Etonians I know have benefitted from it.' Just before their engagement was announced at the end of December 1948, Bill wrote to Shane:

> Dear Sir Shane, As you have heard, Anita has promised to be my wife.
> For me it is a great fulfilment because I have been in love with her for five years of war and peace ... I am not a healthy man, nor ever will be but I have enough to keep her in reasonable comfort until the socialists scoop the pool, when we shall probably become professional yacht hands.

In this letter, Bill made it plain that he intended to remain a Protestant.

Bill was highly amused by the Leslies – 'fun was a word much on their lips', he observed. Arriving unexpectedly at Glaslough – his telegram hadn't arrived – he found Anita and Marjorie arguing about the breeding of greyhounds, 'topply table covered with Ming … the yowls of nervy greyhounds as they slipped on the parquet'. Bill's family had come from County Galway but it was only when he went there with Anita that he discovered this, and that his grandfather had been a professor at what was then Galway's Queen's University, as well as a famous archaeologist.

The bride-to-be was bird happy. To Rose: 'Such a whirl – but I crave protection and tenderness and loving care and am so glad we are going to get married … Bill's radiant happiness and unselfishness has given me a kind of fire – mentally I'm alright again – only physically a bit peaky.' What she was doing may not have struck Anita as particularly odd. As Shane was to point out in his book *Long Shadows* (1966): 'Cherished records have been at the mercy of those whose advantage is to conceal illicit infusions under the façade of wedlock.' The illicit infusions had to remain a secret. Anita made plans: after the hastily arranged wedding at Glaslough, she and Bill would stay with Rose at her chalet in Megève, where Bill could ski. Then Anita would make a furtive return to Dublin to give birth in June, leaving the city before anyone caught sight of the baby, whose official birth date was August. She would lie low until the baby could be shown to friends and family. This concealment would entail taking the baby on a round-the-world voyage on the 24-foot waterline ocean racer that Bill was having built. It didn't seem such an outlandish idea to a woman who had joined the army in order to escape from her first husband.

When Anita was happy she could never recognize someone else's pain. Before her wedding she wrote to Rose from Glaslough: 'Darling Pete arrives for Xmas – he is glad too.' Peter was far from glad but tried to cope with the situation by joining in with the wedding plans. During that fraught December, he wrote frequently to Rose, leading her to believe that he and Anita together had decided on her marriage to Bill, and that Bill himself understood that he would have Anita's companionship only on a part-time basis. At times, in this flurry of correspondence, Peter, now divorced, is convinced that Anita would have married him had not the Bishop of Galway and Peter's own antipathy towards the hypocritical Catholic church made this impossible. He believed that Anita was marrying Bill for his, Peter's sake, and this made him even more devoted to her than he had been for the last ten years. At other times he tells Rose that Anita is unable to love anyone and that he pities Bill, whom he recognizes as loving Anita as much as he, Peter, does. He insists that he must attend the wedding, since he is the only person who can lace Anita into her corset to hide the baby, whom he refers to as 'little Rose'.

He rails against the Leslies, whom he considers theatrical, publicity-mad show-offs; the Jews in Palestine who, he claims, are fighting the Arabs with American and Russian weapons; and the situation in France, which he considers makes the country unsafe for Fleur, Rose's little daughter, who Peter suggests should be sent to Oranmore. He writes to everyone who he suspects might think that Anita has callously thrown him over, and claims to have had his ego boosted by two offers of marriage since the announcement of Anita's engagement. The cascade of letters, flitting from Anita's corset to the war in Palestine to his complicated financial situation, make him sound raving mad rather than heartbroken and bereft. Anita ignored his true state of mind. To Rose: 'Bill and Peter want me to have a white wedding to annoy Paul! They are both so sweet and tender and loving and want to look after me – such big love.'

Like a little girl playing dress-up, she raided Glaslough's attics for her bridal attire. 'Can I wear the old lace veil symbol of virginity or will my friends laugh!!!' Her dress was first worn by a Leslie bride in 1890, the bodice now let out by the blacksmith's wife, the orange blossom headdress 'woven with wire by Monaghan's "modish coiffeuse"'. There would be a bower of flowers from the greenhouse and a dispensation for the mixed marriage by the bishop. Marjorie was in America and would miss the wedding, as would Rose, but this didn't dampen Anita's spirits. She was ready to face the future. To Rose: 'If I think more about other people's happiness I won't get so wrought up in myself ... I am getting excited ... at being able to give so much happiness by just stopping my distressed sulks.' Distressed sulks were a bit of a euphemism to describe the recent suicide attempts. She insisted that Peter felt as happy as she did: 'Pete looking 20 years younger and in terrific spirits is enjoying the shooting here.'

The Rt Hon. Winston Churchill, had he remembered that less than a year ago Anita had asked him to meet her then fiancé, Colonel Philip Parbury, may have been surprised to receive an invitation to her wedding to Commander William D. King. He and Mrs Churchill were unable to attend but sent a congratulatory telegram. In spite of his plans to supervise the fitting of the corset, Peter couldn't go through with it. He couldn't face the church service either but for Anita's sake, he told Rose, he went to the reception at the flower-bedecked castle, which, to add to his distress, was full of Bill's relations. Living a lie was beginning to tell on him.

From Megève, Anita wrote to Shane to thank him for organizing the wedding: 'I don't think any wedding could have been nicer and it has given a happy aura to the old place where our family has been loved and respected for so long.' At the end of this letter, rather ungraciously, since a bishop had accommodated her mixed marriage, she took a snipe at his profession. Irish bishops were 'pompous tyrants with no knowledge of world affairs'. She also wrote, provocatively: 'Don't you really approve of partition? I do,' although she must have known that Shane didn't. He was both a Catholic and a royalist, who wished to see a united Ireland on warm terms with England. At Megève Anita skied all day, although Peter had begged Rose not to let her. She planned to stay with Rose until April, while Bill went to Austria for some more serious skiing with his old friend Ruck-Keene. Unusually, perhaps because he felt lonely at Glaslough, Shane wanted to know his daughter's future whereabouts. Anita produced an itinerary that didn't mention the forthcoming stay in Dublin. She told Shane that after April she was going to Oranmore while Bill finished building his yacht. Bill had asked her whether she needed a lavatory on the boat, 'or could one just throw buckets overboard as it sails faster without a drain!!!' She had insisted on a drainage system. She gave her father the impression that the yacht, when ready to sail, would be moored in the south of France, close to the villa that Rose would be renting for the summer. Naturally, she did not mention her plans to give birth, secretly, in Dublin or to take the unannounced baby on a long sea voyage.

Rather bossily, she instructed Shane on how to talk about her marriage: 'Be sure to tell everyone how pleased the family is at my marrying Bill and what a hero he is and what a darling too. It's so important that everyone should know what sort of person Bill is owing to last summer's dramas.' The Philip Parbury fiasco had not done her reputation much good; one of Bill's many assets was that he was able to provide her with respectability.

15
'He Enchants My Every Moment'

'I don't know how we can call this premature' were the first words Anita heard as she came to from the chloroform that she'd had during the very last stages of a twelve-hour labour. Tarka Leslie King, as he would later be called, was born on 27 June 1949 at 23 Mount Merrion Avenue in Blackrock, Dublin, in the middle of a heatwave. The house belonged to a Mrs Burke, who rented rooms to country people who came to Dublin for medical examinations, but rarely to give birth soon after arrival. Six days after Tarka was born, Anita wrote to Rose:

> Never has she [Mrs Burke] known such tenants – Bill appears half ship-wrecked and starving and vanishes in a little boat – Peter and I appear with a van of lettuces and produce a baby! – Nurses and doctors arrive – She kept staggering up with sandwiches and coffee and Solomons charmed her so she did not quite faint when he met her on the stairs in his underpants only prior to slipping on his white gown – It was a broiling hot night.

So charmed was Mrs Burke that 'she spent the afternoon saying hail Marys in the garden and sending me up roses!'

In his memoir, *One Doctor in His Time* (1956), Bethel Solomons mentions Anita – her elegance and literary achievements – but not the circumstances of her son's birth, when a man who wasn't her husband waited with her for the baby to be born. Anita, because of her precarious health, had been Dr Solomons' patient for some years. He would have seen the photographs of her wedding in *The Irish Times* and realized that the man who stayed with her during her long labour was not Commander King and that her nine-pound baby boy had inherited this man's very large hands and feet.

Following Betsan's advice, Anita had followed the methods of the obstetrician Dr Grantly Dick-Read, who advocated relaxation, deep breathing and an understanding of the birth process long before these procedures became widely acceptable. When Anita's labour began, she 'went into the fray fit as a fiddle' and managed without pain-reducing drugs for the first seven hours. She wrote to Rose about the birth of her little son: 'What a moment it was – rapturous – I never knew I wanted a baby so much – in fact never felt maternal before – the emotion came with an inordinate rush! He enchants my every moment.' This unanticipated state of bliss complicated things. Before Tarka's birth, it had been understood that Peter would mainly take charge of him while Anita and Bill travelled but the rush of maternal feelings changed everything. Anita who, a year previously, had been planning to leave both Peter and Oranmore, now clung to both. Parenthood 'gives us both something to work for – a reason to mend the castle leaks, to improve the garden.'

This change of attitude affected Bill deeply. On 6 July he wrote a five-page letter to his wife from Portsmouth where he was fitting out *Galway Blazer*. He assured her that he was not writing 'in a haze of unhappiness jealousy or emotion but the result of long and careful thought.' He proposed that, in order to provide a stable upbringing for the baby, Anita should remain with Peter at Oranmore, even though their relationship was not ideal. Bill suggested that, for his own mother's sake, he and Anita should keep up a pretence of staying together for some time. He was doubtful whether he himself could ever sire healthy children since, in the past, 'with great misgivings', he had tried to – with three miscarriages as a result. 'Who knows that my weakness may not have contributed to that.' He urged Anita not to consider his proposal emotionally but 'to give it careful thought and consideration.' He then dismissed Anita's plans to stay with Tarka on *Galway Blazer* in September in the Mediterranean to keep the obviously full-term baby out of sight. 'Its first few months are the most important, to look after it in a tiny boat might prove disastrous.' He would allow Anita and Tarka to join him on the boat in the West Indies in the winter. This letter had a sobering effect on Anita, as it was meant to.

On 18 July Anita wrote to Rose from Mrs Burke's hospitable house:

> I can see I've done great wrong to both Peter and Bill ... men have only meant disaster in my life – and I have only dealt out unhappiness ... I'll cope with the future as best I can, remembering one can't go on getting married and unmarried and having babies – and just saying one does not realise what one is doing.

It was no hardship to remain hidden in Dublin, successfully breastfeeding but able to leave Tarka with a competent nurse in order to go to the ballet with Dr Solomons. For these outings, Anita dressed chicly but practically 'in the Schiaparelli cardigan and all Aunty Anne's old camisole tops as nursing mothers have occasional difficulties at meal times'. She planned to stay in Dublin until 1 August and then return to Oranmore, claiming that the baby had been born prematurely on 27 July – 'no one notices or cares about time in the West'. Tarka's birth would be formally announced on 12 September 'when I'll have been married 8 months'. She and the baby would then travel to Gibraltar and keep out of Ireland until the following May.

One of the first things that Bill had noticed about Anita was that she always managed to get her way against all odds. She was doing it now: what she wanted was to stay married to Bill, so she simply ignored his letter. Towards the end of her stay in Dublin, he came to see her. The nurse who had been looking after Tarka had to leave for her next case. Bill and Anita tripped over wet nappies, heated supplementary bottles and, over the following three days, after which Bill had to leave, seemed to have put their marriage together again. 'I do love him,' Anita wrote to Rose, 'and having made a wrong decision must try to play it right.'

Bill left; Peter came back to help Anita during her last five days in Dublin. On 30 July Anita drove back to Oranmore, Peter holding his son in his arms. To Rose: 'What a moment for Peter bringing his son to the home he built so much with his own hands.' Mother and baby were installed in the tower room, the sunniest place and with a bathroom beside it. With Margaret Glynn, 'our stalwart peasant maid who dotes on children', to help her look after Tarka, Anita was able to spend the next two days in bed. To Rose:

> It is strange to be here in the great vaulted hall where a year ago I lay in a vacuum of weary despair and now be utterly obsessed by a new devotion – And here, in the turret with its great stone corbels at which I used to stare and its narrow carved windows where Peter strove to bring me back to health I have brought him something – He is mad about the boy – we share the enchantment – He is all plans for the future – to teach him to ride and swim and sail and dig and farm and know wild birds.

In this undated letter to Rose, which must have been written soon after the return to Oranmore, Anita revealed how she came to marry Bill:

> All that last summer I was completely finished – the main spring broken so that I did not care about anything … So disjointed was my mind that it seemed quite normal and feasible to ask Bill to 'invent' a husband for me, call him Cochian, announce he'd fallen overboard and sail me around the world in a tiny boat – it never struck me questions might be asked or any of this considered extraordinary.

Out of this strange plan had come her marriage to Bill, a marriage that she had gone into lightheartedly – 'so much of my life was charades – the idiocy of my mental engine at this time can be gauged in [*sic*] the fact that I thought it would all be fun for Peter'. Bill's heart-stricken letter, offering to give her up, had amazed her: 'After breaking myself I can't realise there are other people in the world still to break afresh.' She had clearly learned nothing from Peter's distress over Philip's visit to Oranmore the previous year. Somehow, things began to work out. Peter became the involved father of the child he'd longed for. Bill could sail away for months at a time, knowing that Peter would look after Anita. And Anita? She was determined to atone for her previous thoughtlessness towards both men. To

Rose: 'Although my whole being is centred on the child ... I am conscious of two other children dear and sweet who also depend on me.'

Marjorie was still in Santa Barbara, where she found the climate good for her health, and Jack was in San Francisco, looking for a job and sampling the nightlife, particularly the bars. Unfortunately one of the men he met in a bar and to whom he had given Bill Vincent's address, broke into Bill's flat late at night, to Bill's fury. Jack had a new plan: to get up a brochure for Glaslough and let it out to rich Americans, an idea he soon abandoned, to Anita's relief. She was, as always, worried about her brother, writing to Rose of 'the mixture of Catholic chastity – suicide and the other extreme'. She didn't explain what the other extreme was.

That August the Ruck-Keenes stayed at Oranmore for three weeks. Anita was so slender that they thought that she had miscarried until they saw Tarka, who was two months old and large for his age. Unusually for August, often the wettest month in the west of Ireland, the weather was perfect. They swam, rowed out to seal islands and the Ruck-Keenes, perfect guests, did all the cooking. Anita, now 'strong and calm' and with an organized life, wanted Rose and Fleur to visit too – 'Come and have a real rest in good air' but Rose was ill and exhausted again and Oranmore didn't sound like a good place in which to recuperate – 'If the autumn gales blow we just sit indoors (plenty of air even there).' As well as the possibility of gales, there were nine new greyhound puppies who needed a hundred saucers of milk a day. Rose stayed away.

Peter's health was a worry too. To Rose, on 3 September:

> He is so tired as to be almost gaga ... has organised a sort of Chinese coolie life for himself – slaves from 7am till nightfall – unshaven – dressed in rags – a plate of porridge for breakfast – bread and marmalade at 3 for lunch – cocoa and bread for dinner at 10 and goes to bed too tired for a bath. And all for about £30 in profit from the farm ... He's so tired I haven't the heart to ask him to carry the baby upstairs even – and he weighs 12 lbs.

Peter had toothache and a swollen face – and post-divorce problems. His ex-wife, who lived in Limerick, had appealed against a judgement 'giving her ONLY £700 a year'. She lost the case but wanted Peter to pay her legal bills. Anita suggested paying them in kind, 'long to ship off a cart of puppies and little pigs to Limerick'. She still felt twinges of guilt: 'Perhaps it was terrible of me not to marry Peter after the wonderful way he behaved last summer but he seemed to have purposely made a life which it was impossible to share.'

Tarka, on the other hand, was pure pleasure, sleeping through the night and waking 'all yawny and stretchy and almost talks'. Anita was looking forward to taking him to join Bill in Antigua in the West Indies, to spend a sunny winter on the *Galway Blazer*. Unusually for such a self-centred man, Shane wrote to his daughter, objecting to the plan to take the baby on a long sea voyage. Anita replied huffily: 'I am not taking the baby on any long cruise. Solomons recommended sunshine, sea bathing and fruit juice for us both so I am hoping to get on a French steamer in November direct to Guadaloupe and Bill can sail over from Antigua to fetch me.' Shane had obviously reproached her for neglecting Marjorie – a major case of the pot calling the kettle black – for Anita told him: 'I do realise how ill Mummy is and I am therefore planning to join her in USA in April. If she feels well enough to return for the summer we can return together with baby – if not she will at least see him and I'll be back on May 1st.'

Shane also wanted to know who was going to take over the running of Glaslough. Anita's tone remained tetchy:

> It should be you. You have no other home but you won't stay there long enough at a time. Otherwise Desmond but he only wants to make films. However, we all decided a year ago to leave the final decision until October 1950 and I'm sure that is best. We'll all have a jolly summer there to discuss.

In a PS, she told Shane that she didn't think Marjorie would ever come back to Glaslough permanently and that Bill, who was planning to represent England in the Bermuda Race in the summer, would be back in England by October, 'just in time to decide if and on what basis he could farm Glaslough'. To his family's embarrassment, Jack had proposed marriage to Anita's friend Grania Guinness, who was astonished and angry at the proposal, as Jack was clearly not the marrying kind. Anita told her father: 'I agree with her. A wife without love living in that large freezing house would be macabre beyond words. Glaslough only makes sense as a lovely family home with a young happy gay couple whose hearts are in farming and family life.' She meant herself and Bill but this was the first time she'd mentioned the idea.

On Tarka's supposed date of birth, 27 August, when he was actually nearly two months old, Anita had sent wires to Marjorie in America, Shane at Glaslough and Bill's mother, Ina, in Angmering, West Sussex. Anita to Rose:

> Bill's sister Diana would go and have a son 3am morning of [August] 22nd – 6 hours after my supposed 'landing'!!! A 9lb 6 oz boy – 2 weeks overdue – she'll never forget the date. His mother knows all but I sent her a wire too to show to family etc. Her head must be spinning – 18lb of grandson in one night.

Richard Tarka Bourke Leslie King was christened in the Franciscan monastery in Galway on 11 November 1949, in the painted tin that was the temporary font. Old ladies with black shawls over their heads jangled their rosaries at the baby – 'those who had no beads waved cigarette cartons and his poor bewildered little face turned purple with disapproval', his mother noted. Clare, who adored the baby and was delighted that he was named after her late son Richard, appointed herself Chief Sponsor and wore a flowing cloak. Peter was godfather to his own son, and one of Tarka's Protestant godmothers, Diana Daly, was, impressively, able to say the Creed. Most of the godparents were unable to be present: Patsy Jellicoe, General Gruss, the Governor of Strasbourg, Rose Gardner, Hermione Ranfurly, Admiral Ruck-Keene and Henry McIlhenny, the owner of beautiful houses in Donegal and Philadelphia. The christening was a simple little ceremony and, since the Franciscans weren't allowed to accept money, Peter gave the friars two ducks and twenty eggs.

On 19 November Peter drove Anita and Tarka to Cobh, where mother and baby boarded the *Britannic* for New York, where Henry McIlhenny sent a car to bring them to his house at Lincoln Drive, Philadelphia. There life was rather different to the rugged existence at Oranmore. Henry lived life on the grand scale. There was a party to celebrate the opening of the opera and a dinner for Anita. 'Henry has certainly given us a wonderful time,' Anita wrote to Marjorie who was spending the winter in Tucson, Arizona, 'theatres and operas galore and his sister whirled me to her coiffeur and I had my hair done in a new way which everyone praises as very becoming.' Tarka had a slightly snivelly nose and a doctor was called. He pronounced the sniveller

> a beautifully healthy baby [who] should thrive in the West Indies, where he can kick bare and absorb vitamin C through his skin from the sun-drenched air. The doctor said this was a difficult climate [in Philadelphia] for babies as it's cold and changeable and hard to give them enough air.

Fresh air was something of an obsession of Anita's. Her childhood had been made wretched by asthma, which made it difficult to breathe.

Bill cabled that he had reached Antigua after about six weeks' sailing from the Canaries, and Anita and Tarka set off to join him from New York. Until the following April, when not on board the *Galway Blazer*, her address would be the idyllic-sounding Beach Hotel, Parham, Antigua, West Indies.

16
A Sea Change

The story that Anita told in *Love in a Nutshell*, which was published in 1952, was that she and Bill decided to set sail in a 31-foot ocean racer to escape both the wildness and wet of the west of Ireland, and the eccentric household at Oranmore Castle. This included Peter wearing a bowler hat in an attempt to stop the rain dripping though the eight-foot-thick walls from also dripping down his neck, Clare dangerously swinging a mallet in the great hall as she hewed a limestone Madonna, and a clutch of thieving greyhounds.

This is how the tale unfolds: '"Bill," I exclaimed, "you are a sailor! Let's go away. Let's go around the world in a little boat!" "All right," he replied slowly.' The announcement that a baby would be the second mate was later made to the boat builder. 'I was glad not to be present on the day when Bill announced he wanted a swivel-cradle hung over the chart table.'

The book is a delicious – to use one of Anita's favourite words – romp, rather in the manner of a nineteen-thirties screwball comedy. Anita is hopeless at sea, ditsy and forgetful, while Bill is organized and masterful, and Tarka thrives in the sunshine. It strikes both Bill and Anita that after years in a submarine (Bill) and sleeping in an ambulance (Anita) that it was odd for them to choose to live for months in a small boat. It seemed somehow fated, as was the lack of decent food, similar to the situation at Oranmore when, on the rare occasions that Anita remembered to shop, the dogs got to the dinner first. They couldn't always escape the rain either. On Christmas Day, in what was meant to be the dry season in Antigua, it rained without cease. Anita, typically, had not yet organized shore marketing, so Bill was put in charge of the festive meal, which turned out to be Bemax and raisins with rancid tinned butter mixed with rum. When Anita grumbled, Bill said: 'I thought you liked simple fare. There wasn't much to eat at the castle as far as I can remember.'

There are jokes and banter and gossip about life on the more than a dozen islands they visited and glamorous episodes when Anita, in a slinky, sequinned dress, and Bill, in a white dinner jacket, are guests on sleek yachts and at airy villas, while Tarka is looked after by doting native maids. Towards the end of the voyage, Bill decides to enter a yacht race in Bermuda, and Anita and Tarka are flown home. Anita accepts that her husband will always choose a life at sea whenever he can and reflects: 'I infinitely prefer good-tempered men emerging occasionally from dangers they enjoy than thwarted hearties who stay at home and are cross.' *Love in a Nutshell* is all sunshine and blithe spirits, as the couple sail through five hundred miles of blue-green waters.

While they were happily afloat, Marjorie was fretting in Tucson. She wrote to Shane, at Glaslough:

> When Anita and Bill get back from this foolish yachting trip, I think they would be the ones to take on Glaslough. She would make a wonderful hostess, Bill had always been mad to farm and it's a grand place to bring up a child. Then Jack could stay there when he liked.

Marjorie alluded to some scandalous behavior of Jack's. 'He swears, however, before God, that never never again would he do anything the way he did before at Glaslough, and I know he wouldn't, the terrible lesson sank in too deep.' To ensure Jack's future good conduct, Marjorie was going to 'keep an eye on a widow, however if a celebate [*sic*] life in the Glaslough climate should appeal to one'. Marjorie was ill; even the mild, sunny Arizona climate didn't relieve her pain. She hadn't left her cottage for a month and spent part of the day in bed. She complained to Shane that all he did was to get cardinals to pray for her 'and put in the papers that I am dying ... But if I were able I would gladly come back to you at Glaslough, in fact, wouldn't have left if I had thought you were going to settle there.'

At the beginning of 1950 Jack was in New York but wrote to Shane that he was planning to return to Glaslough in the middle of February, when he intended to plant some more trees on the estate. Later on, in the summer, he planned to bring over five daughters of leading American families, 'for twelve dollars a day a piece!' He asked Shane to see that the piano was tuned. Desmond and Agnes were also laying claim to Glaslough That year, *Picture Post* magazine sent one of its most celebrated photographers, Haywood Magee, to photograph the handsome couple at Castle Leslie. In one picture Agnes is asleep in a Venetian baroque bed; in another Desmond holds Titus, a live owl, while striking a pose in the Long Gallery.

Alone at Oranmore, Peter was planning his future. He wrote to Rose that he would never give up Tarka and was determined not to let any offspring of Bill and Anita live at the castle. Since Anita owned the place, it is not clear how he intended to do this. He had always poured out his heart to Rose and now, in a series of letters, told her how much he loved her and how close he felt to her. Anita, from Grenada, in April, on the last leg of her voyage, also had plans. She wrote to her father:

> If you go to Eton on June 4th, you can put down baby's name as Bill does not want him to go to Dartmouth [Bill's alma mater] – says too young to decide a career – and says all his friends who went to Eton were glad they had. His official name is Richard Burke Leslie King – and we may put a hyphen between the last two.

Anita was growing impatient with Shane's eccentricities; she warned him not to wear his kilt when he visited her friend Diana Daly in Grosvenor Square, 'as they are conventional and the Duke does not wear Scotch clothes in London'. Shane had always made his daughter feel that she was dull and uninteresting, and she had always taken his reputation as a brilliant conversationalist on trust. Now, her self-confidence boosted by marriage and motherhood, she recognized that her father was a pompous buffoon with his kilts and faux-Celtic traditions.

Meanwhile, the unusual set-up at Oranmore was causing comment. Anita, after her long trip, was staying with Bill's mother, Ina, at Angmering, when Peter wrote to Rose that people were beginning to guess at the real circumstances of Tarka's birth and that he didn't care, but Anita did and was worried that Philip might find out and laugh at her. Peter admitted that if Tarka was kept from him for too long he would threaten disclosure and, disingenuously, told Rose that he wasn't a good liar. Anita was coming under criticism over her behaviour, Peter Gardner being among those who had taken against her. Anita wrote to Rose:

> As he feels as he does, I will never spend a night under your roof – for it is his roof also and I want him to be told this immediately. If there is no question of his ever seeing me there [the Gardners' chateau at Fontainebleau] there should be no danger of disagreement between you on my account – I have done enough harm without causing argument between you two.

Anita wrote to Peter Gardner by the same post, telling him that she would never stay under his roof and asking him not to divulge anything about her that Rose may have told him for, as Anita told Rose: 'He knows that which I wish he did not and has spoken of it to my great detriment.' Dan Ranfurly also expressed his disapproval of Anita. Anita to Rose:

> I suppose one ought to notice one's friends have husbands but Dan and Peter [Gardner] have never really existed for me until suddenly they become preventatives of my seeing you or Hermione. Let's hope that Peter does not object to your visiting me in Ireland or we shall never be able to meet – not even once in 18 months.

Rose and Anita continued to write to each other. Anita often referred to the subject of her marriage to Bill: 'I did not want to marry either Pete or Bill – but felt it imperative to marry someone.' Life with Peter would, Anita felt, be spent picking potatoes, so 'Bill seemed a better idea and at least he was a companion to go ski-ing with and he was thrilled to sail off in a boat. At the time it seemed a good plan to me and the marriage at Glaslough gave enjoyment to our faithful old employees.' She and Bill were not sure about their future plans. They would be prepared to run Glaslough as long as they were given carte blanche, or Bill might take up the offer of being the skipper of a trading schooner, running from Bermuda through all the West Indies. Bill had also expressed an interest in climbing Mount Everest. Anita disclosed to Rose that the voyage on *Galway Blazer* had not been quite the way she would depict it in her forthcoming book, *Love in a Nutshell*: 'We were so busy and often over-exhausted on the boat there was no time for discussion – it was all baby's next meal and drying sails and the time we could stay at each island.' She had wanted to call the book *Life in a Nutshell* but her publisher had insisted on 'Love'. 'Well, well, who cares.' At the time, Bill was in New York, fitting out *Galway Blazer* with new racing sails and a shorter keel in preparation for the Bermuda race. In this uncertain autumn, Marjorie, to her family's surprise, came back to settle at Glaslough. Anita to Rose on 20 October 1950: 'So Jack feels he must clear out but Bill does not want to run it for him.'

Marjorie knew that she was coming back to die. On her death on 7 February of the following year, Anita wrote to Rose: 'Her poor sick body was an impossible burden – it tortured her – she longed to go and only wanted to be surrounded by affection and love.' A few days before Marjorie died, Peter had brought Tarka to see her. 'In Tarka she saw a sort of resurrection of herself – something she had created through me – "never was there a child with such a soul", she kept saying, "he's unique."'

The kidney infection that caused Marjorie's death worsened so quickly that Desmond, Jack and Shane, who were in London, could not reach Glaslough before she died. By the time the doctor telephoned them, the last scheduled flight had left and the private plane that they then hired arrived too late. Agnes was in London too, nursing her son Sean, who had mastoiditis. As she was reading to the little boy at 5 am, doors opened and shut, the temperature in the room dropped and rose again and Sean reported that his pain had gone. When Desmond rang to say that his mother had died at 5 am, Agnes already knew. For Shane, his wife's death was an occasion for high drama. 'Pa drove us all demented,' Anita told Rose:

He wore Mummy's black velvet teagown as a toga over his belt, laden with black sealing wax – the most important thing he could think of. Thank heaven the kind Alexanders have taken him off our hands and he can use up all their note paper writing lamentations for Shane Leslie.

Marjorie had been much loved. The oldest gardener at Glaslough left his sick bed to say a rosary in her room and there were tributes from everyone who had known her, from the Queen of Spain to a kitchen maid who had benefitted from Marjorie's kindness when the girl had given birth to an illegitimate baby twenty years before. The President of Ireland, Sean O'Kelly, walked for two miles behind her coffin. The first Catholic member of the Leslie family to be buried at Glaslough, she was laid to rest within the grounds of the Protestant church in a separate enclosure, which she had had built by the churchyard wall.

Soon after his mother's death, Jack decided to move to Rome and a company was set up to run Glaslough, of which he was managing director. The other directors were Anita, Bill, Desmond and Agnes, Anita holding fifty-one of the shares, an arrangement that would cause trouble in the future. Clare, aware of the muddle and uncertainty at both Glaslough and Oranmore, told Anita comfortingly: 'Destiny has a queer way of working out tangled threads.' Clare was convinced that Tarka would inherit Glaslough, in spite of Desmond and Agnes's hopes of securing the inheritance for Sean.

It had been two years since Anita had seen Rose, who now, for the first time, visited her at Castle Leslie. The house was bitterly cold so Rose took Anita to Dublin, a visit which was far more enjoyable than their stay in Paris, when Rose had been ill and Anita suffering from morning sickness. Rose was much stronger now. After she left Anita wrote, somewhat enviously: 'You really can see things clearly and decide what you want and do it.' This letter, which Anita wrote at Easter, was full of woe. Peter was being intolerable in spite – or perhaps, because of – having a willing redheaded girl helper. As for Oranmore Castle: 'I thought it was going to be a small project – a sort of little base one could close for six months of the year – A place to have my own things in and perhaps let! Not an encampment for Peter and his incredible serfs.' A note of martyrdom creeps in:

> Now one must just make the best of things and both Glaslough and Oranmore which have sapped the last of my youth and been the backgrounds to my own unhappiness take on a new meaning – They are both wonderful places to rear

Anita as a small child.

The schoolgirl Anita.

Anita in bomb-ridden London in 1940, wearing her Hardy Amies-designed Mechanised Transport Corps (MTC) uniform.

German troops surrendering to the French Army in 1945 with a Red Cross ambulance alongside.

Anita with her MTC ambulance.

Anita with friends during the war.

Anita with donkey in Syria, now Lebanon, c. 1943.

Anita with her co-driver, Geneviève, in front of the ambulance. They are both wearing their recently awarded Croix de Guerre, summer 1945.

Anita and Shane and Lionel Leslie, studio shot from the 1940s.

Anita's commanding officer Jeanne de l'Espée and fellow officer.

Colonel Peter Wilson, Commander of Transjordan Frontier Force and later on Churchill's staff in Berlin and London.

Colonel Paul Rodzianko CMG, Anita's first husband. They were married in 1937, divorced in 1948.

Anita and Colonel Peter Wilson at the Potsdam Conference, July 1945.

Clare Sheridan and Anita in 1940, before Anita sailed to Pretoria with the MTC.

Commander Bill King arranging a picnic, probably in Lebanon, where he first met Anita in 1943.

Anita with her children, Tarka and Leonie.

Anita and Bill on their wedding day at Castle Leslie, with pageboys, 1 January 1949.

Bill, Leonie, Tarka and Anita at their home, Oranmore Castle, Co. Galway.

A glamorous pre-war Anita.

Anita with art-gallery owner Roy Miles in London in the early 1970s.

children … There does not seem any escape open and I am too old to try forcing the issue … For Tarka it's alright – I can't ask more.

Bill, too, came in for criticism.

He says he's 'expended' finished with any attempt at a career and just ready to drift on the sea, or plod up mountains or dig a compost heap! How can I help him do any of these things? It is better he should lead his bachelor life and leave me in peace to organise the real nursery.

Paul was on this list of unsatisfactory men. 'Someone said to me once in Cairo "never hesitate about getting rid of Paul – he'll always find his feet." And he has.' Paul was back in Ireland, training the country's Olympic team at his friend Colonel Joe Dudgen's equitation school. One of the young trainers, Elspeth Gailey, remembered Paul fondly because he supported her use of spurs when Colonel Dudgen questioned it. And Paul had married again, perhaps for the fourth time. His new wife was the former Joan Freeman Mitford, nicknamed 'Rud', a cousin of the famous Mitford Girls, and the widow of Guillermo de Udy, who had died in 1941. According to Mary S. Lovell, author of *The Mitford Girls* (2001), Jessica Mitford, a great friend of Joan's, and her husband Bob Treuhaft, disliked Paul intensely. Jessica referred to Paul in a letter (22 April 1959) as 'Rud's ghastly husband'. 'Well, of course, men are a rotten lot,' Anita went on to write in *Edwardians in Love* (1972). This comment came from the heart. Anita's doleful account of her uneventful and confined life in the letter to Rose didn't mention that *Love in a Nutshell* was about to be published, or that she had started on another book, or that she was having a baby.

She was in London on 13 April for Marjorie's Requiem Mass, which was held at St James's Church, Spanish Place in the West End of London. It was a sunny day and the church was filled with Marjorie's friends. Not her husband, however. Shane was in Maryland, trying to drum up rich American customers for the hotel that he was planning to run at Glaslough, an idea originally mooted by Jack. That spring, Anita suspected that Rose's third marriage was in trouble. Rose appeared to have left the chateau that she had spent years restoring and moved to the Place Vendôme in Paris. Anita skirted round the issue, writing only, 'Let me know what you now call yourself – Vincent or Gardner.'

Anita spent the summer at Angmering with Ina. Anita loved this house, both for the central heating inside and the balmy Sussex air outside. Bill, who now took organic farming seriously because of its perceived benefits to Anita's health – she suffered constantly from bronchitis – was studying farming at Honey Tye Farm in Leavenheath, Colchester. He described himself as 'an Irish peasant farmer and single issue organic maniac'. He intended to build a four-room thatched cottage with, Anita delightedly told Rose, 'an Ideal boiler – central heating and bath water and all electrified as well – as the chief misery of life in Ireland is the complete inability of the houses to cope with the climate – the castle is really only habitable for 6 months a year.' Peter, oblivious to cold and discomfort, 'is there for ever as far as I can see'. He was building a series of what Anita called hideous, untidy sheds that ruined the landscape. In Ina's warm, comfortable house, Anita was outlining a life of her great-grandfather, Leonard Jerome, a project that had previously and disastrously been embarked upon by Shane and then, in the face of Winston's disapproval, abandoned. Anita understood that she would have to seek Winston's approval at an early stage of writing.

Leonie Rose King was born on 10 October 1951 in the Red Room at Castle Leslie, in the four-poster bed in which Marjorie had died eight months previously. She was the first, and so far the only, baby to have been born at Glaslough. Soon afterwards Anita and both her children moved in with Ina. Bill was still in Colchester but he and Anita had acquired a 334-acre farm in Drumlargan, County Meath. The land belonged to the Leslie estate and was given to the couple as part of the 1951 business arrangements. A photograph of Leonie's christening on 11 December at the Brompton Oratory shows Shane, kilted and sporranned, and Anita in a chic, full-length coat and a very Parisian-looking hat. Leonie's two godmothers, Winnie Carlton Page and Mary Soames, Winston's daughter, are wearing drab 'utility' suits with sagging skirts, perhaps the only kind available in a still-rationed England. Six years after the end of the war, Anita and Ina had been grateful for the nylons and food parcels that Shane had sent during his American visit.

At Oranmore the centrally-heated cottage, built for £3000, a ten-minute walk from the drafty castle, was taking shape. From this cosy base,

Bill would be able to farm and hunt, and it was close enough for Peter to see Tarka every day. The children could have the freedom of the castle during the summer months and live in the cottage during the winter. Anita to Rose: 'We can all farm, make compost, have lovely fresh food and hope for happiness – not in nagging each other's souls out but in making a busy healthy background for a new generation.' Although Peter was still cause for complaint – 'it only depresses him when I try to explain the unbearableness of life with him not only for me but for any woman' – Anita sounded positive about the future and her spirits rose further when *Love in a Nutshell* was published in 1952 by Hutchinson in the UK and Greenberg in the US and was well received on both sides of the Atlantic. *The Field*: 'An uncommonly good narrative, enchantingly described in a language always witty and often wise.' Guildford, *Connecticut Times*: 'The book is highly recommended to any reader who wants laughs and some down to earth opinions on the business of living together, family style.'

1952 and 1953 were bumper years for Leslie publications, new additions to the autobiographical 'rows of books upon the shelves', which Swift had disparagingly noted. Desmond, together with an eccentric American flying-saucer enthusiast, George Adamski, wrote *Flying Saucers Have Landed*, a successful book, which, according to Agnes, made Desmond 'a household name with the lunatic fringe', and much in demand for lecture tours. Shane published *An Anthology of Catholic Poets* to a somewhat quieter reception. The Leslie authors were put in the shade by Winston who, in 1953, won the Nobel Prize for Literature. He was also governing the country for the second time, the Conservatives having won the October 1951 election, when Winston was seventy-seven years old.

Jack now lived in Rome in a small, beautiful palazzo at 19 Piazza in Piscinula, Trastevere, but was still nominally in charge of Glaslough. 'Jack's sole instruction to new agricultural manager being to erect the Venetian chandelier he was sending from Mexico!' Anita grumbled to Rose. Shane was unhappy about the situation but Anita pointed out that he had only himself to blame: 'You signed it [Glaslough] away twice which would have been most unwise had you wanted to really live there and run it but now I have to take Jack's orders because he is legally the managing director.' She then told Shane something that must have given him mixed feelings: 'My article on Leonard Jerome has expanded into a brief biography. Clemmie writes me Winston approves the first 20 chapters. I do hope Mifflin publish it – dedicated to LJ's three famous grandchildren, you, Winston and Clare.' This was guileful of Anita. She had, for a long time, intended to write a book about Leonard Jerome rather than an article and this one, at over three hundred pages, was hardly brief. Shane, whose own effort had been so strongly discouraged by Winston, might have been mollified by being bracketed with his cousin as a dedicatee but, when Anita's book was published in 1954, it was dedicated: 'To Bill, my husband, who helped, and to my children Richard Tarka and little Leonie, who did not.'

In the autumn of 1953 Anita tried to finish the book against heavy odds. She had bronchitis again, brought on by sheer exhaustion, partly due to an ill-timed ten-day visit from Clare. To Rose: '[A]ll the evening cooking falling into my hands – Clare wanting greasy meat pie and Bill only salads and Peter only coffee and marmalade – the two nurses only cabbage and bacon and the children their sort of food.' After Clare left for Dublin, 'tirades of abuse arrived addressed to Peter – They included lack of tablecloths, no style of living, brackish water from the taps.' A further complaint from the departed guest: 'Anita brightened up so when she heard I was leaving she even made an effort with the food the last two days.' 'A sort of pneumonia' followed the bronchitis and Anita spent two weeks in bed before going to Glaslough to recuperate. She told Rose that she weighed eight stone, without indicating whether this was a weight loss or gain – very little for such a tall woman. She hadn't heard from Rose for some time and was worried about her. 'I pine for your company – to hear you laugh and talk … Write cos we're all worried and Bill has dreams about you.'

Xandra Frewen, the wife of Clare's nephew Roger, had her first baby that autumn and Anita offered advice: 'I am an awful bore about baby's health but my own childhood was so wrecked by American stuffing of starch that I've taken immense pains to start mine right.' Anita's recommendations to avoid white sugar and bread and to eat home-grown vegetables are commonplace today but were revolutionary in the 1950s. Anita also asked Roger for letters from his grandfather Moreton Frewen, as well as 'amusing photos ... Winston has just passed as "suitable for publication" [in *The Fabulous Leonard Jerome*] my chapter on Randolph [Winston's father].' This had come as a relief since Winston was very touchy on the subject of this brilliant and unstable man, a rotten father who, like many an unsatisfactory parent, was loved by his neglected son. Winston's vetting of Anita's manuscript was kept secret. Anita told Shane: 'We decided long ago it would be much better if Winston did not appear to approve or know anything whatever about this book – that it should have leapt spontaneously from OUR family coffers.'

At the end of 1953 Jack made another decision about Glaslough: to leave the estate to Anita. Anita wrote agitatedly to her father:

> I fear it may make Agnes imagine that I want to get something away from her children - I DON'T if it's going to cause ill feeling. I would like to refuse acceptance as the place has NO meaning save as a family BOND. Please write me Desmond's feelings on subject – IF you know them!

That troublesome estate, retitled Doomsland in Shane's novel of that name, looked set to bring disorder once again.

17
Complicated Chronicles

Bill and Anita decided, after all, to take over Glaslough. In January 1954 Anita wrote to Shane: 'Bill is trying to work out a method whereby he can run this farm [Oranmore] and at the same time spend May 1 to September 1 at Glaslough – THE important farming months.' She and Bill wanted to set up a syndicate to organize pheasant raising and shooting, to plant Scots pines and Sitkas and to reduce 'the immense estate loss [that] exists despite the fact that Reynolds [the farm manager] has reduced the farm loss by £1000. I think it lies in the actual layout of the desmesne – roads, walls, rates.' The usual problems relating to badly managed estates in the mid twentieth century.

Anita's life of Leonard Jerome was going to be published, with Winston's approval, in both the UK and the USA. The ructions surrounding Shane's earlier attempt – 'that ill-fated life of Leonard Jerome which you induced me to take out of print', as Shane accused Winston in a letter on 14 March 1954, marked 'Very confidential' – went on. Winston seemed to think that Shane had sold some papers relating to the enterprise but not belonging to him to a dealer called Jimmy Dunn. Shane had form in spiriting away other people's books and papers. From 1928 until 1952, he had worked as an agent for A.S.W Rosenbach (1876–1952), the famous Philadelphia book dealer. During that time the owners of at least one Big House kept an eye on Shane whenever he visited, aware that he might make off with a book or two. Shane admitted to his cousin that he had sold some manuscripts to Jimmy Dunn for £500 because the Leonard Jerome project had left him in debt, but offered to give Winston everything at Glaslough that related to Winston's mother, Jennie – 'my only wish is that these papers should reach your archives.'

However, when Winston's son Randolph came to Glaslough to retrieve his grandmother's papers, they weren't there. Shane wrote to Winston: 'I remember now that most of the papers are in banks and perfectly safe' but didn't say which banks. To prove his integrity, he continued:

> I might add that I returned to the late King [George VI] three tin boxes of my mother's letters from the late Duke of Connaught which the Princesses believed contained intimate secrets of the Royal Family. H M asked for them and Seymour took them to Buckingham Palace and gave them to the King.

These thousand or so letters, written by the Duke over four decades, are held in the Royal Archives at Windsor and, although they were supposed to remain under seal only until 1993, access to them is denied. Leonie's letters to 'Pat', as she called the Duke, were destroyed after his death.

Anita had resigned herself to an uneventful and frustrating life spent in two icy castles but in 1954 everything changed. 'My life has become so interesting that I simply must recommence a diary.' She finished writing *The Fabulous Leonard Jerome* on 29 April and flew immediately to Geneva to join Betsan on a motoring trip through Yugoslavia – a voyage she described in a travel diary. On 1 June she met Bill in Athens and they joined Bobby Somerset's yacht for a four-week cruise of the Greek islands. After three nights in Rome with Jack, she spent a rainy July and August with the children at Glaslough and then flew to New York for the launch of her new book. The diary that she began that year was a sketchy, spasmodic affair and no substitute for the letters to Rose, begun in their debutante days and revealing Anita's life in detailed instalments but which had now come to an end. Anita's worries about Rose were well-founded;

her friend had disappeared. In 1953 Winston had appointed Dan Ranfurly as Governor of the Bahamas and Peter Gardner went out to join him as his ADC, taking Fleur with him. Rose was supposed to follow a month later, when her clothes would be ready. She never arrived and Fleur didn't see her mother again until, in Rose's old age, Fleur became her guardian. Rose had become a drug addict, something that Anita mentioned briefly in a diary entry in 1958. Apart from this, nothing. What was probably Anita's most intense relationship ended almost without comment.

It had been Winston's idea to have his cousin Shane write a biography of Leonard Jerome during the Second World War, in the hope that by stressing Winston's American connections it would persuade the USA of the need for a special relationship between Britain and America. In Winston's first speech to Congress, on 26 December 1941, three weeks after the USA entered the war, he spoke of being able to trace unbroken descent on his mother's side through five generations, from a lieutenant who served in George Washington's army, so 'it was possible to feel a blood-right to speak to the representatives of the great Republic in our common cause'. Towards the end of the war, in a speech given on 16 February 1944, he said that it was his 'deepest conviction that unless Britain and the United States are joined in a special relationship, another destructive war will come to pass.' Leonard Jerome, his American grandfather, whose three daughters married Englishmen, was an ideal figure to promote this idea of kinship.

Shane, half-American like Winston, looked like the perfect biographer but, having worked on the book for two years, he wrote ominously to his cousin: 'I have finished a life of Leonard Jerome which will startle you.' It certainly did. Instead of a portrait of a captivating sportsman, financier and opera-lover, Shane had 'given our grandfather a creditable if pathetic setting. Otherwise he would be dismissed as a total failure.' Winston was outraged; Shane was mortified. 'I have been so unhappy over upsetting you that if it were not for my publisher I would suppress it totally.' He didn't have to do this because Winston did. Although 'The Life of Leonard Jerome of New York' had already been set up in galley proofs by MacDonalds, it ended up among Shane's papers in Georgetown

University in Washington. A small tag attached to the proofs reads: 'This book was stopped publication by WSC.' When her own book on Leonard Jerome was published, Anita thanks her father in the acknowledgments for his notebooks, scrap albums and anecdotes about Leonard but does not mention Shane's suppressed book. With hindsight, Shane should not have been employed to write a hagiography. His style, although witty and pertinent, was sourly rancorous and he found it hard to resist squelching put-downs of his subject. Winston paid some of MacDonalds' printing costs but Shane was left with debts and Winston's great displeasure.

In a letter to Nancy Mitford in 1984, Evelyn Waugh wrote: 'It cannot be said too often that all Art is the art of pleasing.' If that is true, Anita was a true artist, writing biographies that are the literary equivalent of sitting in sunshine. Her version of her great-grandfather's life was subtitled: 'A delightful and amusing Biography of SIR WINSTON CHURCHILL'S AMERICAN GRANDFATHER.' This Leonard Jerome is dashing, uxorious and a proud and loving father. True enough but far from the whole truth. He was also a chancy speculator who in spite of – or perhaps because of – his lavish and showy spending, failed to gain membership of the 'Four Hundred', a list of the most esteemed New Yorkers of the day. He was also promiscuous. The opera singer Minnie Hauk was undoubtedly Leonard's illegitimate daughter but, in Anita's biography, Minnie was only 'rumoured to be Leonard's daughter through an early romance'. In fact, she was born in 1851, the same year as Leonard's eldest and legitimate daughter, Clara. In private, Anita was more honest. In a letter to Xandra Frewen she wrote: 'Roger [Xandra's husband] must see "La Sonnambula" for Minnie Hauk was Leonard's illeg daughter (and therefore Roger's illeg gt aunt!) and looked so like Jennie C. [Churchill] Made her debut in it aged 16.'

Leonard's flighty, over-indulged daughters also met with disapproval in conservative New York society, one of the reasons, although Anita doesn't spell it out, for the Jeromes moving to a less decorous Europe, where the Jerome girls proved to be catnip to various rackety aristocrats. In England Lord Randolph Churchill wished to marry Jennie Jerome, with whom he had fallen in love at first sight. Anita notes that his father, the 7th Duke of Marlborough, was against the match but doesn't quote directly from the Duke's letters to his impetuous younger son, after he has made enquires about Leonard and discovered that he was 'a well-known man with a fast reputation'. According to the Duke, as the daughter of this rascal, Jennie suffered from a reputation, which 'no man in his senses could think respectable.'

When, after some rather distasteful haggling between the two families over the marriage settlement, Jennie and Randolph married on 15 April 1874, his parents didn't attend their rather muted wedding at the British Embassy in Paris. In Anita's version: 'The Duke could not leave England but he sent a blessing, and the Duchess rejoiced that her favourite son had chosen her birthday for his wedding.' Elizabeth Kehoe, writing about the same event in *Fortune's Daughters* (2004), a biography of the Jerome sisters, considers the absence of the ducal couple a slight, 'a recognition that, although Jennie was accepted by the Marlborough family, this was not a splendid marriage to be celebrated in pomp, merely one that had to be accommodated', and quotes from the Duke's letter to his son, which hoped for his future happiness but pointed out that his bride was 'one whom you have chosen with rather less than usual deliberation'.

Winston was delighted with Anita's book, perhaps because it suggested that Leonard's greatest achievement was to have been Winston's grandfather. The biography ends with the dying Leonard contemplating his grandson, then a schoolboy at Harrow: 'Winston Leonard Spencer Churchill. What would he come to? Where would his road lead?'

At the time of the book's publication, Winston, prime minister once again, had regained his wartime reputation as an internationally recognized Great Man. Anita, promoting the biography in New York, wrote to him: 'The dustman has just swept in (evidently he'd discussed the book with the door porter) and announced "You got just two characters over there that appeal to us Americans – Queen Elizabeth and Winston Churchill – Mr Attlee does not interest us at all." And off he went clanging garbage bins!' Either he was a very politically savvy dustman or Anita invented his conversation in gratitude for Winston's congratulatory cable. Her letter to him ends: 'Your personal opinion means more than anything to me. Thank you.'

From New York, on 1 October 1954, she wrote to Shane about the book's 'unimagined' success. The first US printing of 8000 had sold out in a week and, by October, the second edition was fast selling out too. Shane was mouldering in Glaslough, befuddled by the new managerial arrangements, so may not have been altogether delighted that his daughter was conquering America, 'interviews, television etc and radio every day, lunch with reporters, tea with friends and then theatres which I adore ... Felicitations from everyone including Winston whose thoughtfulness was most touching – Herewith his cable – isn't it splendid.' Then, almost as an afterthought – 'And I could never have pulled it off without your enormous help – so thanks for your endeavours.' After this offhand tribute, she was off again. 'O how restful it is to feel one's hard work rewarded – I am thrilled and letters pour in by every post.' She had lunched with her beloved Barney Baruch – 'he was fascinating on atom bombs and Russians', dined with publishers, given an address at Rochester university – 'I may go to Princetown also.' What a tactless account to send to Shane, whose hard work on Leonard Jerome had not been rewarded at all. Ten days later Anita seemed to regret her boastfulness and told Shane: 'Everyone – every reporter, interviewer etc seems to know you. You certainly made a deep impression over here – But the Jerome book needed to be written by a woman.' She then ruined her earlier flattery by scolding him for his financial ineptitude at Glaslough. 'I would be delighted if you would like to attend meetings and learn the layout of the whole financial side but unless you are prepared to grasp the layout of the new investment plan please do not write me inaccuracies ... ' She seemed to be getting back at Shane for his offhand parenting, when he had made no secret of the fact that he 'would have preferred us not to have been born', had demanded of his awkward daughter why she didn't 'get married and go away', and showed how much his family bored him by closing his heavy-lidded eyes.

During her American tour Anita took a train to Vermont to visit Marjorie's birthplace, St Johnsbury. By this time her diary entries were intermittent but she was so moved by her visit there that she used her diary to write a short biography of her mother's family for her own children to read one distant day: 'The understanding of the other strain which is in us should be there – And it helped me to realise how queer decadent English society must have seemed to my mother Marjorie Ide.' The Ides came from a milieu which 'admired men for their individual achievement and where women were married for love and expected to be virtuous!!' How different from the society into which Marjorie Ide married, 'where inherited titles and wealth were adored, where poor men looked around for heiresses and it was "chic" to sleep with everyone on the right "snob" level.' Anita, reflecting on the Ides' 'sincerity, trueness, lack of sophistication allied to love of culture and instinct for training of the intellect', was overcome by shame and self-loathing. The diary entry is written in a tumbling rush of penitence:

> Could hardworking ambitious cut and dried Henry Ide have imagined his only grandchildren – us three – Jack a dilettante Guards officer who has never earned a penny in his life and is shadowed by the most introverted sexual illusions, Desmond a fly-by-night who lives in nightclubs, makes up to every girl he meets and thinks collecting money for films that never materialise or lecturing on Flying Saucers a man's career – and myself! Of whom the less said the better except perhaps that these New Englanders might have recognised a certain diligence which has resulted in the writing of books – but their code – none of us have had a code we have lived in such different airs and morals – on many subjects we would have been Chinese to each other.

She flew back to Ireland in the middle of October. A diary entry: 'Tarka said: "Mummy, don't go away again. I don't like it" and I knew I never wanted to – not till they are grown up – 3 months away in 6 months has broken my desire ever to travel again – They are in my mind wherever I go – and they need me now – They won't later.' But the next month she flew to London for the UK launch of *The Fabulous Leonard Jerome*, now number thirteen on the American bestseller lists. She went to Winston's eightieth birthday party at Downing Street – 'I was lent a wonderful dress by Worth – Bill said the best there.' She hunted in Galway throughout the winter and returned to London for Clemmie Churchill's seventieth birthday party, the last that the Churchills would hold in Downing Street: 'Winston sad at going – forced to by Eden and Macmillan.'

An extraordinary thing had happened at the end of 1953: Peter Wilson left Oranmore. From being embedded in the muddy, windswept farm, working too hard, unwashed and living on bread and marmalade, he first travelled the world and then settled in the Bahamas at the home of Nancy Oakes. She was the daughter of the tycoon Sir Harry Oakes, whose murder in Nassau, on 8 July 1943, remained unsolved. At the time of Sir Harry's death Nancy was married to Count Alfred de Marigny, who was accused of the murder on the false testimony of two corrupt detectives, brought over from the USA by the then Governor of the Bahamas, the Duke of Windsor. De Marigny was acquitted but because of his contemptuous attitude – he described the Duke as 'a pimple on the arse of the Empire' – was deported from the country. He and Nancy were divorced in 1949 and, in 1952, Nancy married Baron Ernst von Hoyningen-Huene. By the time Peter Wilson arrived in the Bahamas that marriage was shaky and another divorce followed in 1956.

Peter Wilson may have decided to go to the Bahamas because Dan Ranfurly, whom he knew, was then governor, while another acquaintance, Peter Gardner, was his ADC. Dan's term of office ended in 1956, and he and Hermione left for England the following year. Peter Gardner stayed on. He opened a restaurant, Sun And, in Lakeview Drive in Nassau and it became fashionable among the glitterati: The Beatles, Sean Connery, Winston Churchill, Frank Sinatra. For part of the year Peter left the restaurant in the hands of a deputy and ran Snow And, a similar restaurant in the fashionable skiing resort of Kitzbuhl. Peter Wilson also made a life in the Bahamas, working for an unlikely employer, Harold Christie, a property developer and, during Prohibition, a bootlegger. Christie had been a friend and partner of Sir Harry Oakes and was widely believed to have murdered him. He had motive enough: he owed Sir Harry money and the latter had called in the loan because he was planning to move to Mexico. Sir Harry's death meant that the loan needn't be repaid. Christie subsequently became a property millionaire and was knighted in 1964. William Boyd gave a fictional account of this murder mystery in his gripping novel *Any Human Heart*, in which Christie is the main suspect.

Peter Wilson, who had always professed a longing for simplicity and a loathing of corrupting wealth, was a strange employee for the dodgy property developer who had acquired Cat Island, south of Nassau, where, some believe, Christopher Columbus first stepped ashore in the New World. Known as an 'out island', sunshine and tropical lushness apart, it shared some of the features of the west of Ireland: ruins of great houses, poor, decent inhabitants and, something that would have appealed to Peter, 'the feel of true isolation', as described by the travel writer Benedict Thielen in *Holiday* magazine (December 1964). Peter, the only white resident of the island, was in charge of Christie's land there. He planned on returning to Oranmore at some stage and, in a transaction negotiated by Anita, bought Rocklands House, near the castle.

Anita was thriving. Her children were old enough to travel and her diary entries, while short and not very informative, have a sunlit quality. The incessant rain seems to have given way to balmy summers. Tarka and Leonie, the Jellicoe children, and Desmond and Agnes's boys enjoyed 'Heavenly months of sunshine and laughter' at Oranmore. In England there was 'a delightful day with the Lysaghts in the Wye valley', 'a jolly night' with Pooh in Oxford, as well as opera and dinner parties in England, stalking at Glenveagh in Ireland, 'one stag rolling on his back in the sunshine – too sweet to shoot'. In September 1955 the Leslie family gathered at Glaslough to celebrate Shane's seventieth birthday: 'He took it very gloomily with closed eyes and groans' before Anita, Bill and the children moved back to Oranmore and the centrally-heated cottage for the winter.

Tarka was six and his education had begun, with lessons at Monaghan Convent during the summer and home-schooling by Anita, using PNEU teaching methods – short lessons lasting twenty minutes with the emphasis on real ideas – during the hunting season at Oranmore. She was delighted by her little son's unselfconscious religious convictions: 'The maturity of his vision astounds me. Everything I have ever let drop of my own religious beliefs evidently has sunk deep into his imagination.' A letter from Tarka to Peter Wilson: 'Dear PP [Poppa Pete] I saw two dragonflies get out of their skins – just like me when I die.'

Anita's friends were going through harsher times. Sally Perry, who had married the severely wounded Gerald Grosvenor, heir to the Duke of Westminster, during the war, gave birth to a stillborn child and was unable to have another baby. After a visit to the Grosvenors in February 1956, Anita wrote in her diary: 'Sally so lovely and so sad – her twin sister dying of paralysis and herself childless.' And that romantic pair, Patsy and George Jellicoe, were coming adrift: 'Patsy writes miserably about how awful George is – drunk and after floozies.'

In May Anita and Bill took the children skiing in the Austrian Tyrol. Then on to Rome to visit Jack and wave rosaries at the Pope in St Peter's Square: 'I never dreamt how impressive he would be – a radiant personality of love and pity.' Not a universal view; this was Pope Pius XII, whose wartime papacy was, to say the least, controversial. She took the children all over southern Italy, bringing back wartime memories, before they returned to Oranmore and Tarka's lessons. The PNEU school, run by Miss Faunce and Miss Lambert – 'teachers of genius' – had been the only part of her education that Anita had enjoyed. It had instilled in her a love of poetry and literature and 'the sensuous delight of words' before Marjorie's habit of shifting her daughter in and out of different schools had brought this bright period to a close. Anita's next school had been the detestable Convent of the Sacred Heart, which had offered no delight, sensuous or otherwise.

In the summer of 1957 the King family sailed the Brittany coast and that winter, hunting at Oranmore, 'Tarka got the brush.' In March they set off again for three months, the trip beginning with skiing at Klosters in Switzerland with the film director John Huston's children, Tony and Angelica. At the age of forty-four Anita had enough money to give up writing for a few years. Her aunt Anne had left her money to Marjorie, who, in turn, had left it to her children. *The Fabulous Leonard Jerome* had sold well. No longer trapped at Oranmore, Anita spent a lot of time packing suitcases, something that always filled her with pleasurable anticipation.

18
They All Talk Amusingly

Anita now spent more time in London, where she led a heady social life. 'They all talk amusingly,' her diary records, 'but then London lives are unhealthy and to me unliveable.' Patsy Jellicoe had established herself as a patron of the arts, throwing interesting parties for new friends, including the prima ballerina of her time, Margot Fonteyn, and writing and lecturing on Far Eastern Art and garden history. But her marriage to George was coming to an end. Anita's undated diary entry: '[Fonteyn's] amusing, witty Panamanian husband [Roberto "Tito" Arias] sought to cheer up Patsy who was given a black eye by George last night when she refused a divorce (for the sake of her four children).' George persisted in trying to obtain a divorce and, in 1958, resigned from the Foreign Office to avoid scandal. He told an inquisitive reporter: 'Half London must know I want to marry Mrs [Philippa] Bridge.' He was able to do this, and start a new family, in 1966 when his marriage to Patsy was finally dissolved. He resumed a distinguished political career, becoming Lord Privy Seal and Leader of the House of Lords, but it came to an end in 1973 when an involvement with call girls was exposed in the press. George said: 'I behaved with incredulous stupidity.'

All this was in the future. In early 1958 a tearful Patsy waved goodbye to Anita as the latter sailed to New York on the *Liberté* for a social visit to New York, Philadelphia and Palm Beach.

Bill and the children had gone ahead to Andros Island in the Bahamas, staying at the house of Audrey Pleydell-Bouverie, who had created a beautiful garden. When Anita arrived there she was greeted by Bill and Peter Wilson, who seemed to be staying at the house, both men 'dressed in tatters, Eton ties and naval jackets', while her children introduced her to 'a whirl of little black friends'. On 15 May Anita wrote to Shane that this holiday was 'Bill's first real rest since he took over Glaslough', although he seemed to have taken quite a few recent skiing breaks. They had a wonderful time, 'swimming in blue water, coral reef, snorkel-gazing at small brilliant fish, barracuda catching … hide and seek and calypso with negro children in garden! Heaven.' At the end of it, they were seen off by Peter Wilson and Peter Gardner and his small daughter Fleur, 'a brown-eyed Rose'.

This long holiday took place in term time. Tarka was now a pupil at the Boys' National School at Oranmore but Anita took a relaxed attitude about his attendance there. She and Bill intended Tarka to go to Eton but were bypassing the traditional route of pre-prep followed by prep school, which most parents of future Etonians considered essential for passing Eton's entrance examination. Anita paid the Oranmore schoolmaster to teach Tarka English grammar instead of Gaelic. When her son told her that, after four years of lessons, he had learnt only how to stand on his head in the hard playground, Anita decided that he was a natural Huckleberry Finn.

Meanwhile Shane, his Eton days long behind him, and short of money, was selling the library at Glaslough, a collection of books and manuscripts that had been housed at Castle Leslie since the late eighteenth century. The library's contents were sold to John Fleming, a rare-book dealer who, like Shane, had worked with A.S.W. Rosenbach. Fleming paid £1500 and the collection was subsequently resold to the University of Chicago. Later Shane sold many of Winston's books and letters, items much in demand as 'Winstomania', a term coined by Shane, took hold.

Back from the Bahamas, the Leslie-Kings went straight to Augustus John's studio at Fordingbridge, Hampshire. John made two drawings of Anita, both so beautiful that Bill found it hard to choose between them. The one that Anita described as 'tranquil instead of wild-eyed' was shown on the cover of her 1983 memoir, *A Story Half Told*. She wears an expression both world-weary and faraway and has a perfect maquillage – dewy, red lips, long, dark lashes – and a soft cloud of hair. In the memoir published two years earlier, *The Gilt and the Gingerbread*, the cover portrait is by her former brother-in-law Serge Rodzianko, drawn during the 1930s, and Anita's pretty face is a blank canvas, with none of the sexual allure of the later version.

There was less travelling during the winter months, when Anita hunted with the Galway Blazers. The Joint Master of Foxhounds (MFH) was Mollie Cusack Smith, who had given up a successful career as a London couturier during the Second World War to live in Ireland, where for thirty-eight years, from 1946 to 1984, she ruled over horse and hound. Bill and Anita hunted with the Blazers two days a week and with Mollie's own pack, the Bermingham and North Galway Hunt, of which Anita became Joint MFH, for one further day. As well as hunting in Galway, every September Anita stayed with Henry McIlhenny at Glenveagh Castle, Donegal for more strenuous activity: 'Lots of stalking – I seem to get fitter each year.' If she got tired, a 'Nature Cure' diet of lettuce revived her. She had always associated food with asthmatic attacks and ate very little. Meeting her dashing wartime friend Gavin Astor, now 'a plump red faced balding middle aged gentleman', she noted in her diary: 'Food and drink is really the destroyer of youth I suppose.' In 1958 she doesn't seem to have begun a new book of her own but helped Bill to write *The Stick and the Stars*, the first of seven books about his life of sea.

There were two unexpected marriages that year. Peter Wilson married Prim Baker, a former Wren and professional gardener. Audrey Pleydell-Bouverie, Anita's hostess in the Bahamas, didn't approve. Visiting Anita in London, 'she held forth on Peter – his indiscreet tongue and "second rate snob-wife"!!' On 30 May Shane married Iris Carola Frazer, *née* Laing, in London, 'in great privacy in the little Catholic church round the corner', as he described it to Clare. 'Our chief thought is to pray for the souls of our dead spouses.' Unlike Marjorie, Iris regarded Shane as a great literary figure and devoted herself to putting his papers in order, to help a future biographer. Another couple were having marital problems. Desmond Leslie had had many extra-marital affairs and had even fathered an illegitimate child but Agnes had put up with his infidelities. Now, during a five-week-long holiday in Kitzbuhl, he had met and fallen in love with Helen Strong, a tall, beautiful blonde who, it being a small world, had been staying with the Ruck-Keenes. Agnes and Desmond's marriage continued unhappily for the next few years, with Anita an unwilling go-between. Once, when Desmond was lunching with her in London, 'Agnes burst in tearfully to enquire where he was living etc and I tried to sustain a calm discussion of children's holiday plans – it is trying not having any address at which to write to him.'

At Whitsun, at Oranmore, it was Tarka's First Communion, 'thrilled by his new suit and white socks covered with medals and amulets from all the convents around … Leonie was envious and dreadful all day', Anita wrote in her diary. Afterwards the family went to Glaslough, 'frantic with guests and cattle'. Among the guests was Rose's stepmother, Derry Vincent, 'who told me about Rose – that exquisite creature takes drugs – she loves me still but the lack of balance is too intense for us to communicate'. This was all Anita had to record about the woman she had addressed as 'Darlingest' for most of her life. During that Whitsun holiday Charles de Gaulle became president of France. Anita's diary: 'I believe implicitly in de Gaulle – He is so unlikeable and so uncompromising and so admirable – just the iron rod that can save France IF anything can.' She chafed peevishly at the sluggishness of Glaslough:

> Now I long to be in Paris/Algiers with my thumb on the pulse of Europe – oh it is a cage here – a beautiful prison in which one's mind rots – But the children and their blooming fills my creative instinct. Only them – or I'd die of boredom.

Although she insisted that she could never live in London, 'in a milieu of very smart women on stilt heels, their toes ruined by the new pointed shoes', she went there often, having supper at 'a bohemian club in Chelsea', dining with politicians, where the talk was of the Westminster village rather than the cattle pasture.

On 10 June, although Anita and Bill were now in charge of three farms at Glaslough, Oranmore and Drumlargan, the last one needing to be 'entirely rehabilitated', they went to England: 'I had asked Clemmie if I might bring Tarka to see Winston as at nine and a half he will take him in … I was sure the psychic import of Winston's personality would register on a child's mind.' Clemmie had written that Winston was much changed, weak and deaf and that he wouldn't remember what he did in the war. 'I think he will though', Anita wrote in her diary. The invitation for lunch at Chartwell was 6 July, so the Leslie-Kings made a round of visits to the English countryside before arriving at the Churchills' house in its woodland setting in the Weald of Kent. At Audrey Pleydell-Bouverie's home, Julians, in Hertfordshire, whose rose garden was admired as the most beautiful in England, 'the house [was] set like a small jewel in the centre of its fountains and banks of flowers'. Audrey, old and frail, 'whose wit has amused everyone from Queen Mary to Winston', toured her garden in a wheelchair. After a kitchen supper at the house of her friends Aidan and Virginia Crawley, Anita wrote, 'She cooks about like me', which is to say atrociously.

In a long diary entry for Sunday, 6 June 1958, Anita wrote 'Mustn't forget this day!' There was no chance that she would. They arrived at Chartwell to find Clemmie in bed with shingles and too ill to see them and her daughter Diana Sandys acting as hostess. 'Tarka had been warned to be very good and only speak when spoken to and he watched Winston with huge eyes. At lunch he and I sat between Winston and Field Marshal Montgomery! Some company for a small boy to make conversation to!'

At the other end of the table with Bill and Diana sat Winston's literary agent, Emery Reves (1904–81), a distinguished writer, publisher and art collector whom, in 1939, Winston had sent to America to boost pro-British propaganda. Emery was too brilliant for Anita. She described him as a 'Hungarian Jew very clever who has lovely villa at Rocquebrune where Winston stays to the raised eyebrows of proper old ladies who don't approve of Wendy R.' Wendy, also at the table, was Emery's mistress – they married in 1964 – and was a Texan-born *Vogue* model. Their villa, where Winston was a frequent guest, was La Pausa, built in the 1920s by

Bendor, Duke of Westminster, for his mistress Coco Chanel. The 'proper old ladies' may have disapproved of Wendy Russell, as she then was, but she captivated everyone else. Noël Coward, another frequent guest at La Pausa, thought that Winston was 'absolutely obsessed' with this 'most fascinating lady', although he doubted that Winston would ever be unfaithful to Clemmie. Anita admitted that Winston found Wendy 'restful' and then, spitefully: 'She exactly resembles a Peter Arno caricature of a gorgeous poule – huge eyes, huge mouth – startled stare – deliciously brainless and rather sweet.' This waspishness may have been caused by the sight of Bill and Wendy 'making eyes at one end of the table'.

There was a further lapse: 'Monty was wonderful with Tarka – a bit too wonderful as it turned out – Soon the child was laughing and joining in all conversation – accepting the Field Marshall as his particular pal.' After lunch, Monty and the over-excited Tarka romped in the garden. Just before the Leslie-Kings were about to leave, Tarka leapt out of a bush and

> in front of the detectives (and Sunday sightseers by gate) gave the FM a hearty smack on the bottom!!! I nearly died of mortification – Bill didn't see – we snatched the child up and drove off hurriedly leaving Monty with an expression of absolute surprise on his face – the expression Rommel never succeeded in putting there.

Six months later on 9 December, Anita wrote contritely to 'Dear Cousin Winston':

> My little son will never forget his visit to you in July – (I fear 'Monty' will never forget it either but he whirred the small fellow up into such a state of excitement as if it were the eve of Alamein). Next day he said to me apologetically 'But Mummy you never TOLD me General Montgomery was a GREAT MAN TOO!' (But don't tell the Field Marshall this).

Anita and Tarka's next trip was to the south of France, where they were joined by Jack and Desmond. Desmond was a regular visitor to the Côte d'Azur and was able to get free entry for his relations at both the de luxe Beach Swimming Pool and the Casino – 'once is enough', Anita wrote. In France both Tarka and Anita got chickenpox. Weary and poxed, she collected two other small boys, Paddy Jellicoe and Mark Leslie, and took them to Glaslough, 'where I collapse in my large silent green room'. Many years later, when Desmond and Helen's daughter Sammy was running Castle Leslie as a hotel, she retained the family bedrooms as 'heritage rooms', with notes on each written by Desmond. For 'Anita's Room' he described his sister as writing her biographies in bed 'while enjoying a simple diet of smoked salmon and champagne', an unlikely diet for a woman who disliked rich food. Anita would have appreciated the room's current, very restful, décor: white curtains and bed cover and a white-upholstered ottoman. She would also have approved of the generous radiator.

In the winter of 1959 in London, Anita and Bill were guests at a dinner party given by Duncan and Diana Sandys. Also attending were Oswald and Diana Mosley (*née* Mitford), neither of whom seemed to bear any grudge against their hostess, whose father, Winston, had had the pair imprisoned during the war as being 'a danger to the King's realm'. Diana Mosley's cousin, Clementine Beit, had once told Anita that Diana was 'politically calculating and dangerous whereas Unity was only a romantic fool'. Diana was also captivatingly beautiful; Evelyn Waugh said that 'her beauty ran through the room like a peal of bells'. And since Diana was 'the only person of the party not drunk and looking charming I settled on a sofa with her and discussed her "exile" in France', Anita recorded. Oswald, whom Anita had not met before, joined the two women on the sofa. 'It's curious he shows such a good brain and yet is so dislikeable.' Duncan Sandys became provocative: 'Why on earth did you want Hitler ruling here Oswald?' The answer: 'I didn't want Hitler. I wanted myself.'

That edgy occasion took place thirteen years after the end of the war. The sight of two old enemies dining together gave Anita a sense of closure: 'I had a curious feeling of Epilogue – "Here the story of the war endeth."' After the conversation on the Sandys' sofa, Anita found it 'easy to understand Winston's weakness for Diana M. He sent her and her baby "comforts" while she was in prison and tried to arrange for her to have a daily bath, not knowing that there wasn't enough water to ensure this.' In a memoir, *A Life of Contrasts* (1977), Diana wrote, 'It had been a kindly thought of Winston's who had, I suppose been told that this was one of the hardships I minded.' Not everyone took such a benign view of Diana. In *The Sunday Times* (19 July 2009) Max Hastings wrote of her: 'It is extraordinary that some people regard her indulgently as the Mitford family's "fun fascist". She was an impenitent Nazi sympathiser until the day she died.' As was her husband, a fact recognized by most people in England. Oswald's son, Nicholas Mosley, commented in a remark reported in the *New Statesman* in 1979, a year before Oswald's death, that his father 'must be the only Englishman today who is beyond the pale'.

In London again in the spring, Anita lunched with Clemmie Churchill and Diana Sandys at a time when another Churchill daughter, the actress, Sarah, had been on a bender: 'The inevitable publicity – resisted arrest – fighting-drunk in Liverpool and wouldn't pay her 2/9 taxi fare. As Diana said "awfully hard to turn into a plus – one's only hope is that in time it will cease to be news and she'll get smaller and smaller space in the press."' Anita reflected: 'Well we have 3 absolute drunks as Leonard Jerome's great grandchildren – Margaret Sheridan, Sarah and Randolph.' Life was simpler in Oranmore. At Whitsun, it was Leonie's First Communion: 'She drove all over Galway being given 2/6 in each cottage. Came back with 30/- very red in the face and baccante like shouting "They liked my dress the best – I'm the richest and prettiest of all." An eye-opener to Protestant Bill.'

Anita had begun another book. Like so much of her work, it relied on previous research carried out by Shane, discoveries in the Castle Leslie attics and Anita's inventive mind. It was a life of Maria Fitzherbert, the publicly unacknowledged wife of King George IV and, through her adopted daughter, Minnie (or Minney) Seymour, who had married George Dawson-Damer, the father of Anita's great-grandmother, Constance Leslie, almost a relation.

19
Invented Lives

Shane Leslie spent much of his literary life enhancing the reputations of notable Catholics and Maria Fitzherbert was a favourite subject. In his 1917 book *The End of a Chapter*, he had written of Maria: 'Whatever influence in the prince's life was good came from her. Whatever unhappiness entered hers came from him.' In 1939 he published a life of Mrs Fitzherbert and a volume of her letters and papers, taking the same chivalrous approach. Maria was put-upon and saintly; the prince, later George IV, 'the uttermost cad in Europe'. As with so many of Shane's biographies, his subject never came alive. His books were all about him, his opinions, his scholarship, his didacticism. Anita found her father's life of Maria disappointing and knew that she could do better. She never had a problem bringing a subject to life, although her characterization didn't always adhere to the life that was actually lived. She knew how to introduce colour and atmosphere and, unlike Shane, wrote with warmth and sympathy. Her biographies slide pleasantly through your fingers.

In her lifetime, Maria Fitzherbert had been the subject of scabrous gossip and rude cartoons. One of these, by James Gillroy, called 'The

Royal Exhibition – or – A Peek at the Marriage Heads' (May 1786), is of George and Maria, bare-bottomed, with their faces shown on their naked behinds. The twentieth century was more polite towards Maria, although she was still seen as an equivocal figure. Since she destroyed many of her papers and letters – 'Your quest will lead from bonfire to bonfire', Shane had warned Anita – it's still not certain whether Maria's ward, Minney Seymour or her 'niece', Maryanne Smythe, were, in fact, her daughters by the King. George certainly seemed to think that Minney was; he gave her a dowry of £20,000. Anita's Maria had a good head for finance, owning three houses and a fashionable carriage. On their secret marriage in 1785 she had managed to procure an annuity of £6000 from George and, when, after their parting, he sometimes fell behind with the payments, he got a sharp reminder: 'Permit me to receive henceforward the allowance you promised me twenty-eight years ago – an allowance which the times have not increased in value.'

Papers that survived Maria's bonfires were snipped to pieces by Minney's daughter, Lady Constance Leslie, 'in a fit of devotion to Queen Victoria who hated the Fitzherbert story … Scissors have cut out what one most wishes to know', Anita wrote in her book's foreword. But enough documents remained to inspire her to write a biography of the complex woman who was at the centre of the glamorous world of Regency England. Here was a woman who was treated badly by the man she loved but managed to survive pretty well; a story familiar to her biographer. Although Anita's style could be slushy: 'Their eyes met for the first time – untroubled topaz and fevered grey', she skilfully threaded in the love story of 'a dangerously virtuous woman and a rather delightful rake' with an account of what it was like to be a Catholic at the time of the Penal Laws, when English Catholics were 'virtually outlaws in their own country, doomed to a life of secrecy and retirement'. Anita's Maria isn't just a devout innocent, neither is George just a contemptible cad. His failings are traced back to his cold, unresponsive parents, who allowed him to be 'flogged unmercifully for faults in Latin grammar'.

Politics and passion are adroitly intermingled as Beau Brummel, the Duchess of Devonshire, Charles James Fox and Richard Brinsley Sheridan make their appearances. Of a later book, Anita told her publisher that a biography is interesting for what it doesn't say as much as for what it does. This is certainly true of *Mrs Fitzherbert*. Without spelling it out, Anita hints that Maria had a financial steeliness worthy of Ivana Trump and that her tiara, which found its way into a Leslie jewellery box, might have been extracted from a prince whose 'royal rubbery mind' wobbled under the persistent demands of a predatory woman who was all backbone.

Patsy Jellicoe, always an enthusiastic hostess, gave a party in London to celebrate the book's publication on 11 April 1960. The guests included Sally and Gerald Grosvenor, to whom *Mrs Fitzherbert* was dedicated, and 'lots of cousins from the counties'. There don't seem to have been any literary journalists, or publicists or anyone who might have been involved in the book's promotion among the guests. Anita's diary entry for the following day is about taking Tarka to the dentist and the rest of the Easter holiday in London was spent on outings for her own children and those of her friends: the boats at Regent's Park, Disney films, the Tower of London and Tarka's first visit to the ballet: 'He loved it.'

Anita was the least self-conscious of writers. It's as though she wrote books because that is what Leslies did and she didn't suffer much over their composition. This may have been because she wrote biographies rather than novels. Michael Holroyd once remarked that '[b]iographers are like saints: they are always thinking of other people'. Anita didn't have a literary agent or negotiate for higher advances. When her friend Virginia Crawley was given a £20,000 advance for a book on the Commando leader David Stirling, Anita was impressed but not envious because Virginia had 'found it incredibly dreary to write'. She remained with the same publisher, Hutchinson, from 1948 (*Train to Nowhere*) until her death and looked upon her editors there, Harold Harris and Anthony Whittome, as dear friends with whom to enjoy sherry and gossip. To discuss advances would not have been 'amusing'.

What she found increasingly pleasurable, from the 1960s onward, was to spend more time in England, visiting friends who owned well-maintained country houses and gardens, such as the one that was 'all so English and beautifully kept-up with lawn tennis courts – so unlike the jungle-demesnes of Ireland with weedy hard courts deep in water'. Between these visits, she belatedly tried to improve her son's education. In the autumn of 1961 a tutor came to Glaslough to coach Tarka for Eton – 'huge bribes and presents but it all ended in tears over the Latin which he said had "suddenly got so difficult."' With a leaden heart, Anita delivered Tarka to a crammer, Mr Rolls, in Gloucestershire and then 'drove the 4 hours back to Saighton Grange [the Grosvenors' house] so unhappy at making the break with his utterly happy childhood'. Although she would probably have agreed with Nancy Mitford's pronouncement on 'The horror of not having been educated when young', Anita, like her mother before her, could never see education as a priority and was concerned that schooling might get in the way of her children's hunting. In the winter *The Irish Field* published a photograph of Anita, Tarka and Leonie at a meet of the Galway Blazers, and Tarka had 'four good hunts before the frost turned the land to iron'. When the hunting ended, the search for a school began. In February 1962 Bill took Tarka to Scotland for an interview at Gordonstoun, which Prince Charles was about to attend. Suddenly the unfashionable school was oversubscribed. When Tarka told Bill that the interview and test were 'all frightfully easy', Anita wrote smugly in her diary: 'Irish country life has certainly kept him natural and with the right values,' and was delighted when the headmaster told Bill that Tarka

> was so different at the interview from the others – had such a twinkle in
> his eye … so whatever the result one feels he has made his mark and one
> is grateful to the dear old village schoolmaster for giving him supreme self
> confidence without being cheeky. I feel sorry for the 55 little boys from non-
> twinkling boarding schools.

The mother abbess and the nuns of the Poor Clares convent in Galway prayed for Tarka's success but to no avail. Tarka failed the test – 'his MATH paper so very poor! Odd as its [*sic*] his best subject.'

Anita turned to Shane, who was well connected in educational circles, for help. He warned against his own old school, Eton, since he thought it turned out depraved boys – 'This is why I did not send Jack or Des there' – and suggested Stowe or Milton Abbey, implying that both schools had easier entry requirements. Anita understood his reservations about Eton when, disregarding Shane's advice, she took Tarka for an interview at the school and found some of the older boys having tea at the nearby Cockpit restaurant 'drinking tea out of a blonde's slipper'. Anita now regretted that 'the dear old village schoolmaster' at Oranmore didn't prepare his pupils for English public school entrance examinations, instead of letting them practise standing on their heads. A friend assured her: 'You've taught your son more bringing him up in the west of Ireland than any school could,' but she was upset when Tarka failed to get into Eton: 'Tarka's Eton attempt so bad in Latin and French that his housemaster advises not trying again in November.' To her relief, Milton Abbey in Dorset, founded in the 1950s as a 'forward looking school', accepted Tarka. Anita's final diary entry for 1962 is dated 23 August: 'Wonderfully arranged houseparty [at Birr Castle] for Princess Margaret ... She's very pretty and exceedingly intelligent tho inclined to be difficult.' Nancy Mitford, less inclined to deference towards the royal family, referred to the petite princess as 'The Royal Pigmy'.

Anita and Bill were in charge of Glaslough but spent little time there. In 1962 they went on holiday twice with Roger and Xandra Frewen, first a skiing trip and, in August, one to Venice. By then the Leslie-Kings had had enough of Glaslough. The three farms were too much for Bill to manage and Anita, with Tarka at school in England and Leonie about to follow suit, had begun to think about buying a flat in London. According to the memoir of her sister-in-law Agnes the first sign of Bill and Anita's dream of leaving was

> a curious letter from Anita asking Desmond to take over Glaslough alto-
> gether; asking only for Drumlargen in return ...Of course Desmond did
> not turn down the offer nor did he have any feelings of apprehension about
> having to run such a large demesne without the necessary capital.

In his 2010 biography of Desmond, *Desmond Leslie (1921–2001)*, Robert O'Byrne tells the story of the handover in more detail. Trying to keep the estate solvent took up Bill and Anita's time and energy, although they were only jointly co-owners with Desmond and Agnes, who were not involved in the day-to-day management. When the Leslie-Kings offered to transfer the estate to Desmond, he dithered, so exasperating Anita and Bill that they then offered to buy him out completely for £20,000. More dithering. Desmond was doing well in London composing music for films. So was Agnes, her singing career given a spectacular publicity boost when Desmond, in front of eleven million viewers, landed a punch on the critic Bernard Levin during a live television broadcast of *That Was the Week That Was* for having given Agnes's cabaret show a poor review, the amplification system having failed. In the autumn of 1963 agreement was reached: Desmond would run Glaslough, Bill and Anita would retain Drumlargan. Nothing about this was recorded in Anita's diary during the previous spring and summer, when negotiations were getting increasingly frantic. Instead she wrote of her sorrow at the death, from cancer, of Pope John XXIII on 23 June: 'There will never be anyone like him – I have lived in the time of a great saint.' It upset her that the Pope's last days were darkened by 'the tyranny of modern medicine which with drugs draws out a dying and can only alleviate with the false effects of morphia'. She wasn't alone in loving this man, who reached out beyond the Catholic Church to the whole human race and had been named *Time* magazine's Man of the Year in 1962.

Three days after that June diary entry came another:

> From the fascinating elation of Pope John's death to the bathos of Profumo!!. One is wracked with laughter – so sordid – so silly – such an ass and the whole Tory party ludicrous with indignant explanations and trying to make it not matter – MUCH!!

And then: 'Poor Philip P was so easily embarrassed anyway. One really is so sorry for the family – but can't stop giggling.' I have been unable to trace any connection between Anita's erstwhile fiancé and John Profumo, the disgraced Secretary of State for War, whose affair with Christine Keeler led to his resignation on 5 June, followed by that of the prime minister, Harold Macmillan, the following October.

The next diary entry isn't until 1 September and is dramatic: 'Made over Glaslough to brother Des ... A creech owl drowned in the Fountain before I left – I hope this does not mean I have handed the place over to its doom.' Anita's uncle Seymour wrote her a farewell letter, thanking his niece for making it possible for his family to live in one wing of the castle – 'our little hermitage! A sort of link between several epochs

... I think both of you will be happier without this distant burden.' In 1964 the Sir John Leslie Estate Company was wound up. Relieved of the distant burden, Anita began to look for a flat in London. Leonie was now a London schoolgirl, her previous lack of education revealed when she received minus ninety in her first test.

While inspecting a flat at 10 Westbourne Terrace, Anita had a strange psychic experience. The old lady showing her round burst into tears before a photograph of her son who had killed himself two days before Christmas after a quarrel with his wife. Anita wrote in her diary: 'I felt him begging me to say he was sorry and not to cry and that the death anniversary must be a day of joy not grief.' Anita conveyed this experience to the young man's mother who had, it seemed, been longing for some stranger to come with a message. Anita wrote to the grieving woman from Ina's flat in South Lodge, the same block where Marjorie had once owned a flat and where, coincidentally, the young man had spent his childhood:

> I feel he was hanging around trying to send them a message and literally made the greedy little Jewish agent [to Anita, unpleasantly anti-Semitic even after the war, Jews were either 'greedy' or 'clever', by which she meant too clever by half] see this advert in *The Times* and send me hoping he could get me to write from South Lodge and give them a clue.

Anita, perhaps on account of these disturbing portents, didn't buy the Westbourne Grove flat. Soon afterwards she learned that her cousin Diana Churchill, at the age of fifty-four and after several nervous breakdowns, had killed herself on 10 October. Diana had been divorced from her second husband, Duncan Sandys in 1960 and changed her name back to Churchill. Anita's diary: 'Am so flattened by these emotional shocks on top of emotional Glaslough decisions I feel like seeing nobody.' But Christmas at Oranmore, hunting with two enthusiastic children, both 'going like bombs', restored her spirits although, on 18 January 1964, 'children back to school worn out – ditto ponies – ditto me'. That winter she bought a flat at 10 Cleveland Square, near Hyde Park, which she chose because of the leafy street and traffic-free air. As for the rest of the city: 'The noise and smell of London horrify me – AND the people.'

To avoid having to pay UK income tax, Anita put the flat in Xandra Frewen's name. By now, the Frewen marriage was skidding towards divorce. Xandra had fallen in love with another man but was still hanging about Brede Place, the Frewens' marital home, which caused Roger great bitterness. Anita felt that if the Frewens couldn't be reunited, Xandra should marry her lover 'and make him give you a proper home elsewhere. Or if you are sick of him why not marry someone else?' When Xandra pointed out that lack of money was at the root of her morally dubious position, Anita told her: 'BUT my love all morality is based on economics!! The reason such a fuss is made about feminine chastity is because men do not want to bring up other men's children.'

Xandra was beautiful; the head waiter at the Ritz mistook her for the French film star Anouk Aimée, and her adventuresome nature was a worry to Bill and Anita, who took on a parental role towards this reckless young woman. Anita advised Xandra, the mother of four small children, against sailing the Atlantic:

> It just would be so awful if you got drowned my dear – you're so precious to so many. Other people's lives would be terribly spoiled without you … One can't have EVERYTHING – not love and affection and freedom from love and affection … It may be a BORE to be precious but it's not for ever!

There were sitting tenants in the Cleveland Square flat and they wanted to stay in it until November. A new friend of Anita's solved the problem by giving the tenants £2000 to leave. This was Roy Miles, a successful London businessman, who had first met Anita at a party at Lough Cutra Castle in Galway, in 1961, the year that he had been featured in a BBC Radio programme, *New Names Making News*, in which 'young people making their names in the literary, theatrical and business worlds talk about themselves and their work'. Roy had begun his business career by taking over the famous hair salon, Antoine, and its associated beauty products. But his real passion was art, and before long he sold the salon and opened his first art gallery in St James, Piccadilly. He became well known as much for his parties as for his paintings; *The Daily Telegraph* diarist called him 'One of the country's top fifteen self-publicists.' Roy was captivated by Anita. In an interview in 2008, he told me:

I've never met anybody else in my life who could fascinate you with her conversation – who could thrill you. Anita educated me in the ways of high society. She had a way of saying, 'I wouldn't do that.' She was the greatest mentor of my life.

Anita invited Roy to dinner parties attended by duchesses, where dreadful food was served. Roy took Anita and Bill to dinner at the Connaught, where the food was much better.

1965 started with a royal visit to Oranmore Castle. The Countess of Rosse, Lord Snowdon's mother, brought her son and his wife, Princess Margaret, to the castle, where they spent an hour clambering on the roof: 'And I never thought HRH would admire the Red Turret (rather dripping!)', Anita recorded. There was whiskey and gossip and an oyster feast and singing at nearby Clarenbridge. A few days later, an observer 'watching Tony in his odd beatnik shooting outfit pulling out a fabulous cigarette case, said, "He's not a gentleman of course but he will flaunt it."' Anita approved of the unusual royal consort,

> such an alive attractive person – most congenial and such fun for her to be married to – one sees her face in repose is so soft and happy and a gleam in her eyes – after the taut miserable-looking little princess of a few years ago – Obviously he is a good lover and takes trouble with a highstrung temperamental attractive wife – who can't carry on any old how with the press spying and being beastly.

On 10 January Anita recorded, 'Bill left for Kenya – coughing.' She wasn't particularly worried, unlike Bill's old friend Ruckers, who wrote to her that

> the continual coughing and the night sweats (the latter are a bad sign) may well mean his lungs are affected ... I am almost in entire agreement with his contempt for doctors and his faith in nature cures etc but there are occasions when doctors are essential and one is to be screened in case there is the least sign of T.B.

Ruckers intended to give Bill this advice 'but please also add your weight to mine'. It is unlikely that Anita did this, or that Bill would have taken any advice offered; both the Leslie-Kings swore by 'nature cures etc'.

Winston died on 24 January. 'One can think of nothing else but the end of an epoch. All the war revives and runs through one's veins.' Shane was a chief mourner and Tarka, home from school, queued in the cold to witness the Lying in State. Anita wrote: 'He will never forget the Great Hall and Marines on guard with tears pouring down their faces.' Anita attended the funeral in St Paul's and then, from the banks of the Thames, watched 'the little flag-covered coffin leaving us for ever – One was seared by the day.' Inevitably, at Glaslough, there were spooky goings-on. Seymour wrote to Anita: 'Crashes and bangs in the loft overhead and all that week mysterious footsteps in West Wing staircase and Leonie's famous finger-tip drumming, sounded like a typewriter tapping next door!' When Jennie Churchill's grave at Bladon, near Blenheim, was shown on television, 'an awful big bang in our loft! And it's upset Timmie [Seymour's wife]. Twice we've heard together Leonie's drumming finger-tips ... I predicted it would be so.' Seymour's letter concluded: 'Des has FLAG (Eire) ½ mast! Top of castle. Floodlit. The only ½ mast flag!'

There was another significant death on Good Friday, 15 April, that of Paul Rodzianko. After a funeral officiated by his nephew, Father Rodzianko, and attended by representatives of several regiments and the Italian Cavalry School, he was cremated and his ashes spread over the garden of Brayfield Lodge in Buckinghamshire, the house he had shared with his wife Joan and where they had run a school for horsemanship. For Anita, all Paul's sins were forgotten – his bullying, his refusal to give her a divorce. Instead:

> What a character he was. I am glad I could write his book and give him some happiness – tho very little for our penniless garret life was such a strain. It was like being married to a bear – or to the North Wind! Such vitality courage and talent – Farewell Paul. May your best horses await you in the clouds.

It was as though she had momentarily forgotten that she'd spent much of her married life with Paul plotting to run away from him, or pleading for a divorce. By the 1980s she'd returned to a more truthful frame of mind, telling Harold Harris that she could not bear to write about Paul in her forthcoming memoir because of the unhappiness he had caused her. Among Paul's glowing obituaries, one mentioned his marriage to Anita and a schoolfriend of Tarka's brought it to his attention. Tarka was so surprised by this aspect of his mother's past that he was given permission to ring home. Anita assured him that she was going to tell him about Paul 'one day'. Leonie, aged fourteen, staying with Bill Cunningham and his family, heard about the obituary and was deeply shocked that her mother, who had brought up her children as Catholics, was a divorcée.

Several of Anita's friends and associates died during the year: Dr Gillespie, the family doctor at Glaslough, who had delivered Leonie in Marjorie's bed; Montague Porch, Jennie Churchill's third husband, at the age of ninety-nine; Anita's favourite teacher, Miss Lambert, 'the only sensitive teacher of my miserable childhood', and the amateur sailor Bobby Somerset, a close friend. 'I am over 50 so from now on I suppose everyone who has been in my past will drop by the wayside,' Anita recorded gloomily. At a party in July, she met the American former presidential candidate Adlai Stevenson for the first time. He told her that, at his very last meeting with Winston, he'd asked the old man on whom he had modelled his oratorical style and Winston had said that he had learnt all he knew, when he was nineteen, from another American politician: Bourke Cockran. Anita wrote in her diary:

> Only I in all England – except Pa – knew that Jennie had a love affair with Bourke and gave Winston his introduction – Then Bourke married my mother's sister! And left us all his money – And told his wife my aunt the tale! 24 hours after pouring this out for me Stevenson dropped dead in Grosvenor Street.

This was on 14 July; the following weekend, Anita wrote down the entire exchange and brought this record to Randolph Churchill at his house, Stour, in East Bergholt, Sussex, where Randolph was writing his father's life. When the first volume was published in 1966, Anita 'was horrified to find my own ill-written, hasty letter about Bourke inserted verbatim in this most eminent of biographies!' There were more deaths in the second half of 1965: Barney Baruch, Aziz al-Masri, the Egyptian general whom she had known during the war, and Joe Dudgeon of the Irish Riding School. But Anita could write: 'The year ends in great happiness for me personally with both children enjoying their schools and able at 16 and 14 to get the most out of hunting.'

She had been writing another book, once again recycling her father's work. In 1932 Shane had published *Studies in Sublime Failures*, one of the failures being Moreton Frewen, his uncle by marriage and husband of the eldest Jerome sister, Clara. Moreton had had a varied career: cattle dealer in Wyoming, land speculator, financial advisor to the Nizam of Hyderabad, investor in strange products such as a noxious-smelling disinfectant called Electrozone and, briefly, from 1910 to 1911, an Irish Nationalist MP. None of his schemes brought him anything except financial loss, for which he acquired the nickname 'Mortal Ruin'.

Anita's biography of this chancer was published in 1966 and called *Mr Frewen of England. A Victorian Adventurer*. Anita treated her subject sympathetically, writing: 'It has been said of Moreton that he had a first-class mind untroubled by second thoughts.' Rudyard Kipling was harsher: 'He [Moreton] lived in every sense, except what is called common sense, very richly and widely, to his extreme content.'

But not to his family's content. Moreton bamboozled Clara and their children out of every inheritance, which he then lost, to the point where Clara's household goods had to be auctioned. Her two sisters, Leonie and Jennie, who were hardly rich themselves, bought her favourite pieces and returned them to her. With his daughter Clare, Moreton went further: he not only forced her to hand over her inheritance but demanded that she seduce rich men on his behalf, which the strong-willed Clare refused to do. Moreton wrote to her disapprovingly: 'You are a beautiful woman with a mental equipment which, rightly employed, might have helped me infinitely.' He was incorrigible as he launched scheme after disastrous scheme: 'I have got the ball at my feet once more, and this time I'll keep it – you will see.' A philanderer as well as a duplicitous crook, he boasted in his journal: 'Every woman I have ever enjoyed has been completely paralysed by the vigour of my performance.' An outcome which not every lover would relish.

Anita doesn't mention that in spite of Moreton's vigour, Clara's admirer, King Milan of Serbia, may have been Clare's father. Clare herself believed this to be the case. In a letter to Anita on 20 December 1954, Clare wrote: 'Margaret [Clare's daughter] looks so like him and we both so dislike Frewens.' Although the exiled King Milan was devoted to both Clara and Clare and showered them with gifts, Anita was reluctant, as always, to reveal amorous goings-on within her family, a stance not easy to maintain since so many of its members were world-class adulterers. She sprinkled stardust over Moreton as she would do with later biographical subjects, Jennie Churchill and Winston's son Randolph. Ralph Martin, a rival biographer, who will later reappear as Anita's nemesis, preferred another biography of Mortal Ruin: 'The prime source book on Moreton Frewen is *The Splendid Pauper* by Allen Andrews (1968). It is excellent. Anita Leslie has also written a biography of him ... but as a member of the family she is not as objective.' Anita found rascals irresistible, which is perhaps why she was so fond of the Edwardian age, with its randy and rapacious scoundrels and their sultry, adulterous mistresses. To have depicted Moreton as a monstrous cad might have unsettled her readers, who responded to her talent to amuse. Unpleasant aspects of her subjects' lives were kept shadowy. Of her biography of Randolph Churchill, she told Harold Harris: 'That book is full of things I DON'T say.' As for Moreton, she told Betsan Coats: 'I didn't harp on how dreadful Moreton was to his offspring.'

There aren't many diary entries for 1966. One of the most interesting refers to a visit Anita made to Randolph Churchill at Stour.

> Found him weak and doctor said he had cirrhosis of liver. His Vol I so good – warm and well balanced but he knows I think he cannot finish the other 4 vols ... I had to realise he is dying – all because he lives on whisky and plum cake. My heart was aching all the time I tried to jot down notes in the archives for 'Jennie'.

In spite of the state of his liver and his poor diet, Randolph survived until 7 June 1978 when, according to his doctor, he had 'worn out every organ in his body at the same time'. He rallied after Anita's visit and on 27 October 1966 was the guest of honour at a Foyles Literary Luncheon, at the Dorchester Hotel in London, to mark the publication of *Winston S. Churchill Vol. I Youth 1874–1900* (1966). At the top table were Shane, Iris, Anita and Clemmie, now Baroness Spencer-Churchill, GBE. There had been much recent literary collaboration between Churchills and Leslies:

Shane and Anita had helped Randolph, and Randolph had given Anita access to his family archive to help her in the writing of her next book, a biography of Randolph's grandmother Jennie.

At Glaslough there were problems both financial and domestic. Desmond was in Dublin for much of the time with Helen Strong and their baby daughter Sammy. Anita wrote to Betsan:

> Helen maddens everyone by calling herself Mrs Desmond Leslie while Agnes storms around Glaslough, is hateful to poor old Seymour and Timmie stuck in their wing and causes as much scandal and trouble as possible. The farm we worked at for 8 years is ruined and Desmond – who never pays bills – has a huge overdraft and is about to sell the garden as a hotel! I think they are as mad as hatters. Pa spent 3 months there last summer and said they were the most unhappy of his life – with Desmond and Agnes screaming at each other.

Seymour was having a bad time. In a letter of 21 November 1966 to Anita, he referred maliciously to Agnes as '*cette horrible juive à côté de nous*', while Desmond's 'other wife' was 'La Belle Helene'. The war of the wives went on until 1969, when Desmond, despicably, contrived to banish Agnes and her children from Glaslough. Anita immediately took them in at Oranmore until Monaghan County Council found them a house close to Castle Leslie, where Helen and her two daughters had been installed. Sammy and Antonia, Agnes's daughter, were classmates in the local school and became friends. When Antonia was invited to tea at the Castle, she found herself in the room which had once been hers, playing with her old toys. In any ordinary family this would have been regarded as a heart-breaking and scandalous episode but the Leslies had a talent for sliding a veneer of civilized behaviour over their natural ruthlessness, and cordial relations were soon restored between Desmond, past and present wives and all the children. Only Anita continued to find her brother's conduct unforgivable.

20
Jolly Old Age I'm Having

Anita began her biography of her great-aunt Jennie Churchill in 1966. This was the first time that she had written about a member of her family whom she had actually known, although Jennie had died when Anita was only seven. She could make use of her grandmother Leonie's reminiscences about her sister and had access to family papers. What she didn't have was any research on the subject by Shane that she could recycle, as she had done in previous books. In Shane's rare references to Jennie, his tone is one of snooty disdain. On Lord Randolph Churchill's marriage: 'He had married an American in the days when such an alliance was considered as experimental as mating with Martians' (from *The End of a Chapter*); and from *Long Shadows*, on his aunt: 'She could be described as unsuitable as possible for a Bishop's wife or President of a YMCA.' Shane recognized Jennie's dauntless spirit; writing of the Randolph Churchills' last voyage, he wrote: 'She [Jennie] cheerfully crossed the tropical seas, though it was necessary to include a leaden casket among the baggage.' He compared Randolph to Lord Byron, 'they were spendthrifts of their own minds', and describes the former as 'bearded and silent, a cause of trembling to all who passed.' Having to carry out her own research may have been the reason why Anita wrote fewer letters and diary entries than usual and only managed to record the events of 1968 in her 1969 diary, which began 'God what a year to get over.'

1968 had begun with an outbreak of foot-and-mouth disease in England, stranding the Leslie-Kings there and putting paid to their usual Christmas-time hunting in Galway. They were allowed into Switzerland and spent Christmas, enjoyably enough, with Roger Frewen in his chalet at Villars. But Anita mourned the lost hunting season. She wrote to her friend Kathleen, Duchess of Abercorn, 'Hasn't it been too cruel this foot and mouth ruining what promised to be the Blazers best season for years.' As always, she was free with medical advice, advocating to Kathleen the Nature Cure way of treating kidney problems: 'Before breakfast take a "SITZ BATH" – That is put about 6 inches of cold water in bathtub and while warmly dressed on top just hop in and sit for a couple of minutes with feet up on taps and splash the lower back with the cold water.'

Then Bill, the most compliant of husbands, decided, at the age of fifty-eight, to have an awfully big adventure. Anita to Betsan, 10 January 1968:

> Bill to my horror has decided to sail around the world without stopping. I hoped the expenses of his boat (built by a friend for £10,000) might halt him but the Daily Express handed him £4,000 to finish it and have commissioned him to write up the trip – I feel this is really a reaction against the fiasco of being driven out of Glaslough by Desmond and Agnes – who were really too awful to go into partnership with!

This trip was the *Sunday Times* Golden Globe non-stop race and Bill was the oldest of the nine competitors. Even before the *Daily Express* sponsorship came through he had raised £15,000 from selling cattle so that he could get Angus Primrose to build him a two-masted schooner, *Galway Blazer II*. The boat was launched in May from Souter's yard at Cowes and Anita recorded: 'The look of the hull somewhat lightened my leaden heart.' She wasn't in Plymouth when Bill set sail on 24 August but the Ruck-Keenes were there to wave him goodbye. Bill carried his usual frugal provisions: dried fruit, almond paste and green sprouts, as well as instructive books: the New Testament, the Quran and Tolstoy's novels.

Years later, in 2006, he said in the television documentary *Deep Water* that he never got depressed during the journey: 'You are ... alone with God ... there's no opportunity to sin.'

Anita had a bad feeling about the voyage. She wrote to Xandra:

> How I wish the Sunday Times had not turned it into a 'competition' – It destroys all his peace of mind and will force him to slog on with a boat which cannot go fast to windward. Much nicer if he and anyone else who cared had just set off quietly on a great adventure ... Knowing how nervy and wrought up Bill is I fear this will key him up – instead of 'doing him good' after the shambles of Glaslough which took so much out of him.

Her worst fears were realized when she wrote to Betsan:

> On October 31st (Halloween !!) he was turned turtle by a freak wave after a hurricane had blown (out of season) for 2 days and subsided. The wonderful little boat undamaged but the masts snapped off so he crept the 1000 miles to Cape Town with a jury rig – arriving November 21 and Tarka flew out to help him and had a blissful month there.

What she didn't tell Betsan but wrote in her diary was: 'Had he come on deck 30 seconds sooner he would have drowned and one would have just heard nothing EVER. Jolly old age I'm having.' The only competitor to finish the race was 28-year-old Robin Knox-Johnson in *Suhaili*. Bill caught a heavy dose of sea fever and made two further attempts to circumnavigate the globe.

1968 saw the youth of the western world tuning in, dropping out and, in Paris, prising up the cobblestones to throw at the police. In Cleveland Square, Leonie was staging a mild rebellion of her own. She didn't want to go to the Swiss finishing school which, Anita told Xandra, 'I set my heart on so long ago'. Instead, Leonie wanted to attend classes at East London College, at the suggestion of 'a librarian admirer who writes daily poems and hangs around', Anita complained to Betsan. She grumbled that Leonie 'half wants to come out – half wants to be an "intellectual" and sleep on a park bench!!' In spite of every discouragement, Leonie eventually took a degree course at an arts college and became the first member of her family to graduate. It was typical of Anita to put the word intellectual within quotation marks, intellect being something she distrusted as much as cleverness. About this time Leonie gave up hunting, which didn't go down well. But at Oranmore, at Christmas, Anita was pleased to report that her daughter 'was content riding and going to lots of parties'. Although Anita professed shame at having once been 'an idiotic debutante', this seemed to be her ambition for Leonie.

In October of that worrying year, Anita told Shane that she had offered Desmond £25,000 for some of the Glaslough land and added: 'I hope he gives Tarka the whole place and not just a section.' This hope was unrealistic; Desmond had ambitious plans for the estate, most of them unachievable since, as one of his lawyers pointed out, 'he seems to have a foot in each of two clouds simultaneously, if not more!' His latest plan was to build a five-star hotel in the neglected gardens, a scheme that had to be abandoned as the Northern Ireland troubles came closer to the gates of Castle Leslie. Grudgingly, over the years, Desmond, increasingly needy, had to sell parcels of land to Anita, which were put in Tarka's name.

Jennie: The Life of Lady Randolph Churchill was published in June 1969 to enthusiastic reviews. In *The Irish Times*, A. Kingsmill Moore wrote, with unconscious smuttiness: 'Not since I first read Dickens have characters come so bulging and thrusting out of the covers of a book.' *The Sunday Times* called the biography 'brazen and beguiling'; *The Guardian* found it of wide historical interest, while disapproving of the Edwardian ruling class: 'This book is about people who would spend on one party more than a poor man earned in a year.'

By October the book had been reprinted four times. Anita's Jennie was a softer version of Scarlett O'Hara, an optimistic beauty who painted light bulbs yellow to imitate sunshine and tolerantly defined sins as 'exaggerated inclinations'. This Jennie is upbeat, courageous, life-enhancing. It's certainly not a portrait of someone who was thought to be the sexiest woman on the planet; in fact, sex, which played a significant part in Jennie's story, hardly gets a mention. Not for the first time in her biographies, Anita insisted that lovers were no more than ardent admirers and that, since Edward VII referred to Jennie as 'Ma Chère Amie', the couple were no more than close friends, even though His Majesty was a word-class philanderer and Jennie an ambitious sexpot, known suggestively in the popular press as 'Lady Randy'. According to Anita, Victorian girls were subject to round-the-clock chaperonage and, once married, protected from any friskiness by their cumbersome clothing. She doesn't speculate that Winston, born seven months after his parents' marriage, might not have been 'premature'.

Before Anita's *Jennie* was published, its future success in the USA was threatened by the appearance of the first volume of a rival and far more sensational biography; *Jennie: The Life of Lady Randolph Churchill, The Romantic Years 1854–1895*, by Ralph G. Martin, which stayed on the *New York Times* bestseller list for over seven months. Anita wrote crossly in her diary:

> Scribners [her US publisher] much perturbed by Vol 1 of this vulgar Ralph Martin life of Jennie out just 9 months before mine in USA - tries to make a sensation of fact Winston was born 7 months after Jennie's marriage – says 'PROBABLY illegitimately conceived'. What cheek and BOSH! Jerome girls never allowed out of sight – Victorian parents expected all young men to try to seduce their daughters and took NO chances.

Ralph Martin speculated that Winston's younger brother, John Strange Spencer-Churchill (Jack) was the son of John Strange Jocelyn, later 5th Earl of Roden. To refute this suggestion, Anita enlisted the help of Clodagh, Countess of Roden, asking her to inspect visitors' books and diaries to prove that the pair were very unlikely lovers. This was for the benefit of the reading public. Anita knew that Jack's father was Evelyn Boscowen, 7th Viscount Falmouth, known as 'The Star Man'. Clare had told her this in 1956: 'He was Jack Churchill's father but I mustn't write scandal.'

In an undated letter, Shane had written to his daughter, 'As to Star Falmouth ... you can calculate when they [Star and Jennie] first met by when Jack was born.' Anita kept this to herself. Her diary records: 'Rodens send me verification that 5th Lord could NOT have been Jack Churchill's father. Silly Ralph Martin got him muddled up with Falmouth and Jack was most probably Randolph's son anyway.'

Anita was hell-bent on exposing Ralph Martin as an unreliable scandal-monger but she was on shaky ground. Martin was a respected historian, his book endorsed by Martin Gilbert, the greatest living expert on Winston's life. He told the *Sunday Express*, which had published Ralph Martin's account of the Roden connection: 'As far as I know Ralph Martin is the very first person to have gone through the family papers in the archives with any detailed scrutiny. I have no doubt that if he has based his conclusions on the papers they certainly ought to be taken seriously.' Worse, Anita's own family had helped 'this odious American', who, in his book's acknowledgments, thanks 'Sir Shane Leslie and his charming wife, who gave me so much of their time and memory and made available to me letters, documents and photographs.' Shane had also helped Anita with her book and had been similarly acknowledged. Jack Churchill's son Peregrine was thanked by Martin 'for making freely available his large collection of family letters and photographs, and for permitting me to quote from the Reminiscences of Lady Randolph Churchill and other material on which he holds the copyright', a helpfulness that Peregrine would later regret. Like other members of his family, he had allowed access to his papers to the rival biographers, so Anita had been allowed to quote from Jennie's memoirs too. She had also been greatly helped by Winston's son Randolph, to whom her book is dedicated, and her acknowledgments began with thanks to Her Majesty the Queen and King Michael of Romania. Impressive but unlikely to boost sales.

Anita, usually a very self-effacing author, blamed her publishers for the Ralph Martin fiasco. In March 1969, three months before her biography of her great-aunt was even published, in a letter to Harold Harris, she accused Ralph Martin of plagiarism and of lying about Jennie's 'lover life', which, Anita insisted, began only after her husband had withdrawn from her bed on account of the syphilis, which was the cause of his death in 1895, when he was forty-five. Anita also wrote to Hutchinson's managing director, the recently knighted Sir Robert Lusty, criticizing the company for its failure to stand up to Cassells, Martin's UK publisher, or to promote her own *Jennie*. She reminded Sir Robert that Hutchinson's publicity department had not brought a single journalist to 'a champagne press party which she had given for *Mr Frewen of England*.' That book had not sold well but its poor sales may not have been the result of the failure of the press party.

Anita had sent an early draft of *Jennie* to Clemmie Churchill, who had thought it 'fascinating and dramatic', which is true enough, although not as fascinating and dramatic as Jennie herself, who continues to enthral biographers. Anne Sebba's *Jennie Churchill — Winston's American Mother* (John Murray 2007) painted a darker picture of an unrooted woman, disastrously married to a syphilitic, unstable man; beset by money worries and taking bad decisions, financially and emotionally. Elisabeth Kehoe's triple biography of the Jerome sisters, *Fortune's Daughters* (Atlantic Books 2004) is also more robust than Anita's version. In 1969 when Anita's *Jennie* was published, Peregrine Churchill successfully brought a copyright case against Martin, which ensured that the Lord Roden story was omitted from the UK edition of Martin's book. Yet it is Martin's version of Jennie, especially her promiscuity, which has endured. In November 2008, as part of its High Society series, Channel 4 broadcast *Lady Randy*, in which Elisabeth Kehoe and Anne Sebba took it in turns to read out a list of Jennie's lovers, said to number two hundred. The programme also mentioned that Winston, that 'premature' baby, was born with a full head of hair and immediately slept through the nights. Part of this titillating account was filmed at Castle Leslie and featured Jack Leslie discussing Randolph's syphilis. Jennie could no longer be described as a 'Chère Amie', whose sense of decorum forbade participation in what Anita called 'the ultimate relationship'.

Ralph Martin was the least of Anita's concerns in that publication year. In February, she wrote to Betsan: 'I really can't think how to get through the summer with Bill re-masting at Cowes and off again on a solo voyage early Sept and Leonie being a worry generally.' In August from Oranmore, she wrote to Clodagh Roden, explaining why she couldn't go to Dublin to try to find out the truth about the Lord Jocelyn story:

> I am frantic at the moment – a) going to Plymouth to see Bill off … and then back here where I am left with 12 horses and NO groom – Our dear stableman of 23 years service dropped dead (beside poor Leonie) in July. I have got to advertise for a groom for the hunters and arrange for the Connemara mares and foals to be weaned and their feed … All this without Bill or the stableman is half killing me.

In September she told Clodagh that, as they waited in Plymouth for 'a strong north wind to blow Bill out into the Atlantic – my heart is lead but he couldn't NOT do it'.

On 1 November, at the end of that exhausting year, Anita flew to America with her daughter on a two-month lecture tour of Women's Clubs, on the subject of 'Jennie's vitality!!' Leonie was not turning out the way Anita would have wished. A true child of the sixties, she was a left-wing, vegetarian pacifist who had given up hunting, agreeing with Oscar Wilde's view that it entailed 'the unspeakable in pursuit of the uneatable'. She was taken to America to get her away from the London drug scene and her bookish, poetic boyfriend. Tarka, now twenty years old, spent much of the year in Australia with his friend Tony Huston, son of the film director John Huston, visiting Betsan at Paradise Beach in Queensland and making 'a film of the OUTBACK'. The final entry in Anita's sparse 1969 diary is dated 29 April and describes an event which would cast a long shadow. 'We all can only think of Terence O'Neill's gallant battle and sad resignation. John Brooke, once my friend – I really feel I never want to see again.' Northern Ireland's prime minister, Terence O'Neill, had struggled to bring electoral and social reform to the seething province since 1963 but had been forced to resign by a group of dissident Ulster Unionist MPs, one of whom was John Brooke, who later became the 2nd Viscount Brookeborough. Civil unrest followed and, in August, British forces were called out to help restore peace. This marked the start of the Troubles, which affected everyone in Northern Ireland, not least the Leslies, whose ancestral home sat on the border between the North and the Irish Republic.

21

This Leslie Half-World

During the 1970s Anita wrote four books, entered into chaotic negotiations with Desmond regarding Glaslough, managed Oranmore, continued to hunt and did her best to micromanage her grown-up children's lives. In September 1970, waiting in Cornwall for Bill to be able to set sail, in the teeth of gales, on another round-the-world trip, she wrote to Tarka: 'Having waited so long I may as well wait longer – Really I have nothing to do except get the ponies broken and sold – write my new book and buy Leonie birthday presents (I'm trying to get her a black fringed bag to match her boots!)'

During the decade both her children married, and Clare (1970), Shane (1971), Peter (1975) and Margaret (1976) died. Anita abandoned her diary in 1979 but remained a prolific letter-writer, often writing ten letters a day. She increasingly regretted having relinquished Glaslough and tried to buy back land there for Tarka to farm but, although Desmond was deeply in debt, he had other plans. On 4 April 1970, Anita, again in America to promote *Jennie*, wrote to Shane: 'Tarka is seeing Desmond in the faint hope he might be able to buy some of Glaslough farm back before the place is totally sold up to American hotel companies.' She also told her father that 'Ralph Martin's book was a bestseller here for 30 weeks and is still on Book Club adverts.' Perhaps this was to make Shane feel guilty about having helped Martin but it's unlikely that Shane, shamelessness personified, felt any guilt at all.

That October Anita visited Glaslough for the first time in eighteen months to attend a family gathering to celebrate Shane's eighty-fifth birthday. Anita wrote to Kathleen Abercorn:

> I hadn't seen Sammy and Camilla, Desmond's little daughters before and it's very curious the conflicting emotions they evoke – Desmond kept saying 'Aren't they sweet?' and I couldn't say yes – I could see in my mind's eye his sons just that age playing on those same lawns – on that same swing – One is forced to feel that to like these children is disloyal to poor unhappy Shaun and Mark and Antonia.

The birthday celebrations became rather muted when Shane emerged from the Pinetum 'staggering and pouring blood from a gash on the head – Had naughtily gone off alone to chop or clip and had fallen.' Instead of the fiddles and Irish dancing that Desmond had arranged, it was bed for a week and doctor's visits. 'At least we had a NEW WORRY,' Anita wrote. Bill's former farm had been let and was 'a mass of needs and weeds'. Anita wanted to improve the dismal place Glaslough had become but 'All I can think of doing is IMPROVE their LIVES by sending up bridles for my old hunters so they can jog around.'

Her sympathy ran out the following month when Desmond wrote her 'a jeering letter' for offering too little for the land she wished to buy. Anita instructed her solicitor to increase the offer to £200 per acre and to 'ask for access through Farm Gate and hope stewards house and farm buildings can be thrown in.' And then to Tarka on 28 November: 'What DID you say to Desmond on the 'phone?' According to Desmond, Tarka, who had joined the Blues and Royals, had offered to 'contribute' to the upkeep of Glaslough. 'With what may I ask', Anita wrote to her son, pointing out that he had only a small American income which, with an allowance from his mother, just covered the £1200 that his regiment demanded as private means. Tarka's phone call seems to have unhinged Desmond.

He now demanded that Anita raise £60,000 on all her assets to 'invest' in Glaslough. Tarka seems to have also told his uncle that he, Tarka, owned various building sites around Oranmore valued at £80,000. Anita pointed out that much of this land was liable to flooding. She ended the letter to her son: 'Let's STAY FACTUAL.'

Determined that Tarka would own at least a part of Glaslough, she didn't consider how he felt about her controlling his assets or how he saw his future. The letter that Tarka wrote to her on 4 December must have jolted her.

> This Leslie half-world that exists either has to be held together or absolutely forgotten about. It is rather sad that such an interesting old family should suddenly come to such an end but you can see that it is hard for Mark, Shaun, Leonie and I to keep the Leslie spirit as it was when none of the grown-ups talk to each other and are eccentric. The army has provided me with a home and I feel stable for the first time in years. The tension is disappearing from my brain.

'I feel stable for the first time in years.' He couldn't have written anything more wounding. To give her children a more secure childhood than her own, Anita had rooted herself at Oranmore when she longed to travel and given them a healthy, seaside life, free of pressure or the need to compete. It was lucky that, about this time, Peter Wilson and his wife came back to live in Oranmore, at Rocklands, the house which Anita had found for them. Peter immediately took over the irksome business negotiations. Anita was able to tell Tarka:

> Don't worry darling about Glaslough – Peter and I are working like beavers with Desmond who is a very tricky customer and is extremely EVASIVE about selling the Cor Meadows … he may possibly have sold them already … and does not wish to tell me so.

On the last day of 1970 an agreement was formalized between Desmond and Tarka that gave Tarka 'the lands and premises' for £46,924, paid for by Anita. The demesne lands had beautifully soothing names: Mullanlary, Mullaghjordan, Killyconnigan, Telayden, Tullyree, which belied the fraught transactions involved. Anita's letter to her son did not address his concerns about Glaslough or ask if he approved of her purchase on his behalf. Anita tended to ignore other people's desires if they didn't coincide with her own.

Anita, as well as settling land on her son, had also shaped his career. Tarka had left Milton Abbey in 1967 with three O levels, hoping to join the Irish Guards. But without a more impressive academic performance or a hefty private income, he was turned down. Instead, he went on the hippy trail and was drifting around India when, he told me, 'Anita arrived in Delhi in a swirl of sun hats and, within weeks, I was at Mons officer cadet school.' Anita was putting her wartime contacts to good use. Betty Holberton, a friend since MTC days, had, in 1943, married John Nicholas Rede Elliott, an MI6 Intelligence Officer who had known Anita in Beirut where Anita's job on the *Eastern Times* had allowed for some ladylike snooping. It was Elliott, a devoted friend of Kim Philby, who, in 1963, had been sent to Beirut to tell the double agent that the game was up, an episode grippingly recounted by Ben MacIntyre in his book *A Spy Among Friends: Kim Philby and the Great Betrayal* (Bloomsbury 2014). In 1970 the Middle East was getting interesting again. In November the Syrian minister of defence, Hafez al-Assad, had toppled the civilian government in a bloodless military coup. Nicholas Elliott needed someone in the region who could set up an informal network, prior to the intelligence services moving in. He approached Anita, who had kept up several friendships made in the Middle East during the war. She said that, at fifty-six, she was too old for the job but suggested that Tarka might go, if some legitimate way could be found to get him to the region. The army proved to be the way. Tarka was admitted to Mons after being grilled by 'a couple of grey-suited men at a strange office in Berkeley Square'. Impressed by the young man's contacts with Chinese train bombers in Malaya, they were prepared to overlook his lack of academic qualifications and a private income. 'Elliott briefed me privately at his home before each interview. Very good cellar.' The Regimental Colonel of the Blues and Royals, Field Marshall Sir Gerald Templer, who, in the immediate post-war years, had been Director of Military Intelligence at the War Office, invited Tarka to tea at his house in Wilton Street, Belgravia, and said that he had been told that 'I had a brain but no idea how to use it.' After training at Mons, Tarka was posted to Nicosia, Lebanon, Germany and Cyprus. He managed to have a dazzling social life wherever he went.

As Anita fought to secure farmland for her son on an estate that bordered Northern Ireland, it didn't seem to occur to her that this was becoming a place where members of Her Majesty's Armed Forces would not be welcome. Her concerns about his stint in the army were all about his health. She issued lists of confused instructions:

> Don't drink quantities of liquid – weakening to lungs – Remember my tip weak whiskey and water (NOT SODA) ... Remember the BODY BELT! Only heart and kidneys matter ... My chief hope is that you went to bed early, ate well and did not drink anything except wine. Remember BULK is bad for lungs – keep liquid intake SMALL. Don't get in the habit of swilling beer – it exhausts the kidneys which in turn put too much elimination work on the LUNGS. When drinking with the boys can't you – owing to your pneumonia – just order a single whiskey, fill the glass up with water and sip it while they take in the 4 – 5 – 6 pints they think manly. Two single whiskeys a night in a LOT of water are as intoxicating as 6 pints of beer but less bulky. STRONG whiskey is bad for the liver. Learn these things and you will find you can drink a little in full control and yet NOT appear to be unsocial or NOT MANLY. The SECRET is to decide exactly what you want to drink – order your whiskey and pay other people's rounds while making it last their FOUR.

There were more demented letters, full of lurching capitals, as Anita, in London, tried to keep track of possessions and reunite them with their owners:

> WHERE has the Augustus John drawing disappeared to? It was in the hall when I left for Ireland Aug 7 ... I found the cherub head among my shoes. Daddy arriving without pyjamas! What a pair you are! I am sending the rather grubby underwear so you can wear out and throw away ... Nothing I could send from here except those brown boots with sham cowboy look! Can't believe you actually want those?

Packages that Anita despatched to Tarka at his various postings – 'plimsolls and brown shoes – two bath towels'– sometimes failed to arrive:

> It must be stuck in Army PO [post office] as once the parcels reach that stage the ordinary PO can't follow up for secrecy [*sic*] sake!! ... What am I to do

with the heaps of things on the floor? TINS and old underwear? Am I to SORT
IT OUT and THROW ANY away OR keep?

Peter, more calmly, also wrote to Tarka. He and Prim had been
visited by Peter's son Roddy, who was getting divorced, his small child
and a Dutch nanny and had turned the box room at Rocklands into a
nursery. Both Tarka and Leonie realized that Peter was Tarka's father but
the subject was never discussed. It was considered bad form to speculate
on one's parentage. No longer responsible for the Oranmore farm, Peter
enjoyed watching Bill hard at work saving the hay. Peter and Anita hunted
and rode together and went to each other's dinner parties, all past anguish
forgotten. Peter still had a knack of getting things hopelessly wrong. He
thought that the bad situation in Northern Ireland was bound to improve
as more local girls married British soldiers and even that girls from the
Republic were travelling to the North to raid the army for husbands.

1970 ended with Tarka making headway in a new career, Bill
progressing steadily along the world's seas and Leonie at art college in
Brighton. Anita, in between wrapping up parcels doomed, like so many
things she touched, to go missing, had made some progress on the book
which, in 1974, would become her greatest success. The west of Ireland,
like the rest of the country in the wake of the Troubles in the North,
became embroiled in the general nastiness and ill-feeling. At Mollie
Cusack Smith's New Year dance, Gardaí were stationed at the door as
threats had been made and Mollie's daughter, Oonagh Mary, was in tears
in the kitchen. Anita frequently mentioned Oonagh Mary in her letters
to Tarka, hoping that he might marry her. Such a match would have lured
Tarka back to Oranmore and the hunting life that Anita longed to share
with him.

In the spring of 1971 Anita joined Bill in Australia, where *Galway Blazer
II* had put into Perth. She wrote to Tarka: 'Galway Blazer is the first 5 ton
boat to sail non-stop from England to Australia through the Roaring Forties
[strong westerly winds found in the Southern Hemisphere] so Daddy has
achieved one record.' They lived on the boat and were much feted, giving
several interviews. This was pleasanter than the voyage described in *Love
in a Nutshell*. From their complicated wedding when, it seems, Anita

had married Bill just to give her unborn child a name and the Glaslough servants a day to remember, they had settled into a loving and companionable marriage. 'The triumph of love consists, not in winning, but enduring,' as the diarist James Lees-Milne, put it. In *Jennie*, Anita wrote that her great-grandmother, Clara Jerome, advised: '"Never scold a man, my dears. If you do he will only go where he is not scolded."This piece of wisdom was passed on to three generations.' It was certainly passed on to Anita, who never scolded Bill for sailing around the world, leaving her to cope with the horses and to write the books that financed the household, although she insisted that her writing was not a full-time occupation.

While this well-adapted pair were visiting Betsan in Queensland, Desmond was explaining his financial situation to Tarka:

> You can imagine, dearest T, what my inner life has been like these past 7 years, waking up night after night struggling with seeming impossible problems and shortfalling solutions … I have given much prayer and thought to Glaslough all these years and believe that I can see a Guiding Hand at work.

He believed that Tarka had lived at Glaslough in a previous life, perhaps as his great-uncle Norman Leslie, 'Otherwise I don't think you'd feel as strongly as you do, and as I do, about the sacred trust and burden to preserve Glaslough for the New Age of Aquarius.' He would perhaps not have dared to write in such hippy-dippy terms had Anita not been on the other side of the globe.

In August, while Desmond and Helen were in Dublin, Anita and Jack visited Glaslough. She was dismayed by the state of the place, writing to Roger Frewen:

> The golf course scheme is apparently OVER. It looks like stony desert – all thistles – where the topsoil has been scraped off – meanwhile that lies in hummocks of nettles … The house is an untidy shambles – everything moved around all wrong and of course the drawing room ruined by loss of the Bassano.

This referred to the painting of the Flight into Egypt by the sixteenth-century north-Italian artist Jacopo Bassano. Desmond had sent it to be auctioned at Christies in order to raise more money for the estate and, in particular, his latest scheme: a village of artists' and writers' homes. It was hoped that many artists and writers would be lured to the Irish Republic by the then finance minister Charles Haughey's 1969 tax exemption legislation. But although some British artists and writers came to live in Ireland to take advantage of Haughey's scheme, many of them left again, feeling threatened by the increase in IRA activity.

Tarka was now stationed in Cyprus and Anita wrote him almost daily letters, describing the restless goings-on within the family. 'What turbulent artistic blood we Jeromes all have – it's that mixture of Red Indian and pioneer White – infused into English aristocracy – we just can't settle down.' She also instructed her son on how to control hounds and, although Leonie seemed more than capable of meeting men, Anita ordered Tarka: 'Tell your friends to ring her up here [the Cleveland Square flat] from now on and ask her out without letting her know I told you she is here!!'

On 24 June Xandra Frewen remarried. She was thirty-seven and her new husband, David O'Grady Roche, the son of an Irish baronet, was, according to Anita '23 (looking a wan 18) ... I feel it will end in about 5 years – more forlorn infants'. The wedding reception was awkward. Although the bride looked 'perfectly beautiful in new white outfit flowers in hair', Xandra's mother, a classmate of Anita's at Westonbirt and wearing a 'super mauve silk outfit' was drunk and tearful and 'cursing Roger [Frewen] for being such a damn fool and allowing all this to happen: "Why didn't I go to Court and get it stopped – I could have proved he was living with 5 other women!!"' The bridegroom's parents stayed away.

At the Christie's auction the following day, the Bassano failed to meet its reserve of £25,000 and was withdrawn from sale, 'Desmond taking it calmly – champagne parties at the Ritz to cheer himself up.' The painting sold later that year. Leonie showed early signs of entrepreneurship by taking a job as a waitress at the Chelsea Kitchen in the King's Road and 'phoning all MY friends to come and order lots of wine so she gets a "wine bonus", as well as her £20 wages and tips'.

Anita disliked literary gatherings, where she was bound to meet 'clever' people, or people who thought they were clever, but she agreed to take part in a discussion of Irish Writing to be staged at a festival organized by her friend Lady Birley at Seaford in West Sussex. 'The "Irish Talk" was ghastly,' she told Tarka:

> It lasted 2 hours instead of the usual ¾ - Elizabeth Bowen drivelled on and on – gaga and with a stutter … No one spoke properly into microphones and Pa [Shane] walked out muttering 'Are they speaking Irish or English – I can't hear!'

It was a very disorganized festival. Leonie was put in charge of Irish crafts but with 'no prices so she could not sell to fury of visitors'. Later, 'the whole cast of Glyndeborne Opera [*sic*] arrived in COSTUME starving having sung since 5 – to wait an hour for a vast cauldron of burnt rice – which wasn't enough for sixty!'

She had told her son the previous year that he wasn't to worry about Glaslough but now she wrote: 'Now darling concentrate on finance – Tell me exactly how much you have in your current account.' She then explained how things stood with Desmond, which was how things usually stood, with Desmond pressing for payment and Anita holding off as long as possible. To Tarka: 'DO NOT deal with Desmond DIRECT. He is so hysterical.' She was working hard on the book whose working title was 'Edwardian Romantics'. She wrote to Harold Harris: 'When can I have an advance and could it be large? I am buying back the farmland of Castle Leslie for my son and need all available funds – Why do I seem to make so little money?' *Jennie* had sold well in the UK but Anita had given a quarter of her royalties to Seymour for helping with the research and Ralph Martin's book had captured the American market, so it did not make her fortune.

Shane and Iris now lived in the seaside town of Hove, in Sussex. In July, Shane fell and broke his arm. He had an emergency operation and was found to have an enlarged prostate gland. Although shaken, he was still so strong at the age of eighty-five that his family wasn't too worried about him and it was a shock when he died on 14 August. Anita wrote to Clodagh Roden: 'It has left us immensely sad – his going – and curiously surprised.' To Kathleen Abercorn, she described Shane's funeral at Glaslough. To make room for the burial plot, two of Anita's hunters had to be moved out of the orchards where they grazed and 'escaped in the Pinetum where Tarka feared they'd poison themselves.' Tarka, in a borrowed tailcoat, had to coral the horses during a hot morning before taking his place in the cortège, in a rather flushed state. The Bishop made 'a splendid oration' about Shane's lifetime effort to fuse his own Anglo-Irish tradition with the older Gaelic one but he was overshadowed by the interesting presence of both Desmond's wives. 'Helen sat next to Bill in her see-through mourning gown and I saw his eyes rolling nervously towards No 1!'

Her father's death brought home to Anita her folly in handing Glaslough to Desmond, a move that Shane had been against. She was trying to finish her book, scheduled for publication the following spring, but she found time to go with Bill and Tarka for their annual shooting holiday at Henry McIlhenny's Glenveagh Castle in County Donegal. This was after she had spent the summer entertaining up to fifteen people at a time in the old tower at Oranmore, cooking 'a vast meat meal in the Great Hall every evening'. Shane's Requiem Mass was held at Westminster Cathedral on 5 October and then Anita went back to Oranmore, to spend the winter in the restored, centrally heated stables. The castle and outbuildings were now more civilized than they had been immediately after the war when George Jellicoe had complained of the cold and the fish that slithered through the slit windows.

On 21 November, her fifty-seventh birthday, she went hunting – 'jumped more than 57 walls'. She was concerned about the dangerous situation in the North, blaming it on the British governments of Harold Wilson and Edward Heath. In 1971 Heath wanted the Republic of Ireland 'to close 300 mile border to IRA when they [Heath's government] are the CAUSE of all this disaster'. She blamed Wilson for letting Terence O'Neill be thrown out and for sending in British troops and Heath for imposing internment. It was no longer safe for Tarka to come home on leave, 'yet in Cyprus he is with Irish troops for games'. It seemed the right time for Tarka to get an Irish passport which, since he was born in the Republic, he was entitled to. He was advised to wear civilian clothes for his passport photograph.

Bill set off for another leg of his voyage at the end of 1972, from Australia. When he was about four hundred miles southwest of Fremantle, a large sea creature, either a whale or a shark, badly damaged his boat. Bill, hanging over the side, carried out emergency repairs on the shattered hull with ropes, tape and rubber for three days, before he was able to limp back into port at Fremantle. He set out again shortly afterwards but a faulty radio meant that he was out of contact for five months. When *Galway Blazer II* was finally sighted the following May, Ivor Key, a reporter on the *Daily Express*, interviewed Anita in New York where she was publicizing her new book, of which more later. Although it was clear that she had endured five very anxious months, Anita was stoical:

> The solitude and loneliness I go through when he is making these long voyages can be hell but I wouldn't dream of asking him to stop … My nerves aren't in the best of shape after this one but frankly I wouldn't dream of trying to dissuade him – even if going round the world again was what he wanted.

Luckily, for the sake of Anita's nerves, Bill, at the age of sixty-two, had decided against another round-the-world trip.

2 2
The Low-Down on the High-Ups

Anita understood how difficult it was for Tarka to be both a British soldier and an Irish farmer. Rather than give up the idea of Tarka farming at Glaslough, she tried to influence government policy on Northern Ireland. She wrote to Winston's grandson, Winston S. Churchill, the Conservative MP for Stretford, near Manchester, who disagreed with her anti-internment views and was equally unmoved by her conviction that violence in the province was caused by inequalities in housing and jobs. She approached David James, the Conservative MP for North Dorset, with the idea that the British government should pay increased subsidies to Northern Ireland, to iron out these inequalities of provision. His answer was: 'I would far sooner end it [the violence] by assisting the Republic to bring their level of social services up to the standard of our own, as that is the single biggest impediment to a United Ireland.' Anita's friend Aidan Crawley, who had served as first a Labour and then a Conservative MP, had become the influential chairman of London Weekend Television but neither he nor Sir John Foster, the Conservative MP for Norwich, a lawyer who had devoted his career to the advocacy of human rights, seemed to care much about Northern Ireland. Anita received 'an interesting letter back from Michael Foot', but it has yet to turn up in Mr Foot's archive. What unlikely correspondents: the scatty, witty Anglo-Irish woman and the brilliant, intellectual socialist.

Seymour Leslie's views were more radical than Anita's: 'I want the political SF [Sinn Féin] party to be allowed to stand in the Ulster elections,' he wrote in an undated letter to Anita. This was a very bold opinion in the early 1970s. It wasn't until 1983 that Gerry Adams became the first Sinn Féin MP for West Belfast, although he refused to take his seat at Westminster. On 30 January 1972 the event known as Bloody Sunday flared in the Bogside area of Derry, leading to the introduction of direct rule by the British government. Even so, few people in England and even in the Republic of Ireland were overly concerned, at least, not until the start of the IRA bombing campaigns on the mainland.

Anita's new book, published in 1974 and called *Edwardians in Love*, was a nostalgic inspection of a different world, a romantic age that may never have existed in the elegant and passionate manner Anita described. There is nothing rancid or devilish about her Edwardians. When Harold Harris read the manuscript, he thought that she was too enraptured by Edward VII and his circle, which is something of an understatement.

The dedication is: 'For Leonie My Grandmother, died at Castle Leslie 1943 and Leonie My Daughter, born at Castle Leslie 1951'. Grandmother Leonie takes her place among the loved and loving in a chapter called 'Arthur of Connaught and "Beloved Leo"'. Anita would have liked to have written more about this lengthy romance between Leonie and the Duke of Connaught, a relationship described by Anita as merely a loving friendship: her grandmother, 'the amie adorée'. But Arthur's daughter Lady Patricia Ramsay – 'that gaga old Patricia Ramsay' – refused permission to quote from the few letters which had escaped incarceration in the Royal Archives. One wonders, if the relationship was platonic, why the letters between the two are still kept under lock and key. The book was to have been called 'Amorous Edwardians' but Anita wrote to Harold:

My uncle Seymour aged 84 writes 'The word amorous is odious, vulgar-genteel, snide and coy!' Dirty old men paying nubile teenagers are 'amorous'. Granny Leo wasn't amorous ... My grandmother said English girls were taught in the schoolroom never to lift their voices or allow excitement to creep in.

Anita now had a high-powered American agent, a New Yorker, Fanny Holtzmann, 'a leading theatrical and copyright lawyer and friend of the Churchill family'. When Fanny procured a $75,000 advance from Doubleday, Anita nearly fainted and probably forgave her agent for ending her letters 'With my fondest thoughts'. The hefty contract may not have been entirely straightforward since Harold Harris had to unravel prob-lems regarding the US rights. He wrote to Burroughs Mitchell of Charles Scribner: 'Please do not quote me as saying so, but Miss Leslie does get herself into the most fearful muddles.' Nothing more was heard about Miss Holtzmann.

The advance from Hutchinson was £1000 for the hardback edition, plus £300 for the Arrow Books paperback, with a first printing of 30,000 copies. A three-part serialization was sold to *The Sunday Telegraph* while, in America, the book was chosen for the Alternate Selection of the US Literary Guild, and was the *Homes and Gardens* in association with the National Book League Christmas Book Choice. Perhaps the sweetest financial reward of all: Ralph Martin had to pay Anita £500 plus her costs for copyright infringement. When Anita expressed her gratitude to Harold Harris, he wrote back:

> I should like to thank you particularly for your most generous letter about what little help I was able to give you in preparing Edwardians in Love for publication. Indeed, it always seems to me that the greatest service I rendered was in helping you to find the right order for the pages when you dropped the manuscript from the taxi.

When, in 1954, Anita visited her American relatives, the Ides, she had regretted that her mother had left the rectitude and simplicity of Vermont to marry Shane and become part of louche English society. But it was the rollicking, larky and sexually adventurous to whom Anita was drawn, at least in most of her books. *Edwardians in Love* was a success because scandalous goings-on among the upper classes had, and have, universal appeal, as can be seen in television series such as *Upstairs, Downstairs* and *Downton Abbey*. The tone of *Edwardians in Love* is one of fond indulgence towards the cast of adulterers, betrayers, high-class cocottes, racketeers and drunks who were the cream of Edwardian society, people like those disapproved of by St Augustine for living in 'a hissing cauldron of lust'. Characters met previously in her other books make another appearance: the kind-hearted, affection-seeking, amoral Prince of Wales and his acolytes, members of the Marlborough House set, who called their country-house bedroom hopping 'roguey-poguey' and considered other men's wives fair game. 'At luncheon and at tea wives received whom they pleased – it was not husband-time.'

Few of these philanderers were brainy but Anita was suspicious of cleverness; there was something nine-to-five in city offices about it. She admired 'these ... rulers who remained rustic amidst their magnificence and their power, and who did not mix with the professional classes depicted in Galsworthy's Forsyte Saga.' In *Edwardians in Love*, she is more truthful about her great-aunt Jennie Churchill, an honesty which may have been forced on her by Ralph Martin's revelations about Randolph's supposed homosexuality and his syphilis. But she didn't come clean about 'Star' Falmouth. She wrote only: 'although Jennie was a tremendous flirt and always had admirers in tow, there is no shred of evidence to lead one to suppose that she preferred "Star" Falmouth or any other man to her attractive young husband during the years in Ireland.' Some of these badly-behaved aristocrats are sympathetic figures. Lady Aylesford makes the heart-melting remark 'I cannot live uncared for', while her husband, forced to leave the royal party in India to deal with domestic dramas, discovers that 'There is nothing more melancholy, majestic and uncompromising than the hind view of an elephant.'

Macaulay considered 'that the best histories are ... those in which a little of the exaggeration of fictitious narrative is judiciously employed'. This was certainly Anita's style. She heightened the glamour, swept the tawdriness under the costly carpets. And she recounted conversations that may not have existed. '*Se non è vero, è ben trovato*', as the Italians say –

'If it's not true, it's still a good story.' Anita dismissed certain books as being '*Un peu pour les concierges*', a charge that could be levelled at *Edwardians in Love*. One reviewer wrote pithily: 'It is not an edifying theme or spectacle that Miss Leslie presents, but there is always an eager audience for the low-down on the high-ups and she gives us full measure.'

When Anita gave press interviews, she presented herself as a lady dabbler: a farmer and pony breeder who just happened to scribble a bit – no more than three hours a day, usually on the floor with cushions. 'I try to keep [writing] a pleasure', she told *The Scotsman* in October 1972, 'like embroidering or painting. If I had to write more intensively, like a man might to support his family, I wouldn't be able to do that and I'd hate it.' The truth was that Anita did support her family. Bill had only a small pension, Tarka hardly any income and Leonie was still a student. Anita's writing paid for the upkeep of horses, central heating and carpets, a London flat and Glaslough farmland, but to admit it would be to sound like a professional writer, grim and pleasureless.

Sometimes, reluctantly, she had to stand under the literary spotlight. In December she wrote to Xandra that her publisher

> got me to Harrogate for a literary lunch at which I had to spout for 15 minutes – this after a soporific 2 hour luncheon – 400 magnates and wives in feathered hats had all paid £3 each – One woman fainted and another was sick – otherwise a great success.

Far more enjoyable was the premiere of the film *Young Winston*, which Anita attended wearing the tiara that had once belonged to Mrs Fitzherbert. Since Bill was at sea, Leonie accepted the Alec Rose trophy for 'the best individual sailing achievement' on his behalf. Desmond could always be relied upon to cast a shadow. At the end of 1972 he advised his nephew to have a very serious talk with Anita about resigning his commission:

> The name of the British Army in Ireland now stinks to high Heaven ... you must seriously consider the family tradition of nationalism, anti unionism and putting Ireland first above everything. I am sure you will come to the right decision and be very glad that you have done so.

Desmond then described taking part in a bit of 'subversive skulduggery against British helicopter crews.' He would have been superhuman not to have relished the crushing of Anita's dream of Tarka peaceably and profitably farming at Glaslough.

The problems at the estate were endless. Anita to Betsan: 'Things getting for ever worse in the North and Desmond glooming and threatening to sell out if Jack does not support him! I have procured the farm and 300 acres for Tarka – price of BAD Irish land has risen from £30 an acre to £500 in TEN years!'

Anita had begun a new book: a biography of the round-the-world yachtsman Francis Chichester, who had died in 1972, for which she demanded an immediate contract 'because', she wrote to Harold Harris, 'I've seen a beautiful 3 year old ... and the price is £600 – more than I've ever paid for a horse ¾ bred – and her name is to be Daisy Warwick.' Rather fitting to name a beautiful horse after a king's high-stepping mistress. Doubleday, Anita's American publisher, changed the title 'Edwardians in Love' to 'The Marlborough House Set'. In a press release, they claimed: 'Anita Leslie is a delightfully racy old girl who got many of her boudoir anecdotes from her great-aunts and uncles.' In the spring, the delightfully racy old girl hurried back from her American promotional tour for Bill's long-delayed homecoming. She collected Leonie in London and then they waited in Plymouth for five foggy days – Anita with a temperature of 102 – for Bill's eventual emergence through the mist. 'What a moment though when he DID arrive.'

During his last perilous voyage, sea water had affected Bill's circulation, making the skin on his hands peel off. He decided to sell his boat and *Galway Blazer ll* was displayed at the Boat Show in London and sold to Peter Crowther, the landlord of a pub in Devon. During the show an IRA bomb demolished the £18,000 cruiser on the adjoining stand but missed Bill and his boat. 'Really,' Anita wrote to Betsan, 'the last straw to be wrecked at Earl's Court after rounding the HORN!!' Bill invested the money from the sale in buying cattle and started to write *Capsize*, about his 1968 round-the-world attempt. He and Anita were becoming well-known as a bookish couple and, in January 1974, appeared on RTÉ television, discussing their works in progress. Literary pairings were fashionable: the married novelists Elizabeth Jane Howard and Kingsley Amis appeared in advertisements for Sanderson wallpaper.

Anita Burgh, Rose Gardner's former daughter-in-law, wrote to Anita (Leslie) that Rose had collapsed after some kind of overdose, either drink or drugs. The older Anita wrote back to the younger one regretfully:

> I am so sorry that she turned against me when, thoughtlessly I now see – I told her to go back to Peter and Fleur and Bahamas – she resented any advice – it broke the wonderful link between us … I wonder if I had acted differently, might she have been different now.

Rose had been the one person to whom Anita could be 'as awful as I feel like'. After they stopped writing to each other, Anita kept her miseries to herself, and her letters to other correspondents, although interesting, lack the rawness of those to her erstwhile closest friend. It appears to have been a one-sided correspondence, a circumstance that the American writer Jill Lepore describes as 'a house without windows, a left shoe, a pair of spectacles smashed'. Of Rose's infrequent letters to Anita, one that survived is written on both sides of flimsy paper and is indecipherable, suggesting that its writer's heart wasn't in it. So perhaps the loss of Rose's letters isn't significant.

Anita went back to the US in May 1974 in the aftermath of the Watergate scandal and President Nixon's resignation. She toured from coast to coast and gave sixteen lectures in Washington. In an undated letter to Tarka, she wrote: 'They [Americans] seem to regard their president's dishonesty as a major disaster when they ought to be thankful it has shown up the tendency and likelihood of such doings under their SYSTEM!' Back home at Oranmore, so that Bill could finish his book, she took on the job of reselling the cattle, a gloomy task since a wet winter followed by drought had depressed prices. She grumbled about Agnes, who was now living with the eminent architectural historian Maurice Craig, because Agnes, bewilderingly, called herself Mrs Craig in Dublin and Mrs Leslie at Glaslough: 'No one knows or cares who she marries – they just wish she'd stop masquerading.'

What should have been the highlight of the year was the Independent Television production of *The Lives and Loves of Jennie Churchill*, seven one-hour episodes aired to coincide with the centenary of Winston's birth. Anita's *Jennie* was reprinted to take advantage of the television series and sold 25,000 copies. But at the same time, Collins and Independent Television Productions published a book called *Jennie, Lady Randolph Churchill: A Portrait with Letters*, by Julian Mitchell, who scripted the series, and Peregrine Churchill. 'Trying to steal MY sales and pronounce itself as the story of her life,' Anita wrote furiously to Jack. But it was her fault. She had sold the TV rights of *Jennie* to Thames Television for £450 without demanding an acknowledgment. She blamed her publisher: 'Dear Harold, I think nothing of your mouse-sized advert for Jennie while Collins gives 4" x 2" to their hoax, written to accompany the TV series.' She decided to sue the rival publisher for 'passing off' her book; meanwhile she advised friends and relations 'to ask for MY Jennie in bookshops and place it well IN FRONT of any other Jennie they may have been foolish enough to STOCK!'

She approved of most of the casting for the television series, especially Barbara Parkins as Leonie, but thought Lee Remick, in the title role, 'a bit bouncy American rather than a smouldering panther'. In America Remick won a Golden Globe award for Best Actress in a Television Drama and, in the UK a BAFTA award, again for Best Actress. The period details in the series met Anita's tests for accuracy, unlike some episodes of *Upstairs, Downstairs*, where Anita spotted a dinner gong in a London house, when they were only used in the country, and debutantes shimmering with jewels instead of the only permissible adornment of a seed pearl necklace.

In September 1974 Xandra Roche's small son, Standish, died in an accident. Anita believed in a very specific sort of afterlife, where the dead lived in a parallel universe, ageing in the same way as they would on earth. Trying to console Xandra, she wrote:

> If you keep Standish's room and things you MUST NOT FREEZE him in your memory as a little boy – he is a person. Of course one thinks of one's fled children in the form you were accustomed to SEE them in – but that is so PAINFUL – and they are changing all the time just as you are.

In October, a general election saw the return of Harold Wilson's Labour government. Anita wrote to Jack that her friend the Marquis of Duoro, heir to the Duke of Wellington, failed to get elected: 'It's no help to be a duke's son these days – in fact it's almost a handicap – people won't use you because you are CLASS-STAMPED.' Then, bewilderingly: 'I feel that Tarka being a non-intellectual is wringing the best out of what is left to enjoy.' The Marquess's political ambitions may have been stymied because of his class, although he later became an MEP, but the seat he stood for in 1974 as the Conservative candidate was Islington North, which had returned a Labour MP in every election since 1937. Even had the Marquess not been an Old Etonian, married to a daughter of a Prussian prince, there was little chance of his being elected in that particular inner-city seat.

The non-intellectual Tarka, now based in London, was certainly wringing the best out of life. He was now a captain of the Queen's Life Guard, based at Hyde Park Barracks and in charge of training thirty-two black horses to take part in parades. On her son's first day of duty, Anita wrote to him: 'It's really so romantic and UNmodern to trot past your mother's balcony so she can peep over in a nightdress and see you! SUCH a gorgeous uniform you never saw ... and when I think of that little boy in Oranmore village!' Later, when Anita was back in Oranmore, Tarka rang her to say that he had ridden in the Queen's procession at the Opening of Parliament 'and done all his sword salutes right'. In a rare diary entry, she wrote: 'I miss the clatter of his troop in their early morning exercise around Cleveland Square.'

The latest project at Glaslough, following on the failed plans for a hotel and golf course, was for Helen to set up an equestrian centre and a cross-country course of forty kilometres (twenty-five miles) of different rides containing 200 varied fences. Anita predicted another failure. To Tarka: 'I gave Peter Desmond's last letter which he said was too crazy for comment – All about these 'RIDES' and so AIRY-FAIRY.' But, although violence in the North was worsening and Glaslough, with a wall which formed part of the border, was not ideally placed to attract visitors, the equestrian centre was a success. Desmond, chronically short of money, sold the centre in 1984 but his daughter Sammy managed to buy it back in 2004.

By the end of 1974 Anita had received a £2500 advance from Hutchinson for a biography of her cousin Clare Sheridan and had begun her lawsuit against Thames Television. Her children were thriving; Tarka in the army and Leonie, now twenty-three, about to complete her three-year graphic art design course and emerge with a BA degree. In her diary, Anita wrote: 'Nothing in my own life seems to matter except the production of these two so different — immensely dear and interesting children.'

23
Deaths and Entrances

At the beginning of 1975 Anita's lawyers, Rubinstein, Nash & Co, wrote to EMI's legal department, seeking compensation for the 'passing off' of the Thames TV tie-in book, *Jennie, Lady Randolph Churchill*, an action that dragged on for another two years. Meanwhile, both Bill and Anita had new books to publicize, *Adventures in Depth* (Bill) and *Francis Chichester* (Anita), and appeared together on *The Late Late Show*, one of Ireland's most popular television programmes.

In April Peter Wilson died of lung cancer at Oranmore. Anita to Belsan: 'Only ONE day in bed and one hour of desperate illness. 40 years of pipe smoking did it.' Since Peter had wanted to be cremated, which was almost impossible in the Republic of Ireland, his body was flown to Belfast in a private plane. A week later there was a memorial service at the Collegiate Church of St Nicholas in Galway, attended by two hundred countrymen and women, many of whom had never before seen the inside of a Protestant church. Tarka read the lesson. Soon afterwards Prim, Peter's widow, sold Rocklands at a very profitable £35,000 and left Ireland. Anita was preparing herself for another death. To Betsan: 'Rose is dying slowly in Paris ... what a waste of beauty and gifts.' Rose lingered on until 1981, by which time Anita thought she had been dead for years.

Francis Chichester was published in the summer. The blurb read:

> Anita Leslie is the perfect choice as a biographer of Sir Francis Chichester. She knew him, is a close friend of his widow, and has first-hand acquaintance with the sailing background, as she is married to Commander Bill King, the well-known solo sailor.

Sir Francis was a national hero, being the first person to have sailed around the world single-handed, from west to east; a feat achieved in late middle age and when he was in poor health. Anita's writing was never at its best when she strayed too far from the Glaslough attics with their tiaras and parasols, and the Leslie family history revealed in letters from lovers and royal patrons. Her two favourite words, 'amusing' and 'delicious', could not be applied to Sir Francis, whose life, until his sea voyages made him heroic, had been grim. Jonathan Raban in an essay on Sir Francis (in *Driving Home: An American Journey*, Pantheon 2011) considered that he was bonkers, not a word that Anita would have used. It was while she was writing the book that Bill lost contact while at sea, which made describing the perils of solo sailing painful.

Graham Lord reviewed the book unfavourably in the *Sunday Express*: 'Her [Anita's] stodgy style – interrupted by curiously girlish exclamations – suggests that she was as much at sea in writing about her subject as was Sir Francis in his succession of Gypsy Moth boats.' In the *Guardian*, William Golding praised Sir Francis, while scarcely mentioning the book, except to ask whether, since he was a superb self-publicist, 'there is any point in the publication of a biography'. But there was: soon after publication, *Francis Chichester* reached number two in the UK bestseller list. The English like stories about plucky underdogs who succeed against the odds. Anita gave a winsome interview to *The Liverpool Post*, which described her as slim and elegant with pale, ice-blue eyes and, approvingly, as 'not being at all adventurous herself'; the newspaper's research had obviously not included reading *Train to Nowhere*, with its tales of front-line war service.

In October Anita was back on the American lecture circuit. Wherever she went on the ten-week tour, interviewers quizzed her on Ralph Martin's speculations: 'Winston's conception, John's father and when Lord R caught syphilis.' She wrote to Clodagh Roden: 'In Texas the Sunday paper had just had a quiz "Were both Lady Randolph Churchill's children illegitimate" (on the basis I suppose of were they legally so if Martin's insinuations were correct).' When interviewed, Anita offered her usual refutations: the intense chaperonage of unmarried girls, the unlikelihood of Jennie taking as a lover the much older John Strange Jocelyn and her happy marriage.

The violence in the North had spread to the Republic of Ireland. On 12 February 1976, Frank Stagg, a member of the IRA, after enduring a sixty-two-day hunger strike, died in Wakefield prison in West Yorkshire and was repatriated to his native Mayo for burial. The Irish government directed the flight carrying Stagg's remains to Shannon, then he was buried in his family plot at Ballina. To stop the IRA disinterring the body and reburying it in a republican plot, the grave was covered with concrete. Anita to Jack:

> The soldiers had a rough time on Sunday controlling mob of 7000 at Frank Stagg's funeral – 6 gardai in hospital and … if they had not dispersed the Londonderry Derry [sic] IRA who are the real gangsters – with gas and rubber bullets early on they might have had to open fire – such a nightmare and infinitely worse each year – The whole generation which was 7 to 14 when the troubles started now 14 – 21 – armed hooligans.

The Gardaí kept watch on the concreted grave for six months. It became a focal point for violence. When protesters mobbed the Land Rover containing the guards' lunchtime sandwiches and threw the food on the ground, shouting 'Free State bastards', they were severely treated. Anita to Jack: 'You can imagine how furious soldiers [sic] are when deprived of their GRUB!! … The country seems delighted with the STRONG STAND made by the Govt. The IRA is illegal and they just WON'T allow political – demonstration – funerals.' In November republicans tunnelled under the concrete and removed and reburied the body. The violence was getting even closer to home. Mollie Cusack Smith, hunting at Westport, County Mayo, 'cancelled the meet so as not to get involved'.

On the hottest day of that very hot summer, 3 July, Tarka married Jane Forbes, the daughter of a baronet. The bride's wedding dress had belonged to Tarka's great-grandmother, Leonie; her veil was Marjorie's and her tiara the one which had been Mrs Fitzherbert's. Jack, brought to the church in Roy Miles' air-conditioned Rolls Royce, remarked that 'it was a lovely cool day for a wedding'. Roy himself was rather put out. Anita had asked him not to wear a morning coat since Bill didn't own one and Roy, always superbly dressed, regretted not being properly attired. The honeymoon was spent in Italy, after which Tarka retired from his regiment and began an estate management course at the Royal Agricultural College in Cirencester.

On the last day of that drought-ridden July, Comtesse Mary Margaret Motley de Reneville, formerly Margaret Sheridan, died in Biarritz. She had become horribly racist, telling Seymour the year before she died that London had become a 'nigger ridden paradise' and that she never wished to set foot there again. Margaret had led an unhappy life, unable to marry the man she loved because her husband wouldn't give her a divorce, and was inclined to drink too much. Anita was now writing a biography of Margaret's mother, Clare, while, at the same time, buying a larger flat at number 20 Cleveland Square, which was put in Tarka's name. A visit to Glaslough in August was an escape from the London heat. To Xandra: 'Strange to arrive in the silence and peace here for dinner. Ireland is GREEN – there's never been MORE grass for cattle – and MUCH cooler.' She was astounded by the security measures for the Belfast flight,

> everything taken off one and put into plastic bags – so it was 1 hour getting on – 55 min flight – and 1 hour getting off – queueing for plastic bags etc. Desmond was waiting for me behind barricades and soldiers with tommy guns covered one's descent from plane – and went in with the cleaner-gang after! Road blocks – barbed wire entanglements etc must make it the most 'secure' port in Europe.

Tarka was now a married man but Anita went on micromanaging his life and that of his new wife. She suggested that Jane wear a tie-belt on her black pyjamas and questioned Tarka about his finances: 'On Monday I checked all our accounts and you had an overdraft of £465 ... how come you did not know? Don't they send you a monthly account?' She instructed him on buying carpets and, when he told her that he was going to the Royal Ballet, reminded him: 'Don't forget how I opened your eyes to its delights as a little boy, taking you to see Margot Fonteyn.'

Towards the end of the year Anita was invited by the Countess of Rosse, Lord Snowden's mother, to lunch at her London house in Stafford Terrace, Kensington. The other guests were the Queen Mother and the writer Harold Acton. Anita described the occasion to Xandra:

> Q.M in huge mauve picture hat ostrich-plume bedecked (She doesn't mind others being drab – happily as all my clothes dumped in plastic bags and unprocurable). Conversation about Italian sculpture and 'beautiful things' rather than mugging and transvestites! And charming remark from Her Majesty about 'my splendid son-in-law Tony who fights so hard to preserve lovely old buildings'. I wondered for an instant who 'the splendid s-in-law' was!!

It was charming of Her Majesty to praise her hostess's son while he was in the process of getting divorced from her own daughter. Earlier in the year, Anita had marked the end of the Snowden marriage in her diary: 'Queen and Qu Mum upset and Margaret, according to her mother-in-law, "a pathetic child clamouring for love", having terrible nerve fits and worrying her sister to death.'

Cousin Clare: The Tempestuous Career of Clare Sheridan, dedicated 'To Margaret in memory of the golden years', was published in November. Reviewing it in *The Financial Times*, Francis King wrote: 'It is true that in real life people often talk as though they were characters in second-rate fiction; but when so many conversations are given verbatim one would like to know their derivation.' Anita was never averse to inventing scenes and conversations but in the case of *Cousin Clare*, she may have been relying on her excellent memory to record what her outlandish cousin had told her over all the years of their close friendship: details of her affair with Charlie Chaplin and a quarrelsome *tête-à-tête* with an awestruck Mussolini. As newspaper columnists say, 'You couldn't make it up.' As usual, Anita saw her biographical subject through rose-tinted spectacles. Just as Jennie Churchill, a magnificent *poule de luxe*, was presented as a winsome ingenue and the calculating and crafty Maria Fitzherbert as stoically pious, the steely, ambitious sculptor Clare Sheridan was given a ditzy, romantic makeover. Anita's Wilfred Sheridan, tragically killed in the

Great War, is adored by his wife, whereas Clare's own view of her short marriage, as expressed in her published diary, *Mayfair to Moscow* (1921), is more acerbic: 'When it dawned on me that dead clay could be brought to life – a husband who was rather clairvoyant, and doubtless had visions of a neglected home, said "no" – and the flame was suppressed into a rather sullen domesticity.' Anita doesn't quote Clare's stated beliefs that 'Work alone brings happiness and the desire to achieve or to attain is the only satisfaction,' and that 'There are many disappointments in life but the greatest of all are one's children.'

In her autobiography, *Morning Glory*, Clare's daughter Margaret Sheridan has Clare admit that 'she was descended on the one hand from Red Indians, on the other from the Obrenovitches through King Milan of Serbia'. Anita ignored this admission of Clare's paternity; the exiled Balkan king is merely Clara Frewen's 'beau, or in the parlance of the time a cavalier attendant', a sender of daily gardenias and sigher of sighs. Clara accepted him and his lavish gifts because, Anita wrote, 'She had a touch of her mother's snobbism and liked having a Majesty in tow.' *Cousin Clare* and Bill's *Adventure in Depth* were launched as part of Irish Book Week at the new Galway City Museum, which had once been Clare's house and studio. 'People who had known her came in tears of emotion,' Anita wrote to Xandra. The launch, hosted by O'Gormans bookshop, helped the sales of both books. Desmond and Helen visited Oranmore around this time and Anita told Jack, rather triumphantly, that she'd put them in two small, separate rooms.

By the time Anita was able to move into the new London flat in January 1976, she had lost track of several of her possessions, which Tarka was sent out to retrieve:

> Sheila [Chichester] urgently wants you to take away as soon as possible the electric cooker or whatever you left in the cupboard downstairs. Can you remember what you left? ... If you see Patsy [Jellicoe] rescue my red dressing gown and the cherub heads – I think that's all I left with her if you took the pictures and the RED WINE and 2 bottles of champagne!

Perhaps because of all this shifting of household goods, Tarka's back ached. His mother advised: 'So send Mrs A [a very alternative practitioner] a few HAIRS plucked from your head and a spot of your blood on blotting paper

(Jane must have a needle!!?)' At Oranmore, windows blew out, boilers broke down: 'I don't think we DARE let Gerry paint the kitchen while water is pouring through walls from the OUTSIDE.' At Glaslough, bars were stolen off the tractor. Tarka's attempts to help weren't appreciated: 'You hung the garden gate so I could neither get IN or OUT.'

Disagreements with Desmond now centred on rights of way and farm gates. Anita drafted a letter to her brother, supposedly written by Tarka: 'And I would not be prepared to in any way improve the road itself or create foundations.' It didn't seem a very opportune time for Tarka and Jane to move to the violent province but Anita, who could never bear too much reality, urged them to take over the servants' wing at Castle Leslie: 'It could be a most amusing habitation – compact and heatable.' She had become the mother-in-law from hell, writing to Jane: 'I want you to enjoy doing up the [London] flat in your own way and only make these suggestions for economy,' before going on to dictate every aspect of the redecoration, down to the colour of the curtains.

That winter, Sir Alfred and Lady Beit gave their last party at Russborough House, County Wicklow before gifting the house and their six-million-pound art collection to the State. The Beits had bought the Palladian house, designed by Richard Cassels and described by the historian Mark Bence Jones as the most beautiful house in Ireland, in 1952. In 1974 the IRA had raided the house, stolen nineteen valuable paintings and viciously assaulted the Beits, leaving them tied up and gagged. Even after the shaken owners left Russborough, it continued to be burgled, both in 1986 and 2001. After attending the Beits' last party with Bill, Anita wrote to Xandra:

> One realises we are living through a 20 year so-far-bloodless revolution the whole pattern of life changing every year – and what matters amidst the lashing waves is to keep one's health, one's balance and one's own inner calm, – and that is all that has ever mattered even in times of steady security (actually there never has been such a thing – the long Victorian security ended in 2 destructive wars, because all the statesmen talked so elegantly at dinner parties they LOST THEIR eye for DANGER).

Anita's American book tour had become an annual and profitable fixture, at five hundred dollars a lecture plus travel costs. When she returned from the 1977 tour in May, she wrote Seymour a gossipy, eight-page letter, in which she described having tea with the 95-year-old Alice Roosevelt, daughter of Theodore, 'in the same dark Washington mansion hung with Teddy's lion skins that I first visited aged 3!' Mrs Longworth thought the recently elected President Jimmy Carter silly. Anita agreed; she loathed Mr Carter's 'false cosiness ... But a SILLY President of the USA is quite terrifying.' Another interesting encounter: 'Janet Auchincloss, mother of Jackie Kennedy, came to dinner – such a beautiful woman and sweet but so dreamy one wondered if she was gaga with tranquillisers!' It's possible that Mrs Auchincloss was already suffering from the Alzheimer's disease that contributed to her death in 1989. Dinner at the house of a rich biblio-phile, Mrs Hyde, 'started as always in USA with dreadful icy strong drinks ... (I've learnt to totally abstain)'. After dinner, 'Mrs Hyde, fluttering in chiffon, proudly announced ONLY SANKA would be served NO coffee – .' Without the boost of caffeine many of the guests dozed off during a two-hour performance of extracts from Mrs Thrale's journal but Anita 'adored every moment ... how marvellously Americans get up things – how enthu-siastically they collect and how generously they DONATE to colleges and suchlike'. With money from the lecture tour, Anita paid Seymour £800 for a clock that had been in the family for a long time, which she gave to Tarka.

Anita to Xandra, 12 May 1977: 'Now our news is ALL Leonie!' Leonie had, for a long time, been suffering from a chronic pain in her wrist, which doctors in London had pronounced incurable. But that Easter, the Oranmore doctor, Joe Kelly, had X-rayed the wrist from a different angle and discovered what was wrong. After a course of acupuncture and massage, a healthy, rested Leonie was able to take charge of her life again. She got a new haircut – 'So becoming and the first time for years!', Anita told Xandra – and decided to marry Alec Finn:

> He is 33 and very nice and suits her artistic temperament ... of the great Finn clan from west coast ... Has a music group which tours and sells records of Irish traditional not POP ... His very artistic nature-loving temperament suits her and she is happy with him. What else matters!

Alec's 'music group' was the internationally renowned De Dannan, which had been formed in 1973 in Hughes' pub in Spiddal, near Galway and would go on to perform at both the Royal Albert Hall in London and Carnegie Hall in New York. Alec, a founder member, played the bouzouki. On 2 July at Oranmore, the first Leonie's wedding dress and the Fitzherbert tiara got another airing. Anita was due an advance on her next book and David Roberts, Hutchinson's managing director, told the accounts department: 'Could you please rush the cheque off to Anita Leslie. It is to pay for her daughter's wedding.'

A letter from Anita to Kathleen Abercorn on 3 September ends ominously: 'I shall just concentrate on Tarka and getting him to Mollie's meets.' Tarka had completed the estate management course and, during the summer, had moved into Dawson's Lodge at Glaslough, but not for very long, once he discovered its closeness to the village sewerage plant. Jane stayed in England, where she studied at art college in Bristol and Tarka started to convert the old stables at Glaslough into a flat, where he and Jane might live one day. But, for the present, Jane was in England and Anita began to plan a new career for her son: huntsman for Mollie Cusack Smith, with whom he had hunted since he was six years old. Anita to Kath, from Oranmore: 'Tarka is practising his HORN in the kitchen – although not musical he is catching Mollie's notes – He fell in a ditch and lost the hounds first day – Mollie follows by car berating him – a little daunting for a new huntsman.' Although Tarka loved hunting as much as Anita did, he managed to resist the temptation to move back to Oranmore.

Trying to be constantly in control was getting too much for Anita. She wrote to Jack: 'I suddenly feel so old and tired – all I want is one warm light room in which to write my books, in silence. Let the young ones get excited over new doors and windows – it's their turn now to plan and struggle.' As if she would ever be able to stop planning and struggling.

24
No Chance of a
Warm Light Room

Madame Tussaud Waxworker Extraordinary was the only book that Anita wrote just to make money and she probably wouldn't have agreed to write it if Tarka hadn't needed a new car. The book was sponsored by Madame Tussaud's Limited and, under that organization's agreement with Hutchinson, Anita was given a £4000 advance plus £500 for every thousand copies sold, as well as 25 per cent of the revenues from subsidiary rights. The downside of this deal was that the book was to be co-authored with Lady Pauline Chapman, archivist and researcher at Madame Tussaud's, who had spent twelve years researching the life of Marie Tussaud, *née* Grosholz (1761–1850), referred to by Anita as 'the odious subject'.

For a biographer who could always find redeeming features in her subjects, however lecherous (Leonard Jerome), financially idiotic (Moreton Frewen), or promiscuous (Jennie Churchill), Marie presented a challenge. Anita wrote furiously to Harold Harris:

I must ask if a TRUTHFUL biographical representation is desired. (If I were writing for Hutchinson I'd lash out!) or just a nice readable story for school children. Is one permitted to say anything not-all-that-endearing about Mme. T? For instance when the lovely Princesse de Lamballe whom she had known was cut to pieces in prison and her head brought to Marie to model do I tell the TRUTH – that her genitals were mounted on a pike and also paraded through the streets? And even less savoury episodes? You realise she actually did a death mask of the King's severed head (he had been a kindly friend to her for 8 years). And there is not a word to explain her callousness – TERROR? Pressure from her uncle who sounds to me an absolute bastard? The cold objectivity of an artist trained only to 'see' the physical features of people? This is a GUIDE BOOK. I don't leave out what offends. But tell me!

The sickening episode of the paraded genitals made it into print along with other horrors of the French Revolution. But it wasn't Anita's style to present anyone as completely black-hearted, so we have: 'What could she [Marie] have felt as she tinted the hair and painted the wax to exact colourings of the face she had known so well?' This soft approach was all Anita's doing. Pauline Chapman rather admired 'the odious subject' for not letting sentiment stand in her way. Anguished letters from Oranmore were sent to Hutchinson. From Anita to David Roberts, 14 January 1978:

She [Lady Chapman] is certain that Marie was NOT scared of handling the guillotined heads of people she knew well!! I feel that any human being must have been cut to the quick – quite different to handling bits of body of strangers! ... Lady Chapman thinks of her [Marie] as 'the first career woman' but aren't we all rather tired of the avalanche of career women.

And to Harold Harris:

I can't do more with it. As I rewrite – Antoinette and the king become more and more interesting and tragic and Marie Grosholtz a more dismal little bore obsessed with waxworks! ... Being a successful determined business-woman does not make Marie Tussaud interesting!!

Anita objected to Pauline Chapman's preferred title, 'Madame Tussaud – History Maker'. *Waxworker Extraordinary* was substituted but in nearly every other way Lady Chapman's view prevailed: that Marie was an out-and-out professional, concerned only in doing a great job of work, even when her studio was awash with aristocratic blood. The jacket flap sets the tone: 'Shrewd and independent, she [Marie] ranks among the first great career women of modern times, for she built up her business unaided in a man's world.' The book admiringly mentions that Marie seems to have taken no holidays and that 'She deserved her fortune. She had worked every yard of the way.' She was also everything that Anita most despised – a solemn, ambitious workhorse, unlike the feckless aristocrats who lived for pleasure and whom Anita loved for their gaiety, extravagance and wit. But hard-working career women, shouldering their way into a man's world, were currently fascinating: in 1975 Margaret Thatcher had become the first woman to be elected as leader of the opposition and was soon dubbed 'The Iron Lady' by the Russians. The book was an unhappy collaboration, which was perhaps why the authors' correction bill came to £222. One error survived: Marie settled in Baker Street, 'surely next door to Sherlock Holmes'.

The name of Madame Tussaud was internationally famous, so the book was reviewed everywhere, not always kindly, from *The Times Literary Supplement* to *Tit-Bits*. Some reviewers retold the Tussaud story, hardly mentioning the book, while others hurled brickbats. In *British Book News*, 1 January 1979, Carole Angier wrote: ' ... alas, the story is in the "must have been" genre of biography ... it is marred by careless writing and psychological speculation'. This upset Lady Chapman but Geoffrey Chester of Hutchinson reassured her: 'Carole Angier's reservations are at once understandable and "unfair". Sophisticated reviewers may well find the speculations and asides irritating, but they bring the heroine alive for the general reader, which is precisely what was intended.' Other reviewers were as dismissive as Carole Angier. Brian Cleeve in the *Irish Sunday Press*, 1 November 1978: 'They tell us that she "shuddered" or that she was "fairly shaken" and so on. But how do they know?' In *Books & Bookmen*, November 1978, Maurice Richardson predicted snootily, 'It ought to sell like a shilling barrel of oysters.' Although the book didn't find an American publisher, when Anita accepted an invitation in 1980 to speak to a women's club in Chicago, that 'dismal little bore' Marie Tussaud was what her audience most wanted to hear about.

The lawsuit against Thames Television was settled in Anita's favour on 11 January 1978. She was awarded £1100 but, over the five-year dispute, had accrued solicitors' fees of £1800. 'So I won NOTHING – lost a little – but moral victory!' Anita wrote to Jack and she gave Seymour £100 out of her non-existent winnings. This wasn't the whole story. I am indebted to Julian Mitchell, who wrote the book linked to the television series and found himself involved with a litigious Anita. He allowed me to see his diary entries relating to the lawsuit and in 2013 told me, 'I can still feel very angry at the trouble she [Anita] caused me.' While Julian was writing his book, Anita promised to let him see some family letters if she could use a photograph of Lee Remick on the cover of the newly reissued paperback of her own *Jennie* – an impossible request to grant and one that would have caused confusion between the two titles, which was the very situation that Anita claimed she was trying to avoid. Before writs started to fly, Anita was friendly enough. Julian's diary entry for 24 May 1974: 'Tues: dinner at Anita's ... usual raw meat to eat. Anita is so thin, I can't see how she manages to live at all, she looks so brittle.' But by the end of the year, they were no longer on speaking terms, since Anita had resorted to the law, seeking compensation for the 'passing-off' of the tie-in book. A furious diary entry from Julian on 4 January 1975:

> I had to go through all the letters again – Anita's claiming she made it a condition of letting us use the letters that the book was to be called A Portrait with Letters, which is simply untrue ... I have two letters and a postcard from her commenting on the book, and two letters from old Seymour, neither mentioning the title – it's all so mean and stupid, when her book has benefited hugely from the series.

And on 20 October: 'Apparently her claim is based entirely on letters from titled people in castles who got our book instead of hers. Why didn't they buy it before, I want to know.' Anita reduced her demands to complaining only about the rival book's jacket and even apologized to Julian, who remained unmollified.

Anita claimed to want nothing more than a warm, light, quiet room in which to write but, since she gave keys to the London flat to several friends and relations and let everyone know when she was in town,

Cleveland Square was never going to provide comfortable solitude. In June she wrote to her stepmother, Iris, urging her to use the flat whenever she liked: 'I feel the important thing about the flat is availability.' Desmond was about to stay there for one night and so was Leonie, on her way back from Germany where De Danann was touring. Agnes was a regular visitor. Her career was now thriving and she was part of a group called The Radiators, described in *The New Yorker*, when it broke up after thirty-three years, as 'one of the world's greatest bar bands'.

From Oranmore, Anita wrote often to Roy Miles. In 1978 she described the Graham Sutherland portrait of Winston, painted in 1954, commissioned by both Houses of Parliament to mark Winston's eightieth birthday and subsequently destroyed by Clemmie because of its unflattering candour: 'If only Clemmie had left it hidden for 50 years for some other generation to judge – but she cared only for Winston and his moods – that was why she was such a wonderful wife.' Anita and Bill had seen the portrait before its destruction and thought it brilliant: 'Sutherland ... paints the actual psyche – and when a man is old and has lived deeply it isn't the wrinkles and jowliness you see – it is his mind.'

She was cross that Leonie, who was teaching at art college in Galway – 'one day a week only and it is quite enough for her' – had been asked to become a full-time etching 'professor', something that sounded too much like a career woman for Anita's tastes: 'There is no reason why she should not work away with her press for pleasure and because she is creative.' In her letters to Roy, Anita sounds lonely. Oranmore was always kept ready for Tarka to hunt there but, when her son could get away from farming at Glaslough, he went to England to be with his wife. Leonie was often on tour with Alec and Bill went skiing at Kitzbuhel as often as he could. 'So,' Anita wrote, 'all I have to arrange is meals and walks for the dogs.' She was dismissive of the television series on Lily Langtry: 'The LACK of formality in public renders flat the informality in private.'

In spite of her dislike of professional women, Anita admired Margaret Thatcher, although she did not think that she would ever become prime minister, since Penelope Aitken, mother of the Conservative MP Jonathan, had told her that Mrs Thatcher's family thought her health too delicate to stand the pressures of the job. On 28 March 1979 Mrs Thatcher brought a vote of no confidence in James Callaghan's Labour government before the House of Commons. The Government was defeated by one vote – 311 votes to 310 – in what the BBC called, 'one of the most dramatic nights in Westminster history.' Anita was delighted that it was Northern Ireland's SDLP (Social Democratic and Labour Party) MP, Gerry Fitt, whose abstention brought down the unpopular government, which was held to blame for a series of strikes and petrol shortages known as 'The Winter of Discontent'. Anita to Jack: 'It's just like the old days when Irish Nationalists controlled the balance.' Two days later, Airey Neave, the Shadow Northern Ireland Secretary, was killed when a car bomb planted by the Irish National Liberation Army exploded under his Vauxhall Cavalier as he was leaving the House of Commons car park. More violence was expected during the election on 3 May but the day passed peacefully enough. The Conservatives won with a 43-seat majority, making Margaret Thatcher the first British female head of government. Far from being in delicate health, she bloomed robustly and claimed to need only four hours sleep a night.

Anita read the recently published *Irish Country Houses* by Mark Bence-Jones, an Anglo-Irishman after her own heart of whom, on his death in 2010, an obituarist wrote: 'His admiration for the upper classes and grand houses made him seem a man born in the wrong century.' Of the book, Anita wrote to Jack:

> WHAT a plethora of beautiful country houses covered this land but all within demesne walls with the hungry Irish outside – A cruel history unforgotten and instead of pride in the wondrous ruins hatred remains and they all think their hideous bungalows 'lovely'.

At one impressive Irish country estate, Glaslough, the equestrian centre, in spite of its situation on the border, was becoming increasingly popular with European visitors, who enjoyed long cross-country rides, pike fishing on the lake and the superb scenery as well as the weekly drinks parties and barbecues hosted by Desmond and Helen. Guests didn't seem to mind that the house itself was grubby and dilapidated but Jack, who now spent much of the year at Castle Leslie, did. He complained to Iris that 'the house in general has another year's dirt on top of last year's and the windows are still unwashed', but the estate was engaging enough to win, in 1979, a tourism award 'For the best individual effort'.

There were ongoing rows with Tarka over access rights, which some-times stymied Desmond's plans to sell some of his holdings to developers. Under Irish law, Desmond was legally married to Agnes and Helen had no right of inheritance, which, Desmond explained to Tarka, was the reason he had to sell his assets. Anita to Jack: 'Tarka got out his CRYING handerchief.' She had poured money into Glaslough on her son's behalf, selling all of her aunt Anne's jewellery, except for one emerald ring, but Desmond always needed more. Anita to Jack:

> If only I had not made over the estate to Desmond 19 years ago the company would own 1000 acres still — worth £2000 an acre — and we would all be millionaires! But the pressure of family feeling that Desmond and his sons ought to own the family home and Bill's exhausted disgust at trying to deal with Desmond made me take an unwise decision. I felt it in my bones it would be the end of the place and it very nearly has been. BUT I COULD NOT PROVE IT in advance.

Towards the end of 1979 Anita wanted a month by herself in London so that she could finish the first volume of her autobiography, but there were visits from Agnes, now billed as 'The German cabaret legend' and her pianist, who regarded Anita's flat as a convenient rehearsal room, and from Desmond, who, since Anita had given him a key, would arrive without warning. Anita to Iris: 'I'm suffering from fatigue.' She had been booked to give a lecture on Clare Sheridan to an American group staying at Renvyle in Connemara, but she lost her voice due to exhaustion. An icy winter had left Oranmore without fruit or vegetables and a substitute diet of tea, bread and marmalade was not nutritious. Anita was also helping to care for Leonie's first baby, Jessica, who, because of bungled birth proce-dures was brain-damaged. Margaret Glynn, who had looked after Anita's own children, now looked after this special child who brought Anita nothing but joy, perhaps the greatest she had ever known.

Although she was very tired, at the end of September, Anita, with Bill and Tarka, walked the nine miles from Oranmore to Ballybrit racecourse outside Galway to see Pope John Paul II during his three-day visit to

Ireland. Bishop Eamon Casey of Galway, who had organized the visit, and the popular singing priest Father Michael Cleary entertained the crowd of 280,000 until the Pope's helicopter zoomed out of the grey sky. Anita, sitting on a wall, waved her yellow and white scarf in tribute to the white and gold papal flag, then made the long walk home past deserted farms and cottages, whose owners were all at Ballybrit. Some years later, both Bishop Casey and Father Cleary were found to have fathered children with vulnerable women and Bishop Casey admitted to stealing money from the diocese to support his illicit family.

Tarka and Jane decided to move into the old stables at Glaslough for part of the year, although, as Anita told Iris, 'the gloom of farming in that rain is I can see getting Tarka's spirits down'. The London flat was proving to be a financial headache. Tarka was the nominal owner but it was Anita who paid the hefty bills for heating and maintenance and negotiated with the other leaseholders for a share of the freehold. She had given keys to so many people, most of whom didn't keep account of their phone bills, that she had to put locks on the telephone receivers. She also came to an arrangement with one of her neighbours, Joseph Corvo, a leading practitioner of a foot massage technique, Zone Therapy, and nicknamed 'Joe the Toe' by Bill, whereby, on Thursday mornings, he treated twenty patients in Anita's flat, in return for giving free treatments to Anita, her family and friends. Anita might as well have tried to write her books in Piccadilly Circus. At Oranmore she came down with a bout of bronchial asthma, her first attack in years.

At the end of January 1980, three armed men stole a car outside the Castle Leslie equestrian centre and used it to kidnap a Mr Foster, whom they had mistaken for a member of the British security forces. They treated him roughly, before realizing their mistake and freeing him. He was found on the road six hours later, counting himself lucky not to have been shot. Anita to Iris: 'Glaslough has now become horribly dangerous ... Life is one long worry – and over it all looms the likelihood of Word War III.' Lord Rossmore, at nearby Rossmore Castle, 'said that for the first time he felt the absolute hopelessness of trying to live there'. But Anita spent the summer at Glaslough, helping Tarka and Jane get in three thousand bales of wet hay with the help of just one farmhand, Jack Heaney. He had worked there for forty years, couldn't handle a tractor but could lift a bale of hay that Anita only managed to roll along the ground. Jack was entitled to the full agricultural wage of £50 a week, unlike the farmhands of Anita's childhood, who received less than £3. It annoyed her that other people's enterprises were profitable. To Harold Harris: 'The village hotel-pub (which I sold for £1,000) does a roaring trade outside our gates – A turn-over of £20,000 a week – wedding parties – Bar packed every night – and the 1840 Agents house is a Riding Club for continentals at £200 a week! It's a mad world.'

She wrote to Betsan that although Glaslough had 'become the most dangerous place in Europe ... five men were shot dead within a mile of the house last winter', Tarka and Jane loved farming there. She was, as she did so often, deluding herself. Tarka and Jane were expecting their first baby and wanted a safer haven than a home on the Irish border. Tarka did some creative cattle-dealing and bought Pentridge House, in the gentle Dorset countryside. Anita disapproved and showed her displeasure by misspelling the name of the house when she wrote to him. To everyone else she pretended that Pentridge House was a godsend. To her friend and neighbour Tim Gwyn Jones, owner of Lough Cutra castle in Gort: 'Thank heavens! Tarka/Jane have upsticked and bought a house near Salisbury that they fell in love with at first sight – only 10 acres – just right in size. Damnably expensive but just where they want to be.' She didn't visit Pentridge until 1985, when Tarka's daughter was born, commenting only: 'It's really rather nice.'

The police had advised Tarka and Jane to move out of the Glaslough stables, which they had lovingly restored, because the stable block was a ten-minute walk away from the farmyard and screened by wooded avenues. But it wasn't the IRA that torched this dangerously isolated homestead but the brand new flue for the wood stove. Irish wood is the worst possible fuel because it's usually damp and exudes resin, a cause of chimney fires. Malfunctioning heating appliances caused the Leslies more trouble than violent republicans. Fires became blocked, boilers broke down, resulting in icy rooms and passages. The owners of Big Houses spent much of their lives in a quest for warmth. In the early 1980s Desmond described most of Castle Leslie as being 'an energy-saving, environmentally-friendly deep freeze, which is why no one with any pulmonary troubles can survive there in winter'. Oranmore Castle wasn't much warmer. Anita, thin and inclined to bronchitis, would have sold her soul for central heating. She wrote to Tim Gwyn Jones that she would love a visit but although there was a log fire in the Great Hall and the south door had been permanently sealed she advised him to wear ski togs.

On 2 March 1981 a second wave of hunger strikes by republican prisoners began in Northern Ireland. Over the summer ten men starved themselves to death; one of them was Bobby Sands, who had been elected as the anti-H block candidate on 9 April. He died on 5 May after sixty-six days on hunger strike and ten thousand people attended his funeral. The hunger strikes were overshadowed by the engagement of the Prince of Wales to Lady Diana Spencer and their wedding on 29 July. At a ball given by the Welsh Guards to celebrate the royal engagement, Jane wore the Fitzherbert tiara, the last of the Leslies to do so before it was sold at auction in 2010. In May, just before the publication of her first volume of autobiography, *The Gilt and the Gingerbread*, in which the young Rose Vincent featured entertainingly, Anita was told of Rose's death. She had assumed that Rose had died years before, 'And yet', she wrote to Anita Burgh, 'to learn that she no longer breathed on this earth made the most extraordinary sensations arise'. Rose, once ethereally slender but grown plump in middle age, had spent her last years in Rome, moving from hotel to hotel with her borzoi dogs. Anita was horrified to hear this. That month, there was an ominous lull in IRA violence but many people, including Anita, expected renewed trouble in June, when London would be packed with tourists, in England for the royal wedding.

Jack had somehow convinced Tarka that he still had some ownership rights at Castle Leslie, infuriating Anita, who wrote to her son: 'Remember that Jack no longer owns anything at Glaslough ... Jack's assent to the selling of any object he does not actually own means nothing whatsoever ... You must realise the FACTS of legal ownership.' Jack had the same gift of losing money as his two siblings. To help pay off some of Desmond's debts, he had sold a house in Rome near to the one he lived in. Anita continued her letter to Tarka:

> Meanwhile Rome property has soared and if he still owned that house it would be worth 1 million $ but he doesn't! He has over £10,000 sterling a year to live on and the Badia [Jack's country house in Tuscany] – he owns nothing else – Desmond owns Castle Leslie and the gardens and you own the land. I now own nothing but Oranmore Castle and its 16 acres. Pa has sold out and owns nothing in Ireland!

Anita then turned her attention to the dinner party that Tarka and Jane were planning to hold at Cleveland Square on 1 June:

> I suggest starting with avocado pears filled with caviar, then chicken purchased hot and just cooked from Selfridges and salad, then tinned fruit salad strewn with fresh fruit and endless biscuits and cheese? But its YOUR show and you and Jane must do it as you like – I won't appear (except to work in kitchen!) It quite amuses me to see young people stuffing.

And then the magnificent pay off: 'I am dining out on June 1st with my old cousin Duke of Portland – the last duke and duchess – But can help you till 8 pm.'

The summer was darkened by the death of three-year-old Jessica Finn in August. Anita wrote to Harold Harris:

> I feel I must let you know – and NO sympathy is required because it's been the most extraordinary and wonderful experience of my life ... I believe she came to us for a great scoop of love – not for a full life with all its complications and since she left I feel her strong vital spirit as never before.

And to Anita Burgh: 'Since she has gone Jessica means more and more to me – She just dipped into human form for a time to get something she needed – and never for one moment have I felt it was cruel chance.'

In October Anita made a six-day trip to New York, as the guest speaker at the Churchill Library Memorial Lunch, a fundraiser that attracted wealthy sponsors. Not a woman to do things the easy way, she flew back standby on Air India to save the well-heeled committee money. Tarka and Jane's son William was born in London on 22 November and started life in Cleveland Square before he and Jane went to Hampshire to stay with her mother. From cold, damp Glaslough, Anita wrote to Harold Harris that she realized that it was no place to bring a baby: 'I've always ADORED my house but can see that now it's in a war zone ... So I can see that whatever England's problems it has something to offer and the isolation of Glaslough no longer appeals.' She had managed to get back to Oranmore before snow blocked all the Monaghan roads and was enduring the usual wintry conditions of the Atlantic coast. To Harold: 'The gales blew – then we had huge waves and feared inundation by the sea but tide abated just in time – electrics and telephone broken but now mended and the men discovered rats had chewed through the lines as well!!'

As always, Anita had financial problems. Although her biography of Jennie Churchill had been given tax exemption, subsequent books hadn't, the Revenue Commissioners who decided such things having judged them 'non-creative', unaware of how many of the scenes and conversations in them were very creative indeed. Anita intended to fight the judgements book by book, a costly and irksome business. 'It is so exhausting to be suddenly faced with such an unexpected dilemma,' she wrote to Harold. The ways of the tax exemption committee were impossible to fathom; literary biographies could be denied the exemption, while ghost-written memoirs by politicians and sports stars were accorded it.

That winter at Oranmore, Anita and Bill carried kettles and buckets of hot water to the cows' ice-covered drinking troughs. At Castle Leslie, Desmond and Helen tried, and failed, to light the wood stoves with damp wood. Tarka's cattle, under cover in the farmyard, had to be given water from the lake since the water-tank, installed by Tarka's great-grandfather, had cracked from the cold. It was impossible to drive even as far as the lodge gates. In this year of birth and death, violence and change, the September publication of Anita's memoir, *The Gilt and the Gingerbread*, was hardly noticed by the chilled and overburdened family. It was dedicated to Fleur and Rebecca – Rose's daughter and granddaughter. Rebecca was the daughter of Rose's son Peter Burgh and his former wife Anita. The jacket reproduced a pastel portrait of Anita Rodzianko, as she then was, by her brother-in-law, Serge Rodzianko. She looks so dreamily pretty, so untouched by life that it's hard to believe that the portrait was conceived during her hellish first marriage.

Anita's writing was always best when she stayed close to home. The memoir ambles through Leslie family history, not altogether truthfully but always delectably. Only someone whose grandmother constantly admonished 'Smile dear, it costs nothing' and whose great-aunt advised 'One must always pretend the sun is shining even when it isn't' could write with such a determined lack of self pity. Anita had enough material to write a misery memoir but, fortunately for her readers, not the inclination. She shrugged off the general unlovingness of her parents, apart from the observation that her father would have preferred his children not to have been born. As for being abandoned in the detestable Roehampton convent, there is only the mock-tragical comment: 'The incarceration was complete, as if we were in prison.' She doesn't quote from her anguished letters to Marjorie, written from the various unsuitable schools where she had been dumped. Those woeful notes from a neglected and humiliated child would not have been 'amusing' to read.

Anita was not the first writer to describe the nastiness of the debutante Season but was perhaps the first to so exactly pinpoint its ideal in the afore-quoted: 'This was what all mothers hoped of their daughters – maximum sex-appeal with the minimum of sex experience'. She writes lovingly of Castle Leslie, which 'blinked its sixty plate-glass windows at the lake' and, like its chatelaine, Leonie, gave Anita a sense of belonging. 'An Irish childhood does something to one's toes, causing invisible roots to grow into the soil,' she maintained. The last chapter of the book, 'War 1940', noted the end of the phoney war and the start of the killing, which would continue for six years. 'How lucky I was to be husbandless, childless, unloving and unloved.' Not quite true but, to quote Sir Leslie Stephen, editor of the *Dictionary of National Biography*, 'No good story is quite true,' and *The Gilt and the Gingerbread* is a very good story.

'Anecdotal', 'conversational', 'entertaining' were the words reviewers reached for. In *Books & Bookmen* Brian Masters complained that 'There is little sign of a struggle to build a work of literature.' Anthony Powell, in *The Daily Telegraph*, struck by Marjorie's attitude towards her daughter's education, got to the heart of the matter: 'Perhaps the chief point that emerges is how greatly all children dislike not being given an opportunity to learn.' In the Irish *Sunday Independent*, Ulick O'Connor appreciated the stories about Gladys, Duchess of Marlborough, described by Anita as 'hideous yet exotic, surrounded by a moving carpet of King Charles spaniels'. He thought the book was 'a charming autobiography' and looked forward to a second instalment in which Anita would continue 'to paint for us a unique picture of a society in its dying years'. But, when this second memoir was published two years later, there was little about declining Big Houses and their impoverished owners. It was all about troops, prisoners of war, ambulance drivers, battles and wartime leaders – a picture of a society in its fighting years.

25
The War Revisited

Gay Byrne, the popular Irish broadcaster, chose *The Gilt and the Gingerbread* as his top Christmas book buy for 1981 and so did Montgomery Hyde in *Book Choice* magazine. Once the first print run of four thousand copies had sold out, Hutchinson, unaccountably, allowed the memoir to go out of print, losing the Christmas market. Anita, who scorned to use an agent, wrote in anguish to the now retired Harold Harris, who reproached Hutchinson's managing director, Brian Perlman, but to little avail. The situation was made worse when Anita noticed that Molly Keane's novel *Good Behaviour* was on sale everywhere. She and Molly, two quirky chroniclers of a vanished Anglo-Irish world, had appeared on television together but, while Anita's book quickly became unprocurable, Molly's was sold to an English television company and, adapted by Hugh Leonard, aired the following year. In the spring, Anita, a staunch royalist, was cheered up by receiving an invitation to the 'Authors of the Year' party at Hatchards bookshop in Piccadilly, to be attended by Her Majesty the Queen.

In June 1982 Anita brought the sybaritic Roy Miles to Glaslough for a two-day visit. Accustomed to delicious food, he was surprised that Sunday lunch, which Anita cooked, consisted of half-cooked baked potatoes. When these had been eaten Anita disappeared for a while and then came back with 'dessert', a box of chocolates mouldily past their sell-by date. The chocolates had been given to her some time ago by Anthony Whittome, her new editor at Hutchinson. She wrote to him: 'Your chocolates proved delicious and fed us all on Sunday when I blithely organised lunch in the old dining room prior to Roy's departure.' Roy found Anita's frugality as baffling as she found his extravagance. When he flew back to London from Belfast after that unsatisfying lunch he paid £20 for the convenience of a guaranteed seat, shocking Anita, who always flew standby.

That autumn was the last one that Anita, Bill and Tarka would spend a week stalking at Glenveagh; Henry McIlhenny had gifted the estate to the Irish state and was moving permanently to his house in Rittenhouse Square, Philadelphia. 'The only person in Philadelphia with glamour', Andy Warhol called him. Anita wrote to Roy:

> I suffered from the disappearance of all pictures … the Stubbs and all the Landseers have gone to Philadelphia and to me who had grown accustomed over 35 years to look up and see them it was most melancholy – Of course he is right – life must be lived and it's no good as Michael Rosse said 'letting houses kill you'.

Did it occur to her that Glaslough too was a murderous sort of house?

There were two general elections in Ireland in 1982. In the first one, on 18 February, Charles Haughey's Fianna Fáil government was narrowly returned. Anita's opinion: 'Charlie H & Co all crooks but very merry ones'. In the second election, in November, the merry crooks were defeated and Garret Fitzgerald became Taoiseach, for the second time, in a Fine Gael-Labour coalition. Anita's view: 'Fitzgerald is the best brain in Ireland but hamstrung by always being in coalition.' Uncertainty in the Republic, terrorism in the North persuaded Tarka to shed some of his responsibilities at Glaslough. He sold Dawson's Lodge to his uncle Jack for 24,500 Irish punts. The plan was for Jack to rent it out. He commented: 'As a last resort the Gardaí might make suitable tenants.' Tarka, living in Dorset, working in County Monaghan, had double loyalties. In December he attended a ball at Knightsbridge Barracks in aid of the dependants of those members of the Queen's Lifeguard of the Household Cavalry who, on 20 July, had been killed by an IRA bomb as they rode out to Whitehall. At about the same time he contributed to an event, held in County Monaghan, for the destitute families of imprisoned members of the IRA. Agnes, living in Dublin, begged Anita to get Tarka away from Glaslough. Anita wrote to Jack: 'It is such a worry – I really hate him living there at all – and wonder if he realises the constant danger.' Of course, he did; he had told her that he felt like a man with his feet caught in cement but it was hard for Anita to admit that 'the huge effort I made to save something of Glaslough for him is just a handicap'.

Another cold winter. At Oranmore, four big dead rats were found under the floorboards in Bill's bedroom. 'The maddening thing is this,' Anita wrote to Tarka:

> I had arranged with McNally 2 years ago to lay electric cables in the cement so as to have ONE warm room here independent of central heating and he ordered the cables and then went broke and IF we lay cement now it's impossible to lay cables later … we have given up the idea of underfloor electric heating … It is so cold here – the sea frozen and hail showers … the newer roof over the old water tank has cracked … a real job has got to be done with cauldrons of hot tar and it will cost several hundred so do send me that cheque as soon as possible … The really BAD leaks over big kitchen. I can hope that all rain water came in through there and NOT via the exit pipe which is ungettable at.

Oranmore was getting too much to cope with. Even the ponies were irksome – 'I really can't see any joy in riding around here anymore – Glaslough is different.' Hunting no longer appealed to her; there was too much travelling to different meets and the post-hunt parties weren't as lively as they used to be – 'all so old except Min Mahony and his wife! "The county" is vanishing into the mists of old age.' The new owner of one of the old Big Houses failed to put in an appearance: 'She isn't "county" and besides I think she had some row with Anne Hempill over who was most important in the Pony Club.' Sir Oliver St John Gogarty observed that 'The true county families are born concussed' but Anita felt comfortable with them, at ease with their neighbourly gossip and lack of intellectual rigour. In January Anita and Bill were both in bed with high temperatures, rising from their sickbeds to carry feed to the horses and inspect the leaking roofs. Anita wrote plaintively to her son: 'You say you have no time to talk to me here but I've got a lot of things to discuss.' She pined for Cleveland Square: 'I can't tell you how much better I feel in London than here — I think because it's DRIER — If it wasn't for Heather [Leonie and Alec's small daughter] I'd spend most of my time there.'

Anita's wartime memoir, *A Story Half Told*, was published on 25 April 1983 and was celebrated with a party given by Roy Miles at his house 3 Trevor Square in Knightsbridge. Six hundred pounds worth of champagne was served, a rare event at book launches, which are usually held dismally in publishers' offices, with tepid white wine the only drink on offer. Hutchinson paid £100 towards the cost of the party, in recognition that Anita was now a valuable literary property. Her latest advance was raised from £3000 to £3500 and the print run increased to five thousand. Since previous books had not been tax exempt, she transformed her advance into non-taxable expenses. Harold Harris had had misgivings about the book. He had been sent an early typescript, which prompted him to write to Tony Whittome:

> It is bad enough having a dyslexic author without her appointing a dyslexic typist! Both of them use dashes where a full stop, a comma or a semi-colon would be appropriate ... I am bound to say that I found it a very eccentric book indeed ... the whole book is lifted from Train to Nowhere. It is only slightly paraphrased, some of the stories are cut out and some have had one or two comments added, not always to their advantage. I really don't know why she went to the trouble of writing it all again instead of asking Hutchinson to re-publish the old volume. But there it is and this is the result. One can only hope that no-one will notice.

No one did. None of the enthusiastic reviewers realized that *A Story Half Told* was *Train to Nowhere* lite. It had been thirty-five years since the earlier book was published and it had been out of print since 1953. When she wrote it, she had been a disconsolate young woman, adrift in the post-war world. Now she was a well-known biographer of popular, frothy biographies of high-society figures. Readers picked up her books expecting to be amused and Hutchinson knew this. When her publisher sent Anita a rather skittish blurb for her approval, she reproved them: 'My war was with the Fighting Troops – it wasn't a society outing.' But she was aware that her readers expected from her something akin to society outings and the rehashed memoir was more Anita-ish than the original, with more gossip and more detailed character sketches of the terrifying and glamorous Mrs Newall and the glorious Miranda Lampson. Some of the more macabre episodes were left out, such as the exhausted French woman being allowed to shoot dead two even more exhausted German soldiers in reprisal for the killing of her son.

Anita also added an untruthful ending: Bill proposing to her, almost immediately after the war, beside the lake at Glaslough. There had been a marriage proposal in that particular spot: in the spring of 1918, Montagu Porch had proposed to the much older Jennie Churchill, so Anita had just changed the personnel. The tone of the new book, with its touches of girlish gaiety, would have been inappropriate in 1948 but were appealing in 1982, as was the jacket illustration of Augustus John's portrait of Anita, all long lashes and heart-shaped red lips. As in *Train to Nowhere*, Anita's wartime story is less than half told. She doesn't mention Paul stalking her all over the Middle East, her love affairs, abortions and bouts of depression; this is a very upbeat war story.

Critics liked the moments of lightheartedness. Anne Johnstone in the *Sunday Standard*: 'It might not be going too far to say that Anita Leslie has done for the Second World War what Robert Graves did for the First in *Goodbye to All That*. Like that classic, it is both horrifying and hilarious. It is packed with gems of observation.' Victoria Glendinning in *The Times Literary Supplement*: 'It is as if Angela Brazil had collaborated with Noël Coward. Anita Leslie was conspicuously brave and effective, and she was awarded the Croix de Guerre. Yet she has the frivolity, and the style, to describe "her" war as "frivolous" … Anita Leslie was, is, a chic type.'

The chic type was ill again. On 1 May 1983 she wrote to Jack: 'Darling I've been so sick – a virus pneumonia I think.' The cause of the illness was her research on a planned biograpy of Randolph Churchill, who had died in 1968. Anita had gone to Colchester to interview Randolph's last love,

Natalie Bevan. Her return train had been delayed and she had spent hours on a freezing platform. In June she had a temperature of 102° every night for three weeks but refused to see a doctor, not even the one who believed in nature cures and was recommended by Sheila Chichester. Anita applied cold compresses until her temperature returned to normal. The 93-year-old Lady Diana Cooper, who had loved Randolph, rang Anita to tell her that she was praying for her to get well so that she could finish writing the book.

Anita was aware of Randolph's faults: drunkenness, abominable rudeness, an inflated sense of his own importance. But she thought that these character flaws were outweighed by fearlessness and intelligence. As she researched more deeply, she found that dishonesty had to be added to the list of sins; after the war, Randolph had rented a house in Oving and left without paying the bills. In her biography, she writes only: 'Unfortunately, there had been some misunderstanding about Oving,' but she was rattled, having believed Randolph to have an honest nature, the reason for his outspoken lack of tact. She felt that her own health was failing and, that August, made her will, naming her children as her executors, with Tarka her literary executor and legatee. She left her land at Glaslough to Tarka's son William, although she had previously told Tarka that she didn't own anything there, and the Oranmore lands to Leonie's daughter, Heather Oriel. A flawed document, it made no provision for any future grandchildren.

Eccentric Anglo-Irishness was much in fashion, with television adaptations of Molly Keane's *Good Behaviour* and *The Irish RM* by Somerville and Ross. In the greedy, ostentatious 1980s, Chekhovian stories of people in dusty diamonds and threadbare frocks drifting around their half-ruined estates during the last gasp of the British Empire had a nostalgic charm. An Irish media company, McDonagh Associates, thought that Anita, the epitome of Anglo-Irishness, would be the perfect subject for a television series and Tony Whittome agreed. In an internal memo, he wrote: 'I too have long felt that there is enough in Anita's amazing life story and her scatty aristocratic backgound to carry significantly more media exploitation than we have so far been able to arrange.' McDonagh Associates wanted Hutchinson to cooperate in the venture but this was a step too far for the publisher. Although the media company paid £250 for a six-month option on Anita's memoirs, it couldn't raise the production money and the option was allowed to lapse.

Financial success eluded Anita. Not granted tax exemption, she also discovered that, even though she had a British passport and a UK publisher, because she lived in Ireland, she was not eligible to receive Public Lending Right (PLR), a scheme under which authors are paid a small sum on every library borrowing of one of their books. In poor health herself, she gave comfort and advice to a languishing Roy Miles:

> My diagnosis is that your LIVER is delicate. You've played it up with rich banquets and nerve strain combined ... go 2 days on grapes only to purify your blood stream ... only one disease exists – IMPURE BLOOD STREAM. So IMPURE BLOOD AND false values is [sic] all you have to worry about.

The final sentence of this letter to Roy could have been written by Jennie Churchill, it is so chirpily optimistic: 'And remember the Chinese saying that each day is wonderful when the sun rises and there isn't an earthquake or flood.'

By 1984 the 78-year-old Jack Leslie had been living in Italy for thirty years. It had become an unsettling country: in 1978 the outgoing prime minister, Aldo Moro, had been kidnapped by the terrorist group, the Red Brigades, who killed his five bodyguards and, fifty-five days later, Moro himself, leaving his body in the boot of a red Renault car. There was more street crime, robbery and political viciousness. Jack's orderly domestic life was also affected. He recounted in his memoir *Never A Dull Moment* (2006) that, one evening, his manservant, Italo Deidda, 'went out to the nearby fish shop and bought some polpi (small octopi) and ripe nectarines for lunch. After eating the delicious cooked polpi I wondered why he did not bring in the nectarines. Then I went to the kitchen and found Italo dead on the floor.'

Fearful of further calamity, Jack decided to spend even more time at Glaslough. He bought a half-share in the village gate lodge from Agnes and started to negotiate for the paddock behind Dawson's Lodge. But his family was at war. Desmond wrote snarling notes to Tarka:

> All the gates to this estate belong to me ... If you want to make this beau-
> tiful estate look like a tinker encampment, please stick to your own areas.
> But now that we are a recognised, tax-exempted National Monument, a far
> higher standard will be required of you and everyone living within the walls.

Hostility within the walls and increasing danger at its gates. From London,
on 15 June 1984, Anita wrote to Kathleen Abercorn. Tarka had just
arrived with stories to tell:

> A lorry of explosives was captured by the 2nd class gardai who hadn't gone
> down to guard Reagan in Galway! [The US president had visited Ireland
> earlier that month.] Apparently, this lorry was taken at gunpoint from the
> flustered family who owned it ... Apparently, the mortars on it were about
> to go off – they'd intended to point them all at the barracks at Middletown!
> Tarka says the 'boyos' ran away in the dark when they saw a policeman waving
> a torch.

Later that year the entire village of Glaslough had to be evacuated.
'Such incidents do not even warrant a line in newspapers here', Anita
wrote to Kath, 'here' referring to the UK, whose government tried to
ignore the embarrassment that was the Irish border as much as possible,
which was what Anita did too. The letter to Kath was mainly about her
growing collection of grandchildren. Leonie had given birth to a ten-
pound baby boy in March, and Jane was expecting her second child the
following April. 'Bill and I DOTE over all our grandchildren and are I
think – excellent grand parents!!' Bill's book *Dive & Attack*, about his
war years, had been published the previous year and Anita's biography
of Randolph, for which she had interviewed fifty people, was due out
in April – 'I understand him and why he was a drunk.' In the Cleveland
Square flat the balconies, built in 1860, were falling off and the plumbing
didn't work but Anita was used to decaying buildings; they were part of
Anglo-Irish life.

26

Specialists in Survival

Media fascination with the Anglo-Irish continued. They were undoubtedly an interesting race, quirky survivors who were still regarded as usurpers in the country where they'd lived for centuries, and bearing the burden of not belonging with a mixture of insouciance, courage and exasperating insensitivity. At the beginning of January 1985, Channel 4 commissioned a five-part documentary series, *Crown and Shamrock*, an examination of this former ruling class, now financially adrift in their dilapidated houses but with an aura of superiority; players in a slapstick tragedy. The surviving members of the Leslie family were perfect representations of the ascendancy and its dual loyalties and murky heritage.

The researcher for the series was Jeananne Crowley, who would later become a well-known actress. A tall, good-looking girl, devoted to horses and hunting, she got on well with Anita and Bill, who admired the way she fearlessly rode their horses along the icy Oranmore roads. Not everyone in the local hunting set approved of the television crew. At a dance given by the indefatigable Mollie Cusack Smith, a guest referred to Jeananne as 'a vulgar reporter'. 'So glad I wasn't there,' Anita wrote thankfully to

Tarka. Jeananne felt protective towards Anita, who she thought looked frail and in pain but David Hammond, the presenter and interviewer for the series, put Anita on the defensive about her perceived otherness. She snapped at him: 'Well, if you live in a big house and you own a lot of land, you are different to the Irish who don't own land and don't live in big houses.' She told him that she had been refused an Irish passport:

> When I asked, you have to have a grandparent born in Ireland and my grand-father [Sir John Leslie] was born before birth certificates, and so I don't know, I can't prove where he was born. But I have two children who were born in Ireland and so they have Irish passports.

She was wrong about the non-availability of birth certificates – they were introduced in 1837 and Sir John was born in 1857 but she spoke with such authority that the interviewer didn't contradict her.

British passport or not, Anita insisted on her Irishness. 'Well, if you love Ireland, you love Ireland. It gives you a feeling, a sort of pull. How can you live anywhere else in the world except Ireland?' Then a sentence she often repeated: 'My roots have gone down from my toes into the soil.' She compared the Anglo-Irish, deeply rooted in Irish soil as they may have been, to dinosaurs on the verge of extinction. Giving David Hammond a tour of Oranmore Castle, she said that, when she came home after the war, her mother had wanted to see her settled so

> she thought that she would sell a beautiful emerald that she'd got, which she did. It was 19 carat I think, and she got £3,000 for it. And the £3,000 paid for all the windows and the wonderful cement roof and all the plumbing and all the electricity in this castle.

Anita proudly displayed 'the tower to end all towers', half the height of the castle, built with stones, salvaged from a Protestant church, which she'd bought for £300. She explained that the castle walls, although very thick, leaked 'because the wind drives the rain in'. She made it sound the most normal thing in the world for Marjorie to have exchanged a valuable ring for a ruin in the west of Ireland. She and Mollie became a bit fluttery when filming began. At one point Mollie shouted, 'Cut! I haven't got my tooth in,' and Anita, noticing the camera focusing on her, said, 'Oh dear!

I would have put on eyelashes or something.' Jeananne, noticing that the castle didn't have a kitchen apart from a very small scullery, suggested taking Anita and Bill out to dinner, at Channel 4's expense. Anita was delighted for Bill to accept but, worryingly, wouldn't go herself; outings were becoming too tiring.

Then it was Desmond's turn to star. Filmed at Castle Leslie, he went through the family history: the rescue of Queen Margaret by an early Leslie, whereby the family motto became 'Grip Fast'; the indispensable Ascendancy attributes – 'England couldn't run without us. Ireland supplies its generals, writers and horses.' He suggested that Swift, that perspicacious visitor to Castle Leslie, may have been an alien, since he knew so much about magnetic poles. When asked if life on the Irish border was dangerous, he said: 'Certainly one's had a lot of luck in surviving; you become specialists in survival.' He said that he had given up a successful career creating sound effects and music because, 'I thought this place was more important … I feel there's a purpose in everything, and, if I hadn't come here, I don't think this place would still be going.'

Basking in limelight put Desmond in a buoyant mood. On 1 February he wrote affectionately to his sister, addressing her as 'Darling A'. He told her: 'Jeananne Crowley seemed pleased with my chatter … They photographed the dining table spread with ALL the Lesliana from the Dean's tomes, through Anita and Ma to *Flying Saucers Have Landed* in Finnish translation.' Castle Leslie was as icy as Oranmore. Desmond wrote: 'Arrived back from France and have lived in thermals plus ski clothes ever since. Life is simple. When I retire to bed, I take off my cap. In the morning I replace it … Far too cold to take baths or wash.'

The Anglo-Irish shown in *Crown and Shamrock* were an unenviable bunch, living in near squalor in their mouldering houses. At Castle Leslie there may have been a table piled high with literary treasures but the central heating system had broken down years before, replaced by just one smoky, wood-burning stove at the foot of the staircase. Even those who lived in the snug bungalows that Anita disapproved of suffered from the cold that winter. Buses and trains were on strike and, all over Ireland, roads were impassable. Faced with having to fix frozen pipes and a 500 punt bill for central heating oil, Anita complained to her son: 'What has really done me down is having to give you half my income after paying tax here [in Ireland].' She repeated the complaint to Bill, who was stuck in London, unable to get back to Oranmore. 'Tarka hasn't sent me any money – in fact I pay him half my income (2500 punts) until next July.'

Perhaps because she realized that it was her own fault for persuading Tarka to take up a life of unprofitable farming at Glaslough, or because, given the chance to act against her better judgement, she usually did, in dreadful driving conditions she transported a mare belonging to Tarka to Birr Castle, whence it would be sent to Pentridge House. Anita had already paid 1000 punts in stabling charges for the animal. Anita to Tarka: 'We were lucky in 5 hours driving to get there and back without a puncture with bald tyres in front of Land Rover.' Jane and Tarka's daughter Olivia was born on 2 February, making Anita reflect on the complexity of her son's life. A week after Olivia's birth, she wrote to him:

> I can't help wishing Tarka that you were completely OUT of this country [Ireland]. I know Glaslough is beautiful and an old family holding BUT think how simple all our lives would be if run between London and Pentridge! ... I just do feel that England is slightly better than here – it's become a ridiculous country to live in.

Just a few weeks ago, she had said in a television interview: 'How could I live anywhere else in the world except Ireland.'

Anita apologized to Jane for asking Tarka for money so soon after his daughter's birth: 'I really am ready to give T every penny I have but can't extend an overdraft!' And to Tarka: 'It is only the fact that half my income goes to you that has made it difficult for me to pay for the balconies.' And then the never-ending worry:

> I fuss about Glaslough – it seems so far away and such an effort for you to farm and Desmond so difficult and I can well see that Monaghan is a hopeless background for you and Jane – especially not owning the big house which alone made it worth while striving – one will have to see.

This is a new development. Anita, a woman who was often in two minds, now seemed to be wishing for two scenarios; the first was for Tarka to be rid of the Glaslough farmlands, which Anita had bought for him over the years, the second to regain ownership of Castle Leslie. She had never mentioned taking back the castle from Desmond before but she may have felt that the time was now ripe to do so. In 1983 Desmond sold the equestrian centre to Geraldine Bellew, who had been in charge of the stables. The equestrian centre was profitable and looked as though it would become even more successful, so its sale seemed baffling. Desmond's sympathetic biographer, Robert O'Byrne, suggests that Desmond was simply too worn out to continue to run the business. Helen's mother had left her a house in the south of France and Desmond spent an increasing amount of time there. When he returned to Castle Leslie, it was to find that dry rot had begun to ruin the main reception rooms, so that he and his family had to live in a small section of the house. Chronically short of money, he sold paintings, land and outbuildings, reducing the value of the estate. This frustrated and saddened his sister. Anita to Tarka: 'I only wish that I'd either kept the whole show … or moved away. As it is I seem to have tied you and Jane into inexplicable knots for nothing.' The knots became even more tangled over the next few years as Tarka and the Bellews argued over access rights to various parts of the estate.

The Cleveland Square flat had become a money pit and there was confusion about who should pay the bills for crumbling masonry and faulty appliances. Anita to Tarka on 7 March 1985:

> I have paid 3 installments of £1,500 for the balconies. You paid one only (I paid £4,500 and you £1,500). Now who has been paying the electric light and telephone? I have never received any bills – And I don't want to arrive and find the phone CUT off like last year! And the RATES which are at least £300 are due this month.

She was dismayed that Tarka had employed an expensive builder to make new kitchen cupboards and had installed new telephones, and even more dismayed that he planned to cover the cost of these enterprises by letting the flat. Anita to Tarka: 'My one extravagance is to pay service charges of £3,200 a year to have somewhere I can leave everything.' She had planned a long stay in the flat to coincide with the publication of *Cousin Randolph* at the end of April but, faced with another slew of bills, she had had enough:

I can see that the flat has become too expensive for us to keep without letting and so I will move out FOREVER next winter and leave it to you to do what you like with ... I really could not bear to have to keep moving my books and papers to Pentridge – much less all our clothes ... The whole point of the place was to have a base in London where one could leave things however grubby it was.

She was at a low ebb that March, unable to shake off a cold that had plagued her for weeks and which looked like stopping her from attending Olivia's christening. Her dream of the quiet room in which to write seemed to be over, due, like so many other mishaps, to her inability to keep to one plan. She had put the flat in Tarka's name because, had she herself had a London address, she might have been liable to UK taxation. At the time, it appeared that the flat would still be hers in all but name but before long she assured Tarka and Jane that the flat was theirs, although she never seemed clear about who was supposed to pay the bills. In any case, it seemed that the flat was not an attractive proposition to the rich Americans whom Tarka hoped to attract as tenants. When Bill stayed there during the winter, he noticed the inconvenient kitchen, the malfunctioning radiator, the broken handbasin and filthy lavatory and the bags of builders' rubble outside the door. He had made things worse one night when he forgot his key: climbing up the scaffolding, which had been erected while repairs to the balconies were carried out, he had broken a window, which had to be boarded up. He suggested to Tarka that it might be better to get the place 'in first class nick' before offering it to 'luxury' clients.

In April, for the third time that year, Anita wrote a pained letter to her son:

Let me know how much longer I have to send you half my income – or is it for ever? ... After Randolph book has come out we'll see about leaving the flat forever to be let. I don't want to go to London to see friends if I cannot keep my books and papers there in the same drawers.

And then, in the same letter, as though regretting her snappishness, she said that Jane could borrow the Fitzherbert tiara whenever she wanted to and she wished that she, Anita, could afford to pay for extra help for the new baby. Still at Oranmore at Easter, she wrote sadly to Tarka:

I had half intended to reside permanently in Cleveland Square and change my residence once the battle about my books being tax exempt is over but now I feel maybe that this castle is the best place for me to settle down in ... I feel more inclined than ever to leave London for ever and the flat to you to let or not let as you choose.

There was something to be said for remaining at Oranmore. Leonie and Alec's children, Heather and Cian, often stayed at the castle to be doted on by their grandparents and Margaret Glynn. Leonie and Alec, unlike Tarka, were not a source of financial anxiety. Leonie had her teaching job and had a knack for buying property, including a pub in Galway, which she profitably rented out, and six acres of sheltered woodland, a valuable holding on that wind-battered Atlantic shore. De Danann was now so famous, striking record deals and touring the world, that Anita now referred to it by name. To have continued to call it 'Alec's music group' would have been like calling Mikhail Baryshnikov 'a dancer'. When Anita had supper with this successful couple there was champagne and smoked salmon from McDonaghs, Galway's renowned fish shop. The castle was now well heated and, if there were problems with the plumbing or the roof, it was easier to get them fixed than it was at Cleveland Square, where frustrating negotiations with managing agents caused delays.

Bill, who had only a £400 monthly pension, was no help financially. Over the years, he had let Anita take charge of their lives, which left him free to go skiing as often as he could. His boyish charm was irresistible; his boyish irresponsibility less so. Once at Oranmore, he tried to repair a blunted chainsaw without wearing goggles and nearly lost an eye. During the transport strike in Ireland, it was Anita who arranged his passage home by telephoning Dublin Yacht Club and organizing a lift. When Anita came to London to promote her new book, Bill, once again, went skiing. Anita arrived at Cleveland Square in April to discover that some very unlikely items had gone missing. She wrote to Tarka: 'I got very ill in first night here and looked for the cold compresses left in bathroom – but they'd vanished.' So had the towel rail, the rubbish bin and, most oddly, the legs from her bed and the frill for it, which she had made herself. Although she had assured Jane that the latter could decorate the flat in any way she liked,

Anita criticized the result: 'Kitchen – I hate it … I can't bear the cream walls and will paint the colour I most like and always intended … The sofa now looks straight into the mirror – Do take it away. And bring back the small tables.' It was only a month ago that she had written that, after the summer, she would leave the flat for ever. Her plan to repaint the kitchen walls gives the impression that she may have changed her mind again.

Anita had worked on her biography of Randolph Churchill for two years. It had been such a difficult assignment that she urged Anita Burgh to stick to novels, which the younger writer successfully did. The older Anita swore that her latest book, for which she received an advance of £4000, would be the last biography she wrote. It was but, sadly, not in the way she intended. By the time Anita's book *Cousin Randolph. The Life of Randolph Churchill* was published, Brian Roberts' *Randolph. A Study of Churchill's Son*, had already appeared. Randolph's son Winston, his official biographer, was working on *His Father's Son*, which was published in 1997, and wrote stuffily to Anita when she asked if she might quote from Randolph's letters. Winston had been under the impression that she was writing a personal memoir and was annoyed to learn that she was interviewing the same people as he was. He did give her permission to quote from Randolph's love letters to Laura Marlborough and Natalie Bevan. But Anita realized that Winston wouldn't welcome her book and even worse, as she wrote to Roy Miles on the eve of publication: 'Mary [Soames] wrote me rather sourly about not contacting the family – but honestly Roy I couldn't – I had to write my OWN account of Randolph who was very dear to me.' Roy had wanted to give a launch party at Trevor Square but Anita told him: 'Much as I love your house and perfect as it is to give a party in – this particular volume is TOO TRICKY.'

Randolph Churchill, of whom Noel Coward remarked, 'Dear Randolph, entirely unspoilt by failure,' was just Anita's cup of tea. Like her father, the author of *Studies in Sublime Failure* and, according to his biographer, somewhat of a sublime failure himself, Anita was fascinated by men who, starting off fabulously, wandered on to an inescapable downward path. Leonard Jerome, Mortal Ruin and now her beloved Randolph with his mingled charm and boorishness and what Elizabeth Paget called his 'ghastly good looks'. This lovable/detestable man inspired a gripping biography. It also provided a chance to recycle material previously published in her memoirs. So, once again, we have the incident at Blenheim Palace, when Randolph asks the teenage Anita to 'Clear off. Here's ten bob', to leave his path clear for seduction. The footmen in damp white gloves also give a repeat performance, as does Randolph's championship of the manic depressive Orde Wingate in wartime Egypt.

Anita's biography was a heaven-sent assignment for Fleet Street's book reviewers, many of whom had known Randolph, a towering figure among journalists, and were happy to recall their own encounters with him. To M.R.D Foot, writing in *Books & Bookmen*, Anita had done exactly what she had set out to do: 'She manages to prove that boaster and failure though he may have been, he was a personality of tremendous force of character and a most loveable man.' Martin Gilbert, who had worked for Randolph on the official life of his father, wrote in *The Sunday Times* that the biography 'has many insights into Randolph's life'. Gordon Rhodes in the *Yorkshire Post*: 'We are won over to her belief that the man had charm – not the practised art of one who knows how to turn it on like a tap, but the childlike appeal of someone whom we have to laugh about even when he is being infuriating.' Peter Quennell, a friend of Randolph whom Anita had interviewed, wrote in *The Sunday Telegraph*, which ran two extracts from the book: 'Altogether Miss Leslie has produced a candid, able, popularly written account.'

Only Alan Watkins in *The Listener* struck a sour note, pointing out Anita's lapses of style, with which Harold Harris had long been familiar:

> If a name may contain a hyphen but does not, she puts it in and vice versa. She is partial to italicisation and to exclamation marks in a style often described as 'women's magazine', though it refers to a way of writing which went out of these publications about 30 years ago and itself derives from the society remarks, the recollections of a lady of fashion, of the period before 1939.

He criticized Anita's book for being unreliable, inaccurate and eccentric in her judgements of politics. But he conceded: 'It may be full of mistakes but it is also full of life … The imaginative sympathy which Miss Leslie shows with Randolph and his work is admirable.' Anita's own verdict, given to Harold Harris: 'That book is full of things I DON'T say!'

Following the book's publication, Anita got pneumonia again and had to cancel an appearance at a *Yorkshire Post* literary luncheon. Bill came back from his skiing holiday and put an end to too many friends visiting his wife at the same time, which tired her. Seeing how thin she had become prompted her friends to bring food to Cleveland Square: homemade soup and fish from Joe Corvo's wife, Victoria, a smoked chicken from Jane's mother. 'I am still gaga,' Anita wrote to her daughter-in-law on 19 May but 'woolly brained' as she was, she still insisted: 'The fact that he [Tarka] takes half my income stymies me.' She was being unfair; she had chosen Tarka's career path for him, ignoring his reluctance to be part of the 'Leslie half-world' and his complaints of feeling as though his feet were set in concrete. Although, in recent years, she had expressed regret at buying him farmland at Glaslough without considering the financial implications, as well as putting his life in danger, she doesn't seem to have considered pulling out of the estate, freeing her son from the responsibility of farming nine hundred acres in a danger zone and from the frustrating skirmishes with Desmond.

By the beginning of June Anita was on the mend. She attended the private view of an exhibition of portraits at the Mall Galleries, which included a small portrait of her by the Spanish artist Theodore Ramos. It depicts a wispy-haired Anita looking old and ill, but she liked it and planned to commission another portrait by Ramos, in which she would wear a khaki shirt and flashes. She never talked about her war experiences but now, uncharacteristically, she told Jane: 'I was the only woman in the world to get the Desert Star and the Croix de Guerre.' Later that summer, Roy Miles visited her at Cleveland Square. Anita sat, exhausted, on a sofa and Bill told Roy that she wasn't eating. Since their first meeting in 1961, Anita had captivated Roy. She had predicted his future, using a rare old set of Tarot cards, and insisted that he sell his gallery, as she had seen the death card. This persuaded him to sell his Bruton Street premises and operate as an art dealer in a less flamboyant and less stressful way. She had invited him to dinner parties where he had been entertained by three duchesses. She had advised him about his health in letters crammed with oddly placed capital letters and exclamation marks. Now, at what was to be their last meeting, she treated him coldly. She had heard some scur-rilous gossip about him and, although he told her it wasn't true, merely the price of fame, she failed to sympathize. He left Cleveland Square sick at heart.

In September she was back at Oranmore and back at work. She was planning a third memoir, spanning the last thirty-five years and, after that, a novel. She wrote to Tony Whittome: 'I thought of beginning in 1847 before the Famine and then I can roll on indefinitely incorporating my own family history in modern times.' The Famine actually began in 1845. She was also trying to help her uncle Lionel write his memoirs. Lionel was a favourite of hers; when she was in Paris as a young girl, he had intro-duced her to his artistic world and this had led to her writing a biography of Rodin. Anita felt guilty towards her uncle because, when the Sir John Leslie company had been dissolved and Lionel had sold his shares, unlike his older brother Seymour, he had not been rewarded with an apartment at Glaslough. 'Such an interesting life – but he cannot write and one has to remake every chapter,' Anita wrote to Tarka, although Lionel was the published author of *One Man's World: A Story of Strange Places and Strange People* (1961) and *Wilderness Trails in Three Continents* (1931).

However hard she worked, her financial worries worsened. In 1985 tax on her American income rose from 500 punts to 700, insurance of 400 punts was due on the Land Rover and refilling the oil tank required 300 punts. She claimed that she would have nothing to spend on Christmas presents, particularly since her income for the year was £18,000 pounds, down on the previous year's £21,000. 'I must discuss WHY?', she wrote to Tarka, but the labyrinthine complexities of her finances – the American bequest from her late aunt Anne Bourke Cockran, book royalties and horse sales, profits of which were set against the vagaries of the Irish tax system – would flummox the canniest accountant. She had not had a final decision from the Revenue Commissioners regarding the possible tax-exempt status of her books, so she sent a copy of *Edwardians in Love* to Charles Haughey, now leader of the opposition, with a letter asking him if that was what he meant when he passed the [artists' exemption] Bill. But, as she explained to Tony Whittome, her timing was off: 'His yacht struck a rock and sank and after 3 hours on a raft he has not answered me.' Haughey had had to be rescued off Mizen Head by the Baltimore life-boat and perhaps was too distracted to read *Edwardians in Love*, although he would have identified with the luxury-loving adulterers who were its heroes. A frustrated Anita wrote crossly to her son: 'I want you to under-stand the situation I am in ... When are you likely to be able to pay my tax? Don't come here – just write the facts.'

Tarka had just returned home to Pentridge from Glaslough, where the price of cattle had gone down and the barley crop had failed. Pentridge was not cheerful either. He wrote to Anita on 30 October: 'Life here seems to be a state of continuous semi-bedlam.' The mail had piled up, the house and horses needed attention and the rocking-horse business he had started had Christmas orders that needed to be dealt with. At least the Cleveland Square flat had been rented out for six weeks and he told his mother that 'the money should help towards something'. No mention of paying her tax bill but an account of a disturbing incident at Glaslough:

> I was got out of bed at midnight by the Provos as one had a sick child that had to be got to Dr. Gillespie. We reached his door at 1.15 am. On the way home I was told 'You are the only man who can drive safely round both sides of the border at this time of night!' I don't know whether to be flattered or worried.

Anita could not be distracted from her financial problems. On 2 November she wrote separately to Tarka and Jane. To Jane, she sent receipts of the service charges she had paid and, although she had recently insisted that she would not be returning to the London flat, she scolded:

> The whole point of a flat is a place to leave one's books and papers in and know they will be there whenever one gets back. As it is I can't remember half the things that Tarka has moved – and to tell the truth I HATE the new kitchen! Don't buy any more of those odd shaped white plates because they are a nightmare and all the plates I slowly accumulated worked! I suppose the real time for letting is the summer – just when Bill and I need it.

Predictably she ended this shrill letter on a conciliatory note, urging Jane to get her, Anita's, fur coat out of storage and wear it herself. To Tarka, who had returned to Glaslough and its agricultural problems, she wrote:

'Don't bother to come here [Oranmore] for only 1 night ... because it tires me to have you for such a short time!' Having said that she couldn't afford to buy Christmas presents, she now told Tarka that she was sending Theodore Ramos £900, so that he could paint a portrait of her in her wartime regalia. This sounds deranged, as do her constant demands for money.

The last letters she wrote, again separate ones to Tarka and Jane, were dated 5 November. With Jane's letter, she enclosed a cheque for William's birthday, writing wistfully: 'It is cruelly sad for me having grandchildren in two different countries – and such fascinating grandchildren.' To Tarka, she gave some good news: the Inspector of Taxes was prepared to grant tax exemption for the six books published over the previous twelve years. Her accountants had written to her: 'We trust you can appreciate the leniency of the Inspector of Taxes in this matter as there were no receipts to back up the expenses claimed for the years 1974 to 1983 inclusive.' The word 'leniency' didn't play well with Anita; she thought the decision was 'only justice'.

Tarka had hoped that Bill would come to Pentridge in the spring to help with the pruning. Anita reported spitefully: 'Pa says what is wrong with our children? They can't survive on the income we gave them OR do their own pruning!' Hard to imagine pragmatic Bill saying anything like this. After this harsh criticism, Anita wrote: 'Tarka – don't worry about having TOO MUCH to do. Glaslough is a nightmare that I did not expect.' Then, in the next sentence: 'You don't say if you can refund me my tax money? This is the one thing I want to know ... Can you pay me at least £5,000 in punts? Maybe £7600?' The tetchy, unloving, unrealistic letter, the last one she wrote to Tarka, ended there.

27
Back Where She Belonged

'Leslie-King. At midnight on November 5, at Oranmore Castle, quietly in her sleep, the author Anita Leslie, beloved wife of Bill Leslie-King and mother of Tarka and Leonie. Funeral at Glaslough Friday 8 November.' (*The Irish Times.*) Tony Whittome wrote an obituary for *The Times* in which he said that Anita 'represented all that was most captivating and individual about the Anglo-Irish aristocracy', while David Holloway, the literary editor of *The Daily Telegraph*, wrote that Anita 'was at her most effective in her books about her relations.' Anita had left highly idiosyncratic burial instructions:

> In accordance to the beliefs of my Red Indian ancestors I wish to return my body to the earth that made it. Feeling the breath of god in the trees I gladly give my physical remains to the roots of the great Irish forest beside the lake at Glaslough, which I have always loved – the grave to be unmarked. I would prefer to be buried without a coffin – just tied to a board – but if that is complicated take the lid off. And let those who love me not imagine I am where my cast-off body lies. That goes to the good earth. If you wonder where I am, listen to the trees whispering.

The perfect resting place was found, between two young lime trees, standing like sentinels beside the lake she loved. Anita was laid out in Castle Leslie's gallery, surrounded by flowers and candles. The next day, there was a small, quiet funeral at the local Catholic church, before the journey to the edge of the lake. Volunteers had worked frantically to clear fallen branches and potholes from the lakeside avenue, so that mourners could reach the site beside the lime trees. In a letter to Tony Whittome, Desmond described a heavy rain sending everyone scurrying back to the Castle, from where they saw a sudden 100 mph gust of wind bending the trees double. Then the party began, with De Danann playing and the Irish Anthem of Peace sung. On 24 April of the following year, a Requiem Mass for Anita was held at the Church of the Immaculate Conception in Farm Street, Mayfair.

Bill also wrote to Tony Whittome. He said that after the funeral he had stood beside Anita's grave at dusk, listening to the rooks coming home to roost, and had been inspired to write the following: 'Farewell my love/ the spirit flies, we cannot follow/Deep in our bones we know/There is a tomorrow/When we shall fly and meet at Heaven's Gate.' Anita, controlling her family from beyond the grave, had left the written instruction: 'No mourning, no tears.' Bill complied, writing to Kathleen Abercorn, 'We must pick up the bits.' In his case, this meant continuing to hunt with the Blazers, of which he was the oldest member.

He also wanted to get Anita's third volume of autobiography published and sent a typescript to Tony Whittome. Bill told Tarka that Anita had done 'a lovely rewrite of Love in a Nutshell', but her account of more recent events was disappointing: 'I hoped that she would recover and make a better fist of it.' Nothing more was heard of the typescript and, by the time I started my research, Tony Whittome, then still at Hutchinson after forty years, had forgotten about it until I showed him a copy of Bill's letter of 1985, asking for a meeting to discuss it. A search of the Hutchinson files revealed a few typewritten chapters and some handwritten ones, none of them publishable. Anita had pilfered material not just from *Love in a Nutshell* but from her previous memoirs and her diary entries and arranged it in a rambling, chaotic way. Little wonder that Tony, who retired in 2010, put off discussing it with Bill.

The Revenue Commissioners, that fickle outfit, decided that *Cousin Randolph* wasn't tax exempt. A furious Bill drafted a letter which, wisely, he didn't post. It was signed off, 'I hope that God will forgive you your gross trespass.' The 'Revenue Vultures', as he called them, had warned Anita that any future claims for tax exemption must be backed up by receipts but their letter had arrived at Oranmore three days before Anita died, which was Bill's explanation for the absence of receipts. Anita's books soon went out of print, apart from *Jennie*, which a small publisher, George Mann Books, reissued in 1992, paying an advance of £750. More recently, Bloomsbury has reissued *Train to Nowhere*, the wartime memoir that I consider to be Anita's masterpiece.

Glaslough's shaky fortunes improved when Desmond and Helen's daughter Sammy, who had qualified as an instructor with the British Horse Society when she was seventeen, took over the running of the estate in 1991 at the age of twenty-four. She started by opening a tearoom in the leaky conservatory and gradually restored the castle into a prizewinning country house hotel, which became famous, in 2002, when it hosted the wedding of Paul McCartney and Heather Mills. It now caters for about sixty weddings a year. In 2004 Sammy repurchased the equestrian centre, which Desmond had sold, and, in 2005, the Castle Leslie Estate won the *Sunday Times* Best Country House Hotel award. Those former houseguests who remember Anita's lunch of half-cooked baked potatoes and mouldy chocolates must find it hardly credible that Castle Leslie is now a gourmet's paradise. The journalist Kevin Myers listed the dishes served on the opening night of the Castle Leslie Gourmet Circle: 'Quail eggs set in consommé, timbale of Glaslough pike on a bed of spinach … chicken creperettes with lardoons … petit pot de crème with praline.' Until his death in 2016, Jack acted as a very idiosyncratic and popular tour guide at Castle Leslie.

Desmond died in Helen's house in Antibes, in the south of France, in 2001. Agnes died in 1999, after a long and happy relationship with Maurice Craig and professional success as a cabaret singer, collaborating with Marc Almond, Elvis Costello and Tom Waits. Helen Leslie, the inspiration behind the equestrian centre, died in Antibes in 2011. Bill, who continued to live at Oranmore Castle, died in October 2012, at the age of 102. He was buried beside Anita at Glaslough. Oranmore village has spread towards the city of Galway in a rash of new housing estates but, on its seaward side, the castle still soars in grey remoteness under the wild skies.

The Leslies continue to fascinate. Writers, other than themselves, now fill the shelves with books about this extraordinary family. They feature in Agnes's memoir, *The Fun Palace* (1996), in *Fortune's Daughters* (2004) by Elisabeth Kehoe, subtitled 'The extravagant lives of the Jerome sisters', and, in 2009, a further biography of Jennie by Anne Sebba. *Shane Leslie: Sublime Failure* by Otto Rauchbauer appeared in the same year, 2010, as did Robert O'Byrne's *Desmond Leslie: The Biography of an Irish Gentleman*. Anita who, in her lifetime, was the best known of the writing Leslies, has been somewhat overlooked. I have tried to bring this brave, interesting and complicated woman into the limelight.

Acknowledgments

This book couldn't have been written without the help of Anita Leslie's children, Tarka King and Leonie Finn, who shared their insights into their mother's life as well as her letters, photographs, diaries and albums.

I am also grateful to the late Leonie de Barros, Anita Burgh, Lord Burgh, Nicola Beauman, Lady Moyra Campbell, The Chartwell Trust, The Sir Winston Churchill Archive Trust, Thea Courchevel, Jeananne Crowley, the late Elspeth Gailey, Tim Gwyn-Jones, Eoghan Harris, Sarah Henson, the late Patricia, Countess of Jellicoe, Angela and Joe Kelly, Linda Kelly, the Lilliput Press for permission to quote from *The Fun Palace*, the late Fleur Melvill-Gardner, the late Roy Miles, the staff of the National Library of Ireland, Julian Mitchell, James Owen, The Hon. Lady Roche MBE, the Earl of Roden, Jean Rose, Serena de Stacpoole, Caroline Sweeney, the late Bill Vincent, Hugo Vickers, Anthony Whittome, the late Roddy Wilson and Djinn von Noorden, Bridget Farrell and Ruth Hallinan at the Lilliput Press.

Every effort has been made to secure all necessary clearances and permissions. Both the author and publisher will be glad to recognize any holders of copyright who have not been acknowledged above.

Bibliography

Books by Anita Leslie

Rodin: Immortal Peasant 1939

Train to Nowhere 1948

Love in a Nutshell 1952

The Fabulous Leonard Jerome 1954

Mrs Fitzherbert 1960

Mr Frewen of England 1966

Jennie: The Life of Lady Randolph Churchill 1969

Edwardians in Love 1972

Francis Chichester 1975

Cousin Clare 1976

Madame Tussaud (with Pauline Chapman) 1978

The Gilt and the Gingerbread 1981

A Story Half Told 1983

Cousin Randolph 1985

Books by Commander Bill King

The Stick and the Stars 1958

Capsize 1969

Adventure in Depth 1975
Dive and Attack 1983
The Wheeling Stars 1989
Kamikaze: The Wind of God 1997

Further reading

Agnes Bernelle, *The Fun Palace*. Lilliput 1996
Michael Bloch, *James Lees-Milne*. John Murray 2009
Elizabeth Bowen, *The Last September*. Jonathan Cape 1929
R.F. Foster, *Words Alone*. Oxford 2011
Adam Gopnik, *The Table Comes First*. Quercus 2011
Michael Holroyd, *Works on Paper*. Little, Brown 2002
Tony Judt, *Postwar: A History of Europe since 1945*. Heinemann 2005
Elizabeth Kehoe, *Fortune's Daughters*. Atlantic Books 2004
Declan Kiberd, *Inventing Ireland*. Jonathan Cape 1995
Hermione Lee, *Edith Wharton*. Vintage 2007
James Lees-Milne, *Ancestral Voices*. Chatto & Windus 1975
Sir John Leslie, *Never a Dull Moment*. 2006
Shane Leslie, *The End of a Chapter*. Constable 1917
Mary S. Lovell, *The Mitford Girls*. Little, Brown 2011; *The Churchills*.
    Little, Brown 2011
Sinead McCoole, *Hazel: A Life of Lady Lavery 1880–1935*. Lilliput 1996
Ben Macintyre, *Operation Mincemeat*. Bloomsbury 2010
W.J. McCormack, *Blood Kindred*. Pimlico 2005
Roy Miles, *Priceless*. Metro 2003
Mary Motley, *Morning Glory*. Longmans 1961
Robert O'Byrne, *Desmond Leslie (1921–2001)*. Lilliput 2010
Anthony Powell, *At Lady Molly's*. Heinemann 1957
Otto Rauchbauer, *Shane Leslie: Sublime Failure*. Lilliput 2009
Paul Rodzianko, *Modern Horsemanship*, 1936; *Tattered Banners*, 1939. Both
    published by Seeley Service.
Anne Sebba, *Jennie Churchill – Winston's American Mother*. John Murray 2007
Clare Sheridan, *Mayfair to Moscow*. Boni and Liveright 1921; *Nuda Veritas*.
    Thornton Butterworth 1927

Dramatis Personae

Sir Harold Alexander, later 1st Earl Alexander of Tunis 1891–1969
Churchill's favourite general, perhaps because he was always able to dance among the skulls. A long-time family friend of the Leslies, he told Anita in Italy, before she embarked for France: 'Don't falter, Anita.' She didn't.

Agnes Bernelle 1923–99 Fled Berlin for London in 1936 and, aged fifteen, worked for the Office of Strategic Services (OSS) involved in black propaganda, under the code name Vicki. Became an actress and cabaret singer. Married Desmond Leslie 1945. Divorced 1969. Subsequently became very successful, singing with Marc Almond, Elvis Costello, Tom Waits, and The Radiators. Author of *The Fun Palace* (1996), in which she gives laconic descriptions of Anita's wartime 'beaux'.

Rose Burgh (*née* Vincent) 1915–81 The most important person in Anita's life from their debutante days until Rose, long divorced from Lord Burgh and a second husband, disappeared en route to join her third husband and small daughter in the Bahamas. Anita said Rose was the only person she could tell the truth to and Anita's life story is reconstructed in the almost daily letters she wrote to this rich, beautiful, much-married woman, who flitted to and from a series of luxury chateaux and villas in various countries and eventually became a drug addict. Rose's letters to Anita, if they ever existed, haven't survived.

Jennie Churchill 1854–1921 Daughter of Leonard Jerome, mother of Winston Churchill. Said by Lord d'Abernon to have 'more of the Panther than the woman in her look'. Anita's great-aunt and the subject of her biography, *Jennie: The Life of Lady Randolph Churchill* (1969), in which the smouldering panther is declawed and softened to disarming effect. This fascinating woman has been the subject of several biographies, all of them more revealing but less charming than Anita's.

Winston Leonard Spencer Churchill 1874–1965 A very original portrait of her first cousin once removed emerges from Anita's wartime memoirs. Until he became prime minister in May 1940, he was disregarded by many members of his family, who dismissed his warnings of the threat posed by fascism – after he became prime minister his relations asked for various favours. Yet he always showed tolerance towards them, even to his cousin Clare Sheridan, whose idiotic goings-on were a constant embarrassment. Anita, who had flirted with fascism before the war, redeemed herself by providing a link between Winston and the war on the ground in a series of enlivening and intelligent letters.

Commander William (Bill) King 1910–2012 Put in charge of his first submarine aged twenty-nine at the outbreak of the Second World War, the only person to command a British submarine on the first and last days of the war. Exceptionally brave – he was awarded seven medals during the war – he was also exceptionally modest. He first met Anita in 1943 in the Lebanon and became what he called 'her number 4 admirer', languishing behind her husband, Paul Rodzianko, who had followed her to the Middle East, Philip Parbury, whom Anita loved and Peter Wilson, who loved her. He finally became number one admirer and married Anita at Glaslough on 1 January 1949. After retiring from the navy he competed in round-the-world yacht races until late in middle age.

Anne Theodosia (Anita) Leslie 1914–85 When she became a successful writer of witty, entertaining and rather fluffy biographies of her Leslie,

Churchill and Jerome relations, the audiences at her annual US lecture tours described her as 'a grand old girl'. They had no idea that she was a war heroine, twice awarded the Croix de Guerre, a survivor of offhand and unkind parenting, scarred by an abysmal first marriage and tormented by financial worries. Anita was less emotionally robust than she pretended to be, something that is revealed in her letters and diaries but not in her insouciant memoirs.

Desmond Leslie 1921–2001 Youngest son of Shane and Marjorie Leslie. Spitfire pilot in the Second World War but invalided out in 1943 on account of a damaged heart. Pioneer of electronic music, novelist, UFO enthusiast. Cast down by the difficulties of running the Castle Leslie estate, as was his father Shane. Married Agnes Bernelle in 1945 and, after a complicated divorce, Helen Strong in 1970.

Sir John Randolph (Shane) Leslie 3rd Baronet 1885–1971 Catholic convert, supporter of Irish nationalism, philanderer, fulminating critic of James Joyce, whose work, he thought, should be banned from every decent Catholic household. Reluctantly took over the management of the family estate when his son Jack wasn't able to run it. Married Marjorie Ide in 1912 and after Marjorie's death in 1951, Iris Carola Lang in 1958. Although rather flaunting his nationalist leanings by wearing an Irish kilt on most occasions, he joined the Home Guard in London in 1939 and stayed there throughout the Blitz.

Sir John (Jack) Leslie 4th Baronet 1916–2016 Older son of Shane and Marjorie. Joined the Irish Guards at the outbreak of war, was taken prisoner in May 1940 and spent the rest of the war in Bavaria. Released in May 1945, awarded the Légion d'Honneur in 2015. After the war he lived in Italy before returning to Glaslough in his old age. When Sammy Leslie took over the running of Castle Leslie, successfully turning it into a luxury hotel, Jack became a popular tour guide and an indefatigable patron of the local nightclubs.

Colonel Philip Parbury 1910–88 Born in Australia where he returned after the war. He married Eileen Sybil Phipps in 1948 after having been

engaged to her and Anita at the same time. His bravery during the war
– he was mentioned in despatches and awarded the DSO in 1947 – is at
odds with his bewildering, dishonest and despicable behaviour after it,
which, at one point, involved him faking a broken leg.

Colonel Paul Rodzianko CMG 1880–1965 Ukrainian landowner and
soldier until dispossessed after the 1917 Russian Revolution. During the
First World War he'd been an officer in the Tsar's Imperial Guard and
had been married to Tamara Novosiloff, a maid of honour to the Russian
empress, and may possibly have had a second wife too. In 1928 he was
the instructor of the Irish Equitation School and seems to have first met
Anita in 1934. Her grandmother, Leonie Leslie, called Paul 'the NHB' – the
noisy, hungry bore. Knowing that she was making a catastrophic mistake,
Anita married him in 1937 and joined the MTC in order to escape him;
not a very successful ploy since he managed to follow her to South Africa
and the Middle East, only thwarted when she was sent to Italy. He denied
Anita a divorce for many years but she was finally granted one in 1948. He
subsequently married Joan Freeman Mitford, widow of Guillermo de Udy.

Clare Sheridan 1885–1970 Tempestuous doesn't begin to describe
Anita's sculptor cousin, daughter of the dodgy financier Moreton Frewen,
nicknamed 'Mortal Ruin', who was married to Jennie Churchill's sister
Clara. Although Anita in her biography *Cousin Clare* (1976) depicts King
Milan of Serbia as Clara's devoted admirer, he was probably Clare's father.
Anita also bathes Clare's short-lived marriage to Wilfred Sheridan, who
was lost in battle in 1915, in a rosy light. Clare herself, in her memoir *Nuda
Veritas* (1927), writes that she realized early in her marriage that Wilfred
didn't approve of her becoming a sculptor or indeed working at all while
she herself thought that work was the most satisfying thing in life and children the least. Her lovers included Charlie Chaplin, Lord Birkenhead and
Lev Kamenev, Trotsky's son-in-law and a high-ranking Soviet functionary,
a list that reads like the characters in a Tom Stoppard play.

Colonel Peter Wilson 1894–1975 Of all the Mr Wrongs with whom
Anita was involved, Peter was probably the most misbegotten. They met

in 1943, and, although Peter loved Anita devotedly for many years, he also wanted to control her life, including persuading her into unwanted pregnancies that couldn't be sustained. Their post-war life at Oranmore Castle was fraught but in 1949 he gave her the greatest gift she could imagine: her son Tarka, although due to the complications which were always part of Anita's life, his birth and parentage had to be kept secret. It's extraordinary that Anita and Peter's relationship survived so much bruising, but it did. He died, married to someone else, near to where Anita lived in Oranmore, in a house which she had chosen for him.

Anita's Houses

Brede Place, East Sussex A fourteenth-century manor house described by Sir Edwin Lutyens as the most interesting and haunted inhabited house in Sussex. It was bought by Moreton Frewen, Clare Sheridan's father, in 1898 and Clare was brought up there. Her mother Clara spent years of her life restoring the house and creating the garden, and her ghost is one of many said to haunt the house. Her appearances are marked by wafts of the violet scent she used to wear. Clare visited Brede often when her nephew Roger Frewen owned the house, and created several sculptures there.

Frampton Court, Dorset Owned by various members of the Sheridan family including Clare's son, Richard, who was born at Frampton in 1932. Built by Robert Brown in 1704 on the site of an ancient priory, in 1790 the park was laid out by Lancelot 'Capability' Brown. The house carried a curse in response to Henry VIII's expulsion of the priory's monks. The curse decreed that no firstborn son would inherit and live. Clare urged Richard to sell Frampton but the estate failed to find a buyer. Unbeknown to Clare, Richard held on to a single acre where a relative was buried. Touring France on his twenty-first birthday, he died suddenly of peritonitis.

Glenveagh Castle, Co. Donegal Large castellated mansion built in about 1870. Bought by Henry McIlhenny of Philadelphia – the only glamorous inhabitant there, according to Andy Warhol – in 1938. The glamorous Mr McIlhenny was very rich; previous McIlhennys had invented the gas meter and Tabasco sauce. Henry had a dazzling art collection, including paintings by Stubbs and Landseer, and created a lush garden on the estate of 40,000 mountainous and wooded acres. Anita, Bill and Tarka visited Glenveagh every September to cull the herd of red deer. Henry gifted the estate to the Irish nation and moved back to Philadelphia where he died in 1986.

Castle Leslie, Glaslough, Co. Monaghan Seat of the Leslies since 1665. Built by Sir John Leslie, 1st Baronet and a Member of Parliament, in 1870 on the site of an earlier castle. It has three lakes, extensive woodland and a Renaissance-style cloister. As a child, Anita loved Glaslough and begged her parents to allow her to spend all her school holidays there. She and Bill took over the running of the estate after the war but were persuaded by Desmond to hand over the ownership, something she regretted for the rest of her life. She spent most of the money she earned from her books buying Glaslough farmland for her son Tarka, leading to family feuds. As in so many Irish houses, Castle Leslie was prone to spooky goings-on. When Winston Churchill (a Leslie nephew) died, crashes and bangs in the loft, mysterious footsteps in the west wing and Leonie Leslie's familiar fingertip drumming were heard. The estate was on the border between the North and the Irish Republic. In 1980 during the Troubles, after three men were shot dead within a mile of the house, Anita wrote to her stepmother Iris that Glaslough had become 'the most dangerous place in Europe'.

Oranmore Castle, Co. Galway On the site of a Norman keep beside Galway Bay. Dating from the fifteenth century, it may have been built on the site of an older castle. From the seventeenth century it was owned by the Blakes, one of Galway's twelve tribes. The tower, which is half the height of the castle, and the adjoining house were ruinous when Marjorie Leslie, assisted by her friend the lawyer and writer Oliver St John Gogarty, bought it for £200 for her daughter Anita who, after the war, had decided that she wanted to live in the west of Ireland. In spite of the castle's eight-foot-thick walls, George Jellicoe, visiting Anita in 1948, complained that the sea came through the windows. Attractively renovated, Oranmore is now the home of Anita and Bill's daughter Leonie and her husband, the musician Alec Finn.

A Note on the Author

Penny Perrick, who lived for many years in the West of Ireland, was a fashion editor for *Vogue*, a columnist on *the Sun* and *The Times* and a fiction editor for the *Sunday Times*. She is also a novelist and the author of *Something to Hide*, a biography of the poet Sheila Wingfield. She now lives in London.

Index